A THOUSAND EYES

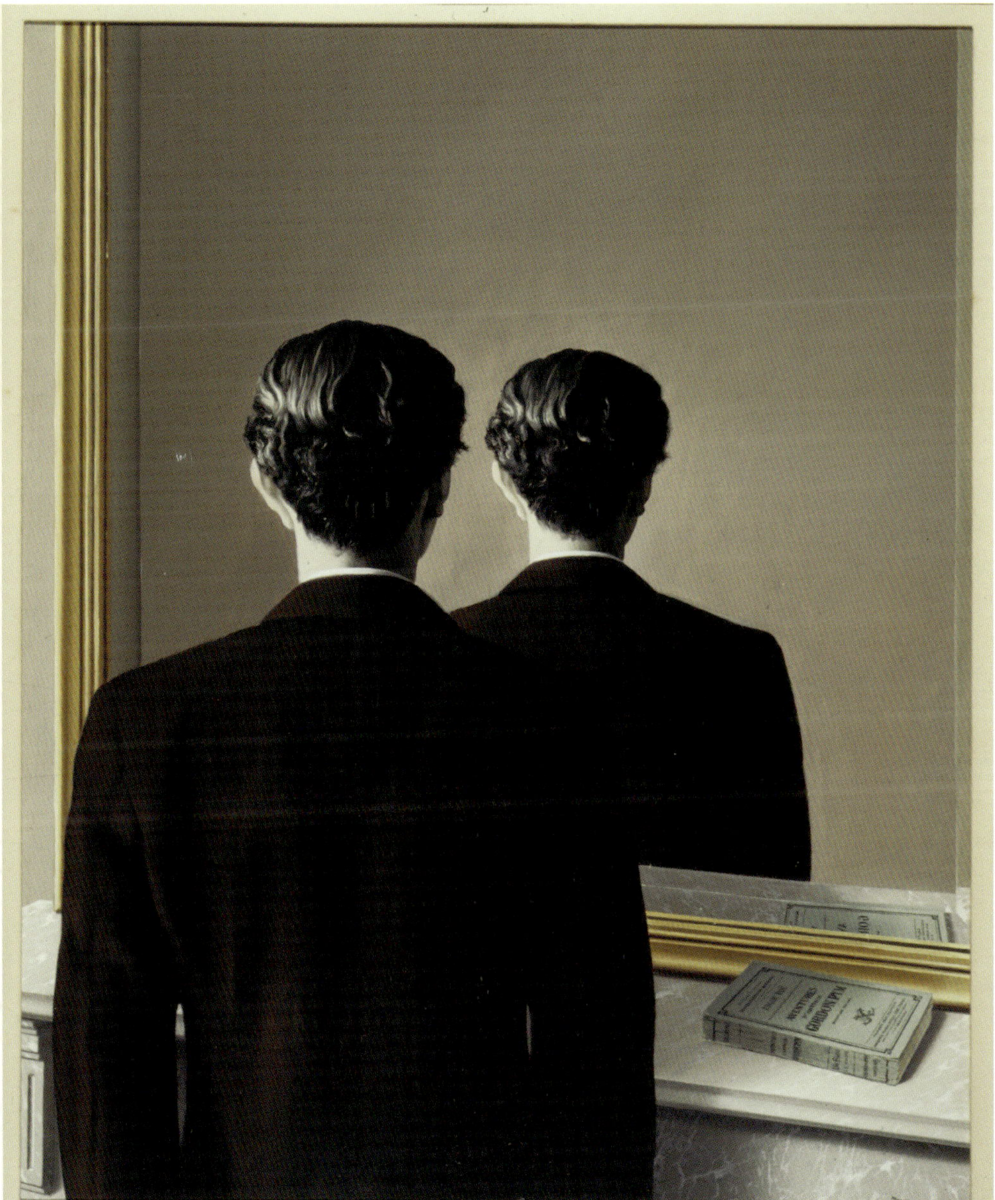

René Magritte, *Not to Be Reproduced | La Reproduction Interdit* (1937).
Stichting Museum Boijmans Van Beuningen.

[See p.245]

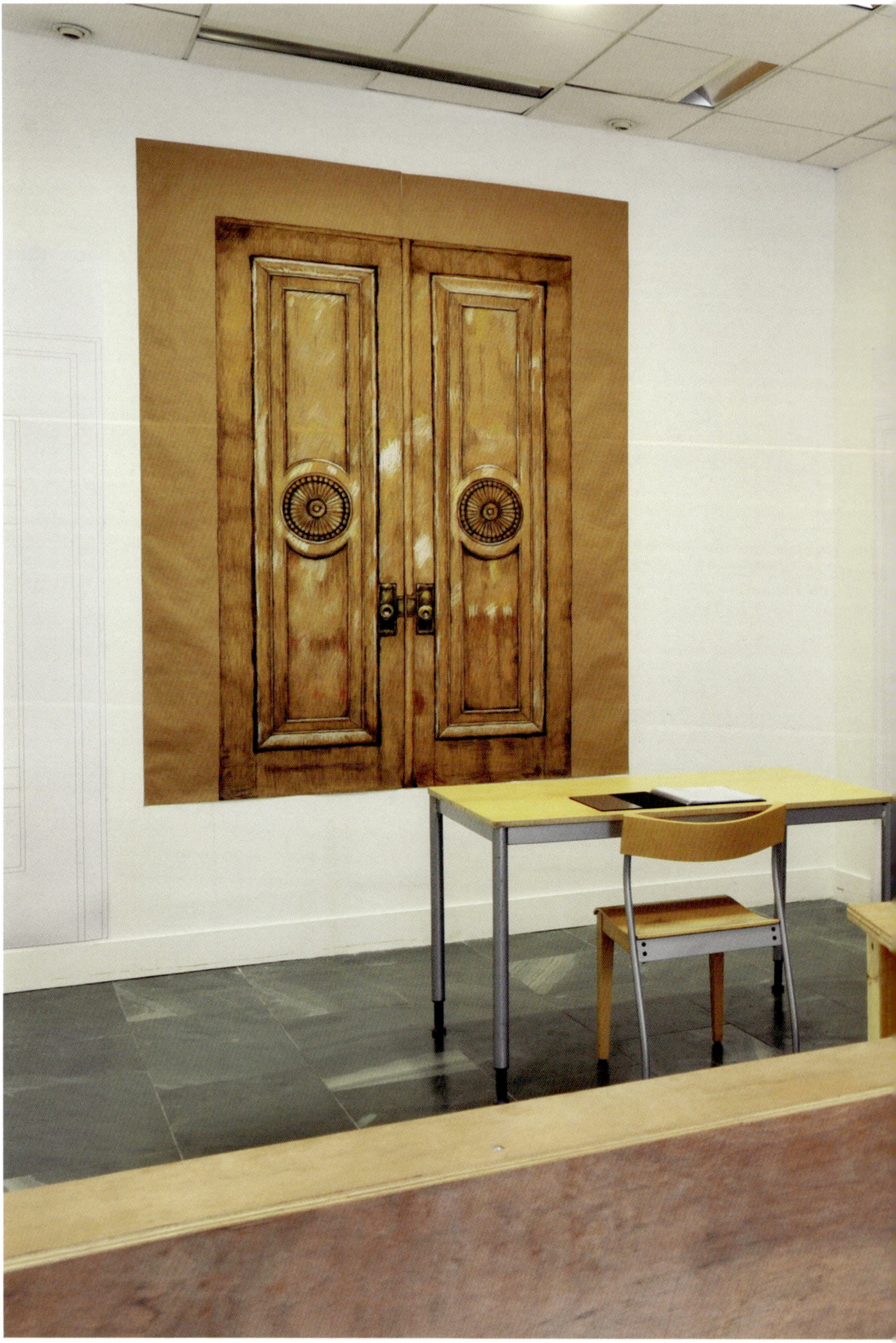

Model Court, Installation, Center for Contemporary Arts, Glasgow (2009).
By Lawrence Abu Hamdan, Sidsel Meineche Hansen, Lorenzo Pezzani and Oliver Rees. [See p.245

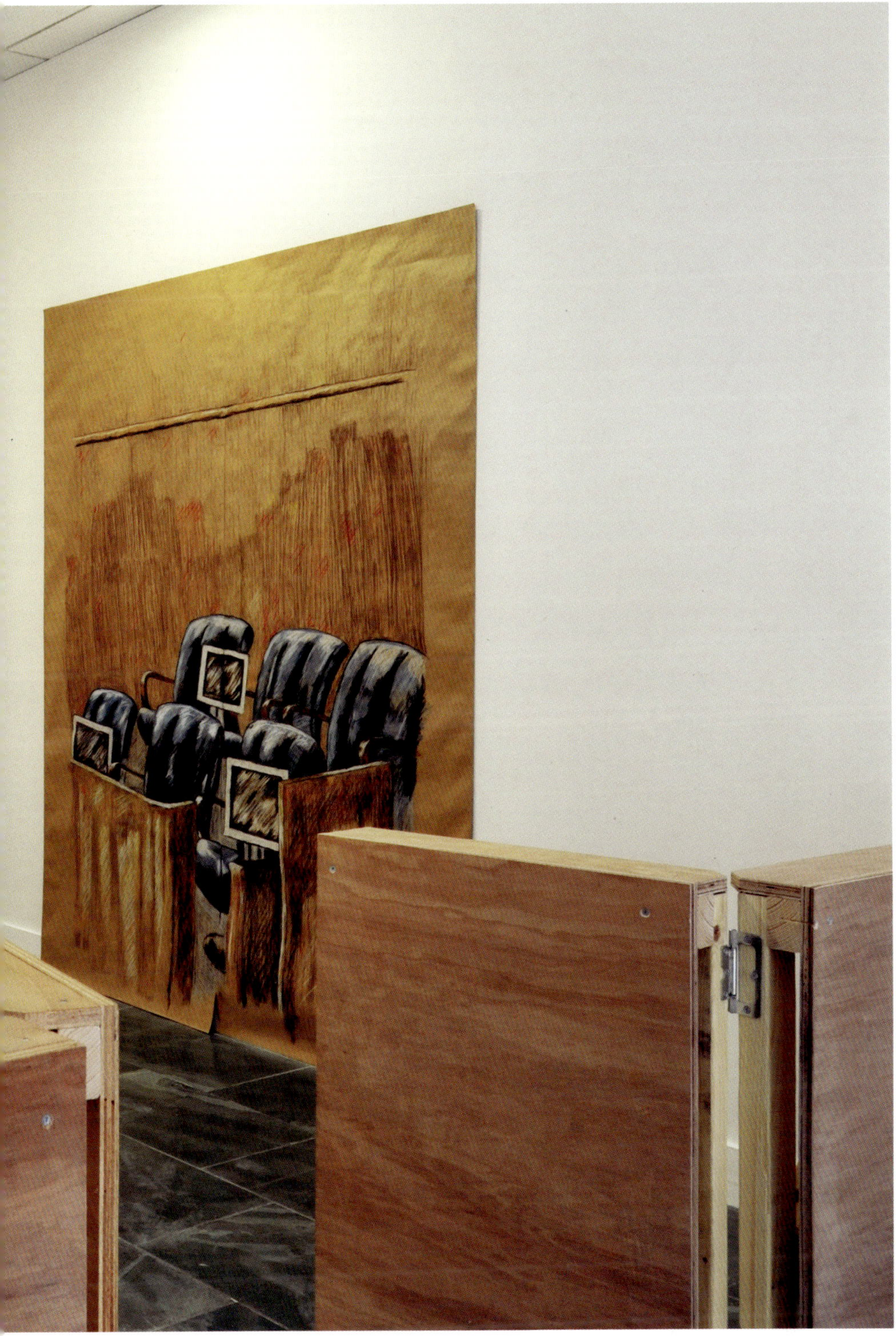

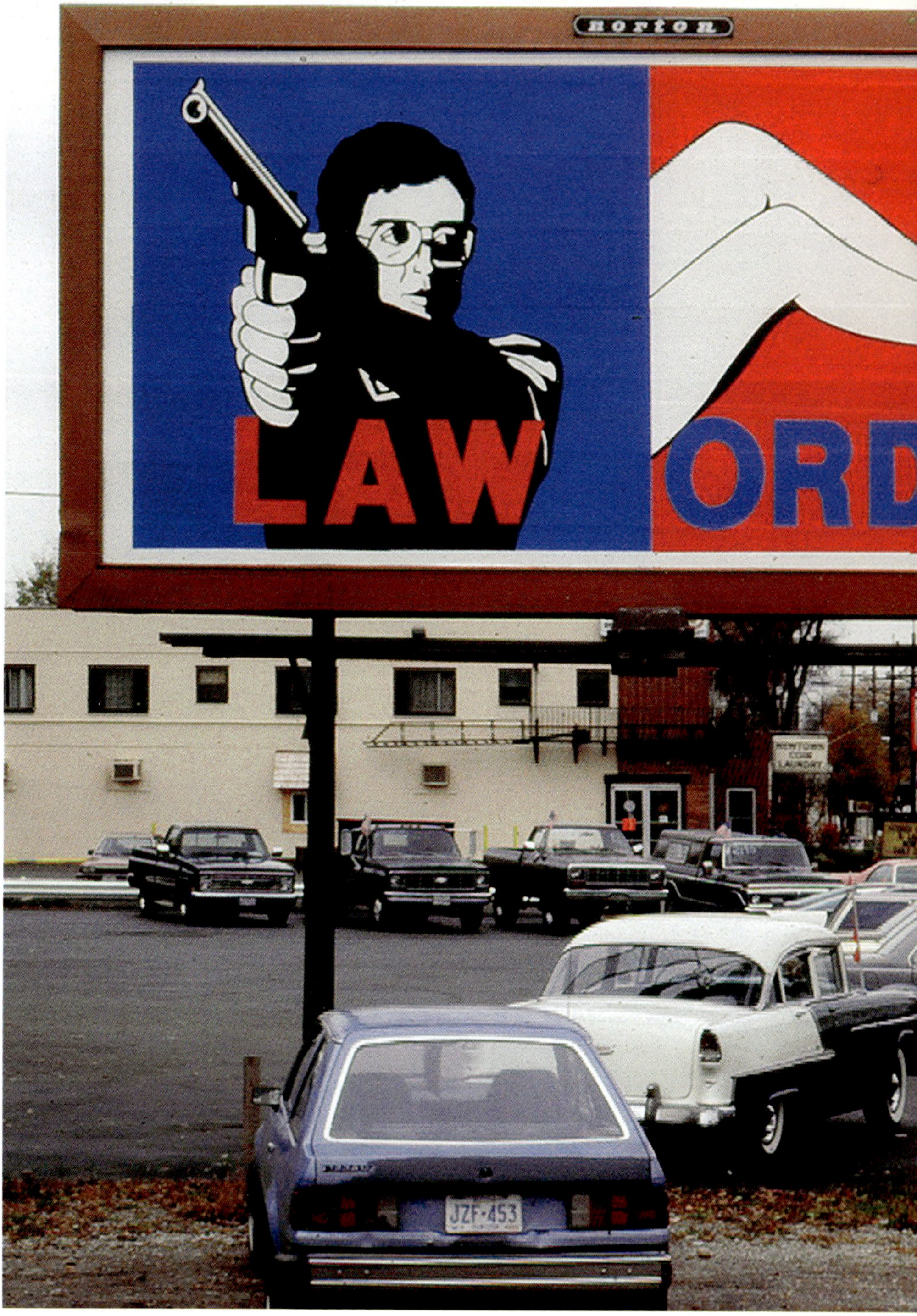

Les Levine, *Law Order* (1992). Media campaign. Cincinnati, Ohio. 100 billboards 10 × 22 feet each.
© 1992 Les Levine. Photo © Les Levine 1992. Courtesy Museum of Mott Art, Inc.

[See p.245]

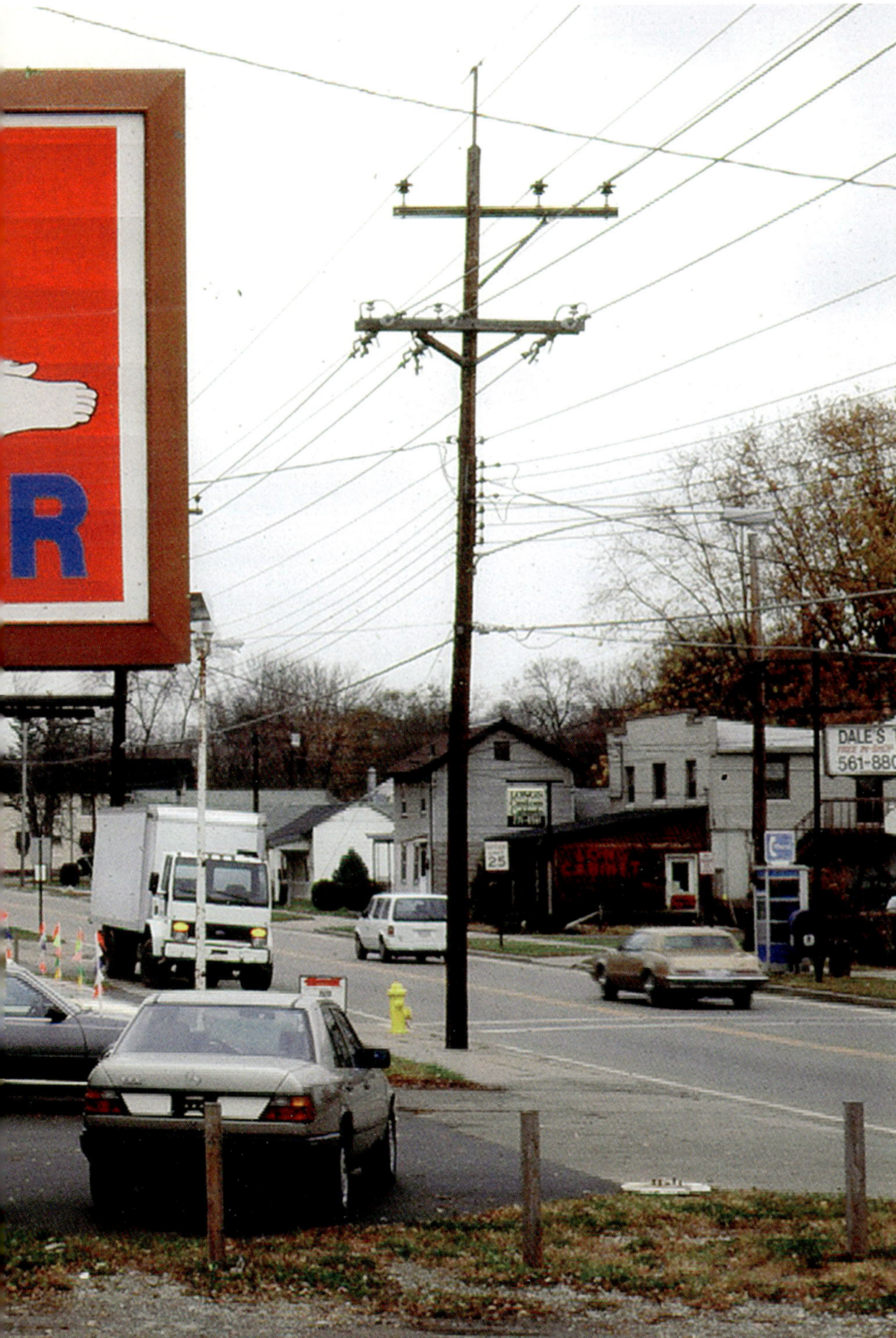
DALE'S T
561-880
25

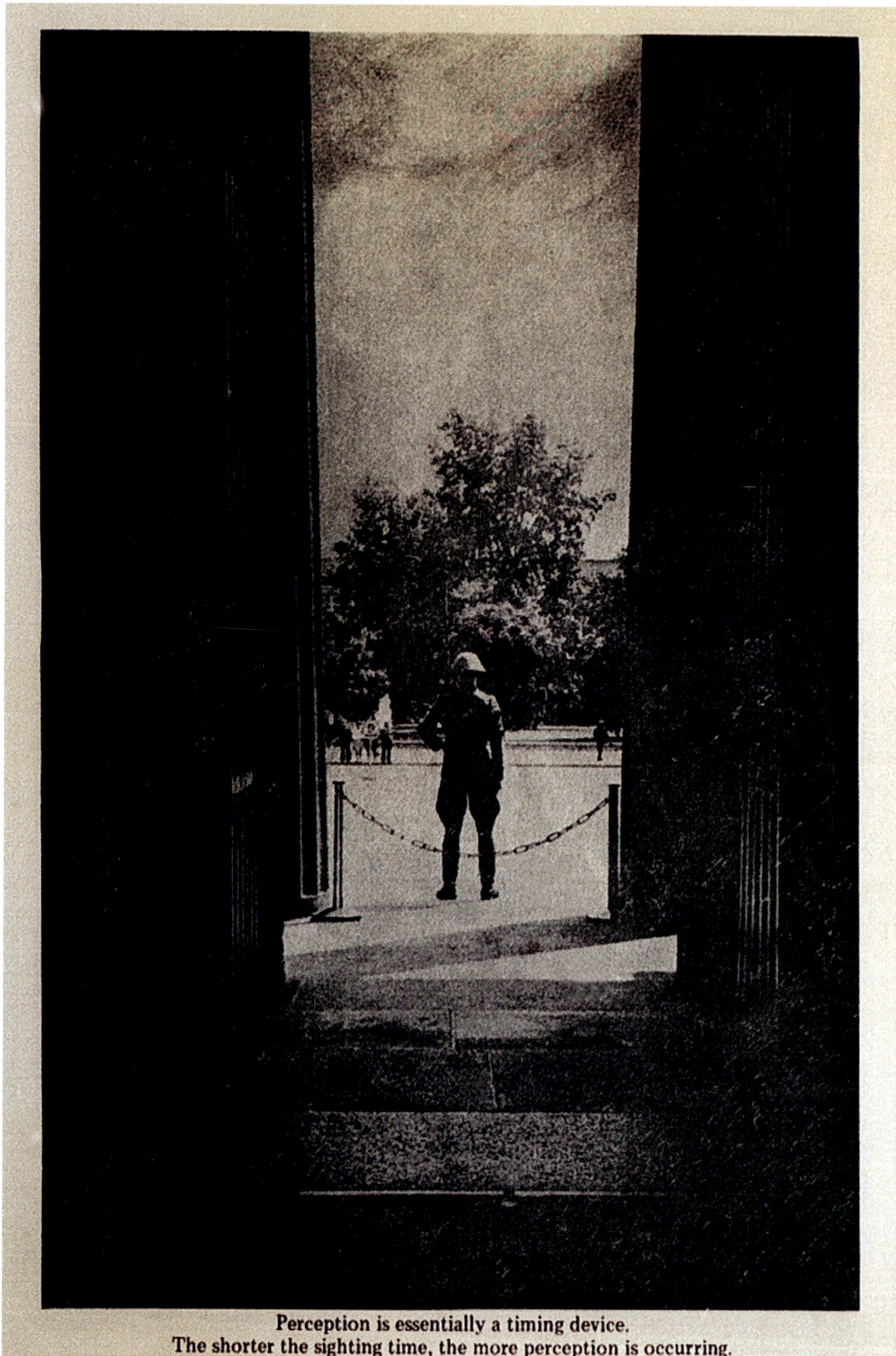

Les Levine, *Using the Camera as a Club* (1979). Intaglio etching on buff German etching paper, 22 × 30 inches.
 [See p.245]

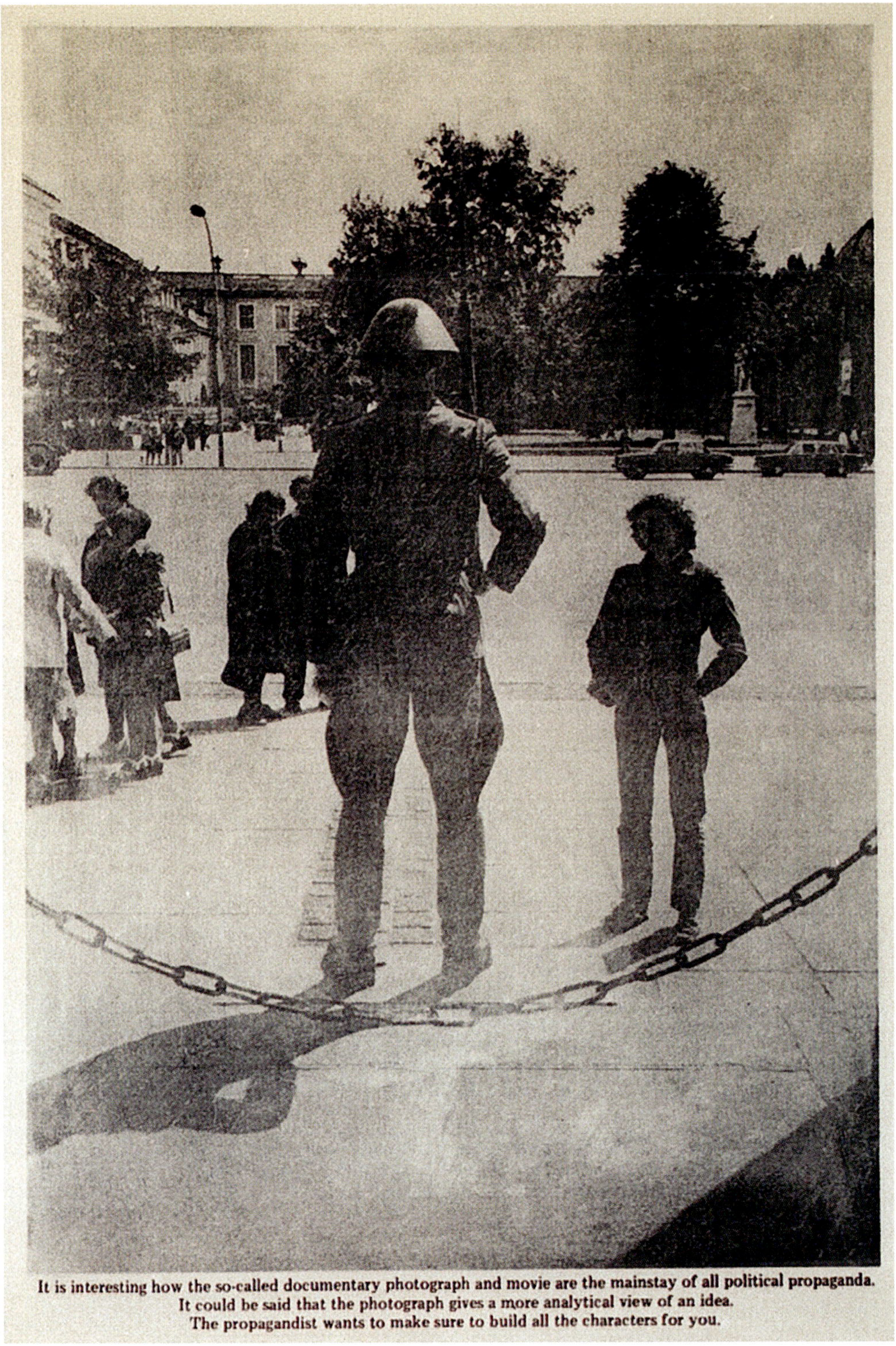

Les Levine, *Using the Camera as a Club* (1979). Intaglio etching on buff German etching paper, 22 × 30 inches.
 [See p.245]

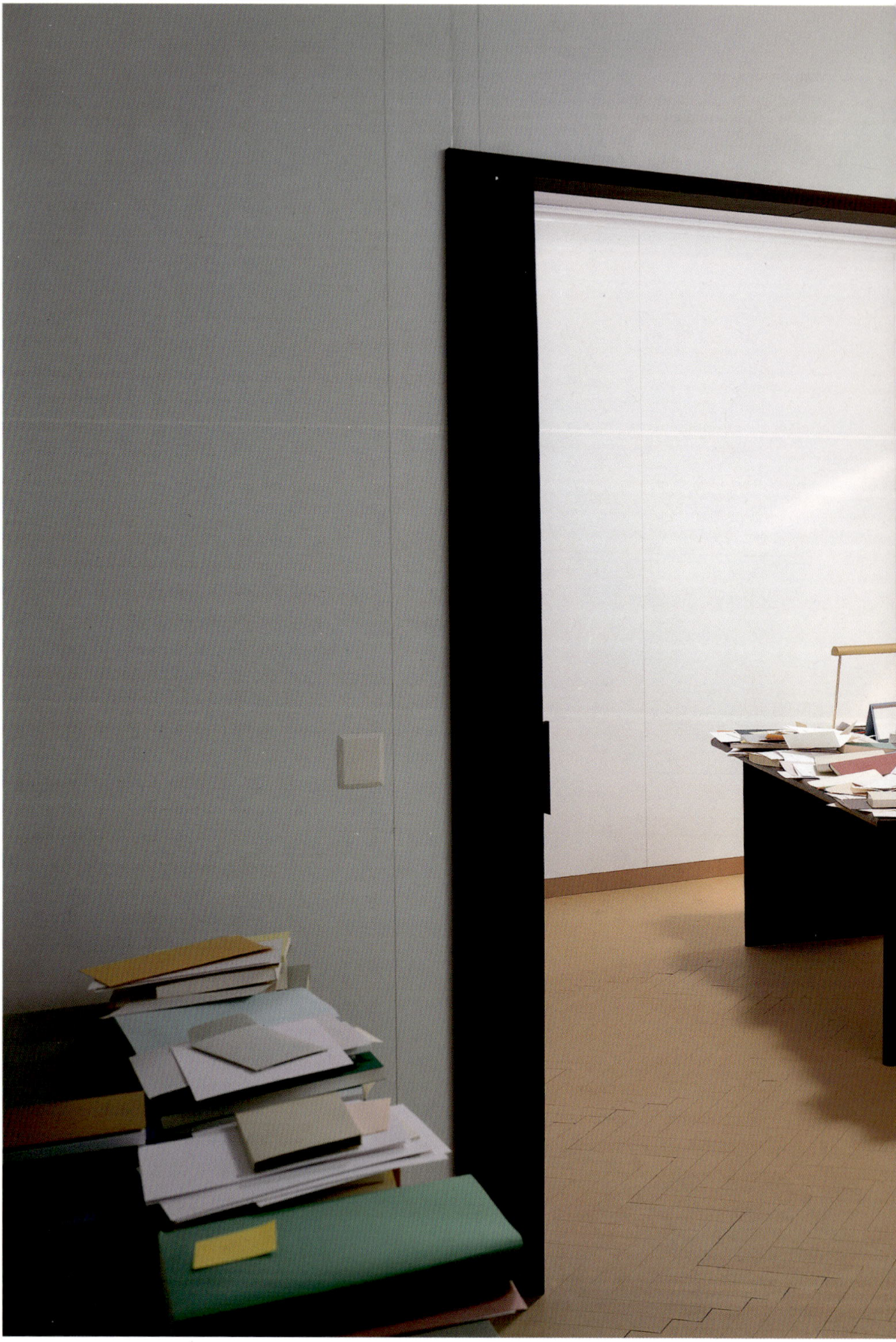

Thomas Demand, *Embassy VI* (2007). C-Print / Diasec, 232 × 180 cm.

[See p.246]

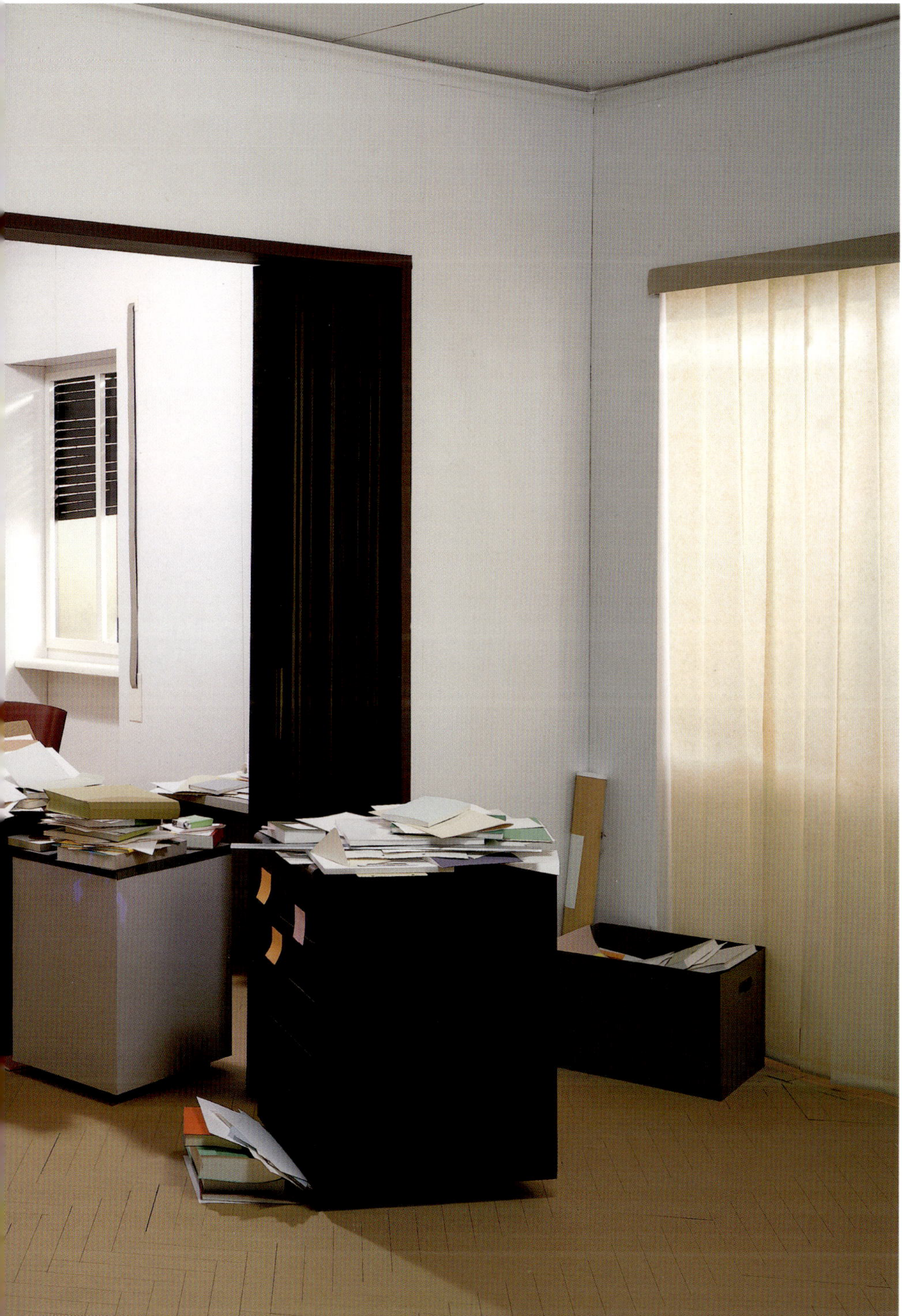

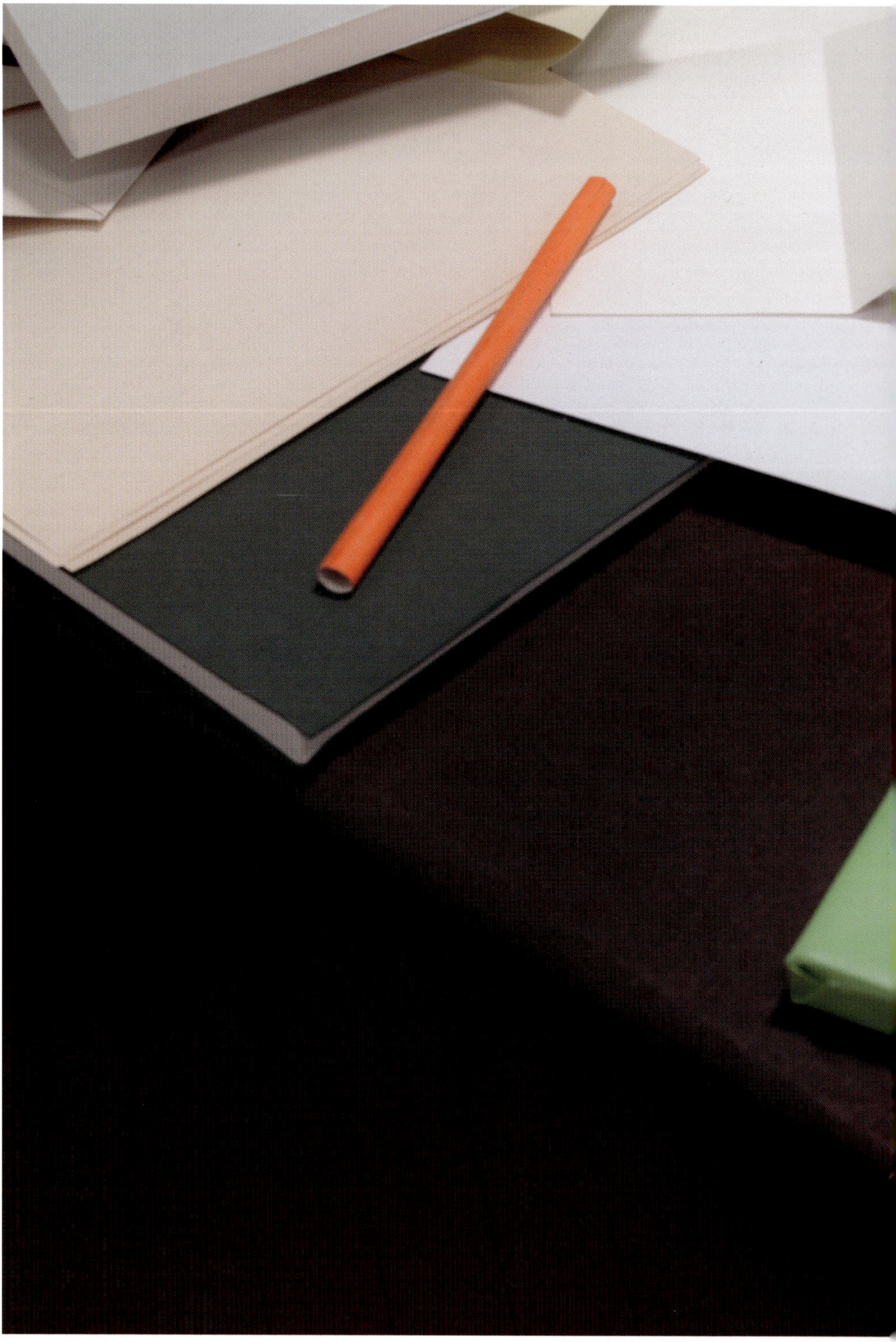

Thomas Demand, *Embassy VII.a* (2007). C-Print / Diasec, 53,5 × 51 cm.

[See p.246]

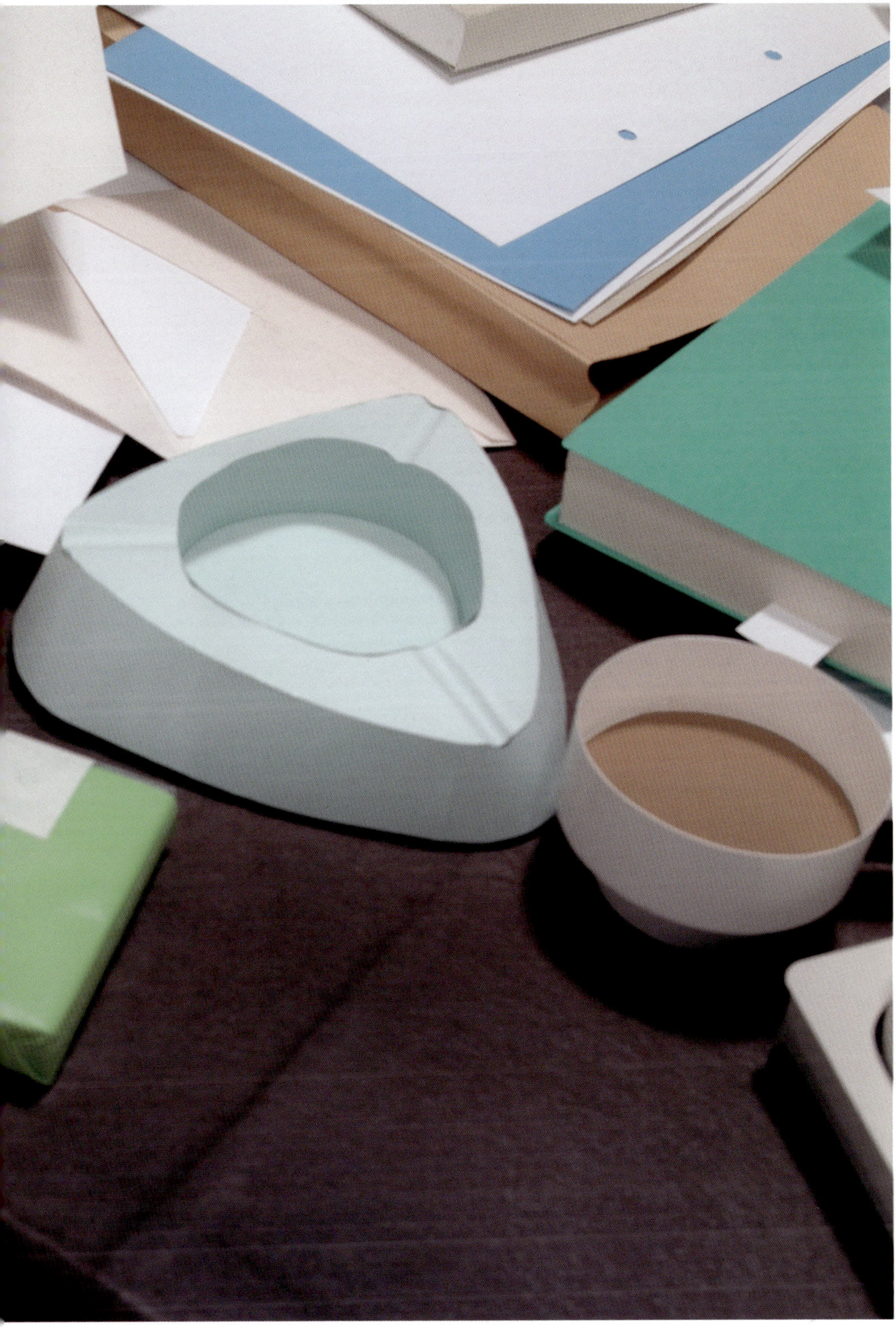

Sotheby's EST. 1744

DE BOELENLAAN 30 1083 HJ AMSTERDAM P.O. BOX 75522 1070 AM AMSTERDAM
+31 (0)20 550 22 00 F + 31 (0)20 550 22 22 WWW.SOTHEBYS.COM

Sotheby's | Cataloguing Preview

20th Century Prints & Printed matter

Graphis 127
The magazine, 1966, printed in colours, lacking the leporello and the subscription card, on 120gm2 fine white Biber-Kunstdruckpapier by the Graphis Press, Zurich, the cover printed by Merkur AG, Langenthal, published by Walter Herdeg, Zurich.

CONDITION REPORT:
A vertical, circa 4 by 1 cm (front) and 2 by 1 cm (back) tear with associated paper loss, creases and buckling running through the lower centre of the magazine, affecting text and images of all the pages. Two ca. 3 cm long, oblique tears, running upwards from the top of the central tear in two different directions. The front cover has a large, 6 by 12 cm piece of paper loss in the lower left part. Extensive paper loss and tears along the spine. Minor wear, rubbing and handling marks at the corners and along all four edges. Some slight paper discoloration along the edges of the pages.

"In response to your inquiry, we are pleased to provide you with a general report of the condition of the property described above. Since we are not professional conservators or restorers, we urge you to consult with a restorer or conservator of your choice who will be better able to provide a detailed, professional report. Prospective buyers should inspect each lot to satisfy themselves as to condition and must understand that any statement made by Sotheby's is merely a subjective, qualified opinion. Prospective buyers should also refer to any Important Notices regarding this sale, which are printed in the Sale Catalogue.
NOTWITHSTANDING THIS REPORT OR ANY DISCUSSIONS CONCERNING A LOT, ALL LOTS ARE OFFERED AND SOLD AS IS" IN ACCORDANCE WITH THE CONDITIONS OF BUSINESS PRINTED IN THE SALE CATALOGUE."

Rana Hamadeh, *G R A P H I S N° 127* (2008 – ongoing).
Official Condition report on Graphis 127, penetrated during the Lebanese civil war by a bullet; issued by the Department of 20th Century Prints and Printed Matter at Sotheby's (Amsterdam) after inspection of the magazine by one of their specialists, Amsterdam 2009. Courtesy the artist.

[See p.246]

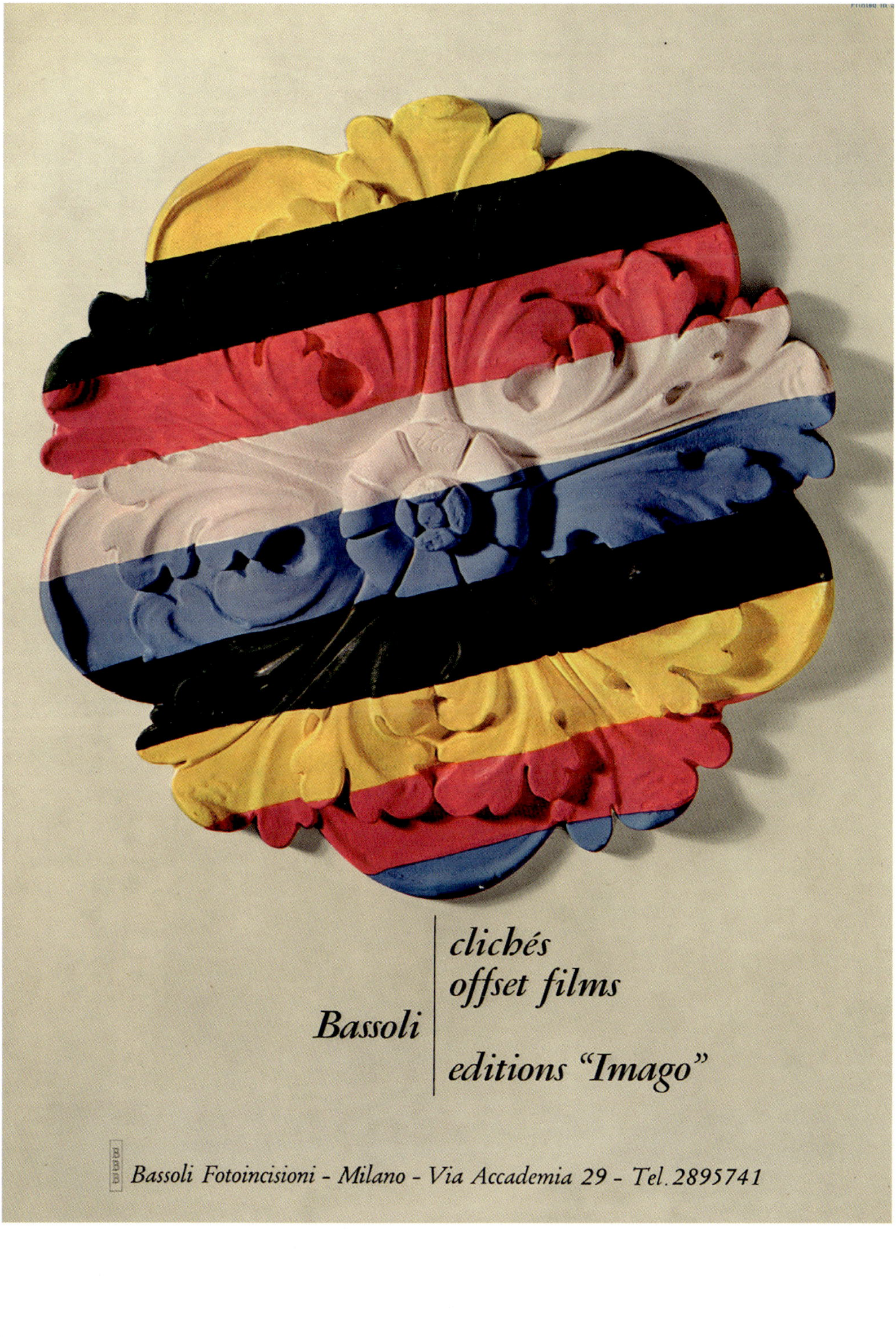

Rana Hamadeh, *G R A P H I S N° 127* (2008 – ongoing).
Backcover of an undamaged copy of Graphis 127 magazine, published in Zurich, 1966.
Acquired from Aya Ohara, Tokyo, Japan, in March 2009. Courtesy the artist.

[See p.246]

Sotheby's EST. 1744

DE BOELENLAAN 30 1083 HJ AMSTERDAM P.O. BOX 75522 1070 AM AMSTERDAM
+31 (0)20 550 22 00 F + 31 (0)20 550 22 22 WWW.SOTHEBYS.COM

Sotheby's | Cataloguing Preview

Contemporary Art

RANA HAMADEH (1983-)

Graphis 127
Readymade: magazine with bullet hole
29.9 x 23.5 cm.
Executed in 2008. This work is unique.

This work is accompanied by a certificate of authenticity signed by the artist.

CONDITION REPORT:
The printed magazine Graphis 127, 1966, with a bullet hole in the lower centre.
In perfect condition as intended by the artist.

"In response to your inquiry, we are pleased to provide you with a general report of the condition of the property described above. Since we are not professional conservators or restorers, we urge you to consult with a restorer or conservator of your choice who will be better able to provide a detailed, professional report. Prospective buyers should inspect each lot to satisfy themselves as to condition and must understand that any statement made by Sotheby's is merely a subjective, qualified opinion. Prospective buyers should also refer to any Important Notices regarding this sale, which are printed in the Sale Catalogue.
NOTWITHSTANDING THIS REPORT OR ANY DISCUSSIONS CONCERNING A LOT, ALL LOTS ARE OFFERED AND SOLD AS IS" IN ACCORDANCE WITH THE CONDITIONS OF BUSINESS PRINTED IN THE SALE CATALOGUE."

Rana Hamadeh, *G R A P H I S N° 127* (2008 – Ongoing).
Official Condition report on Graphis 127, a magazine penetrated during the Lebanese civil war by a bullet; issued by the Department of Contemporary Art at Sotheby's (Amsterdam) after inspection of the artwork by one of their specialists, Amsterdam 2009. Courtesy the artist. [See p.246]

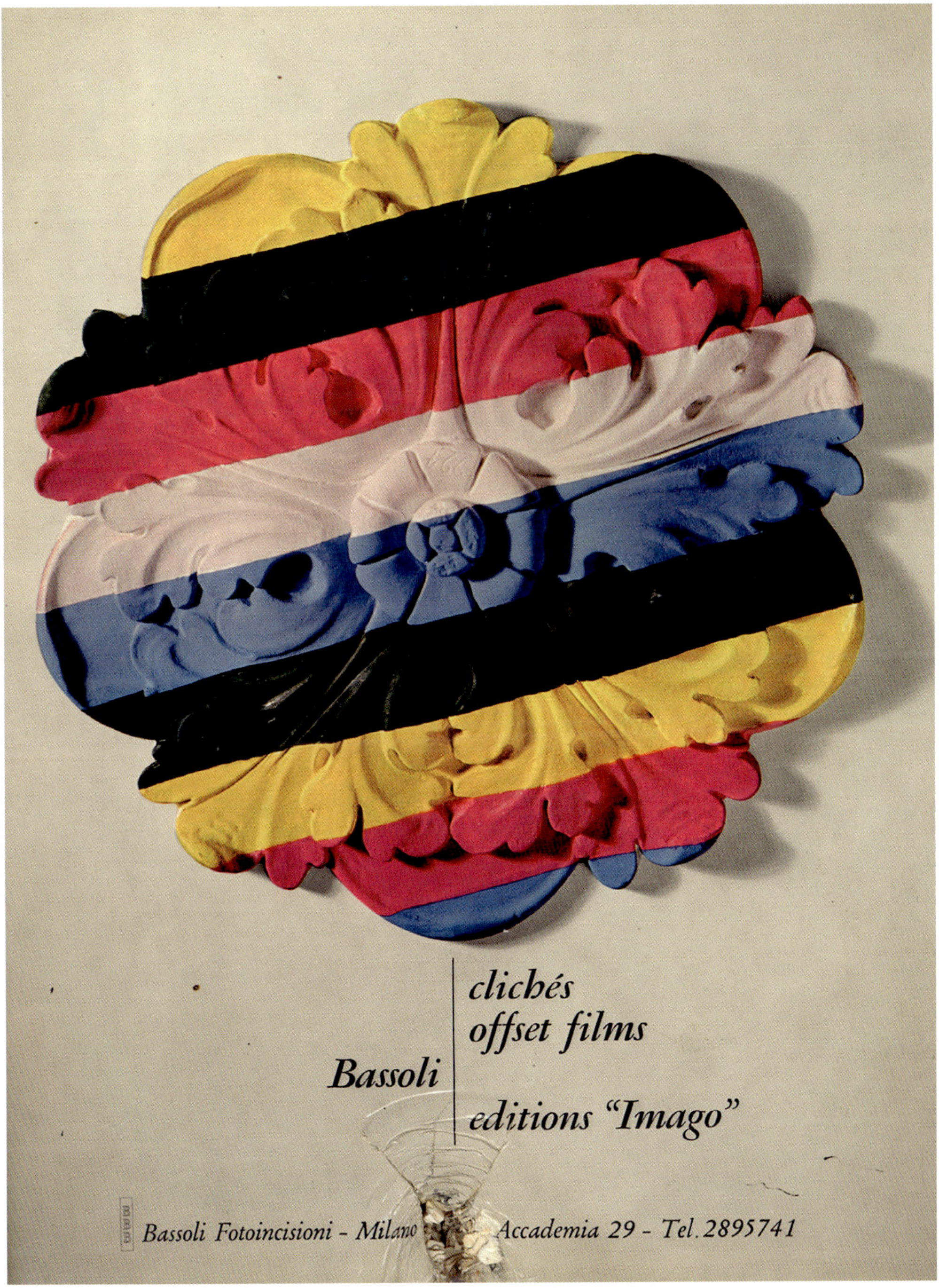

Rana Hamadeh, *G R A P H I S N° 127* (2008 – ongoing).
Back cover of Graphis 127, published in Zurich, 1966.
Magazine with a bullet hole that the artist inherited from her uncle Nizar Mroué, Beirut, August 2005.
Courtesy the artist.

[See p.246]

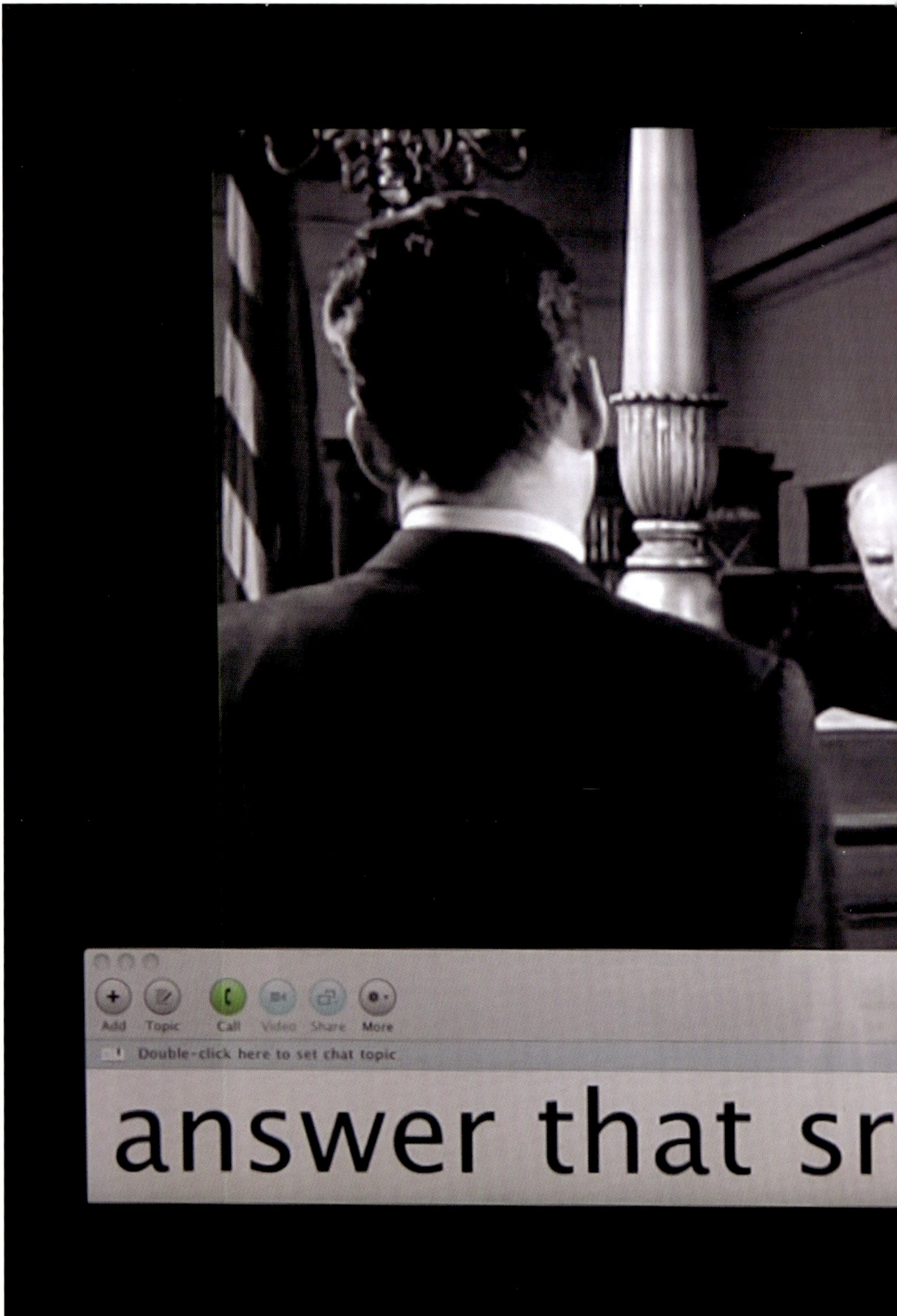

Model Court, Workshop; transcription and subtitling exercise, Helsinki Public School (2010).
By Lawrence Abu Hamdan, Sidsel Meineche Hansen, Lorenzo Pezzani and Oliver Rees.

[See p.245]

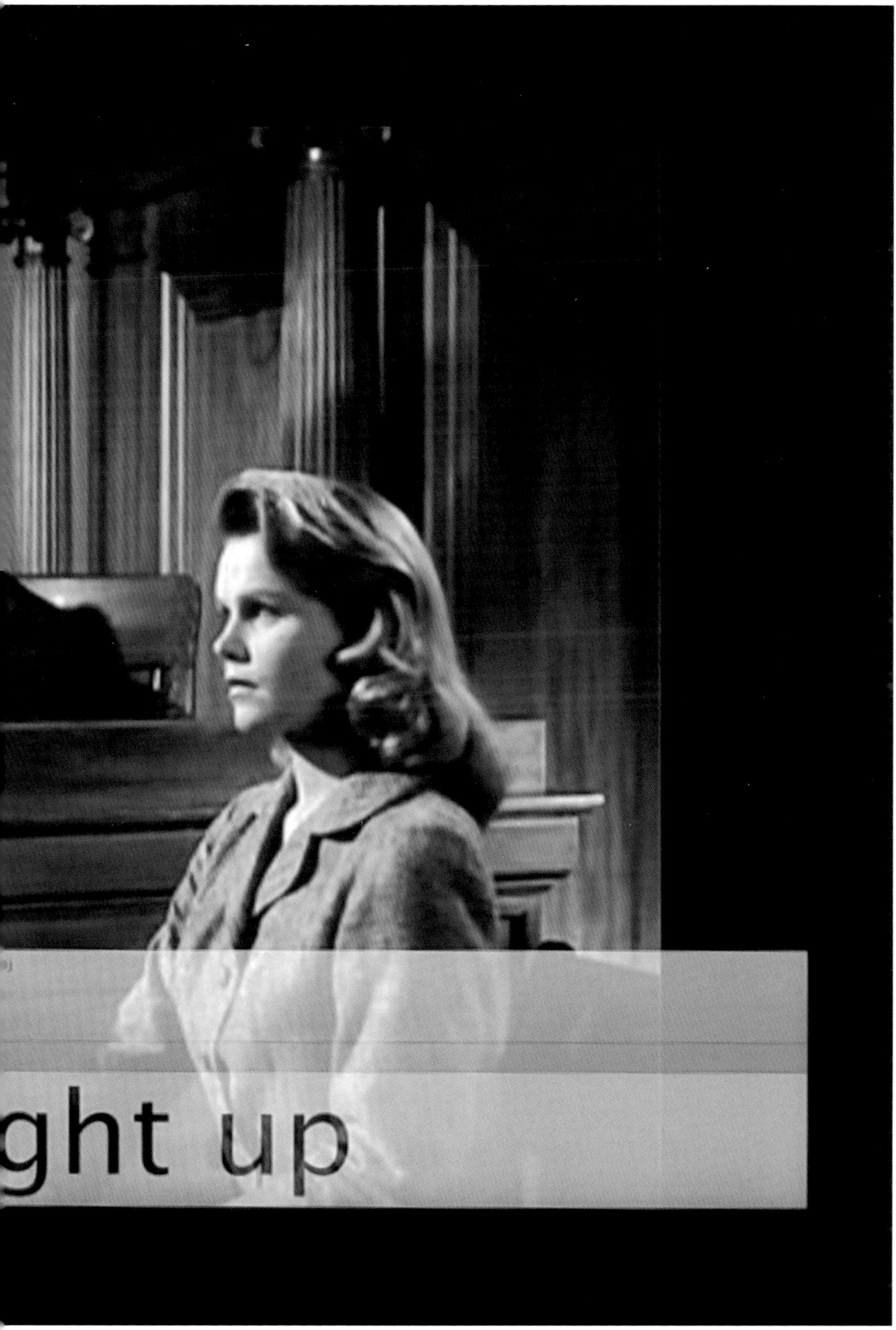
ght up

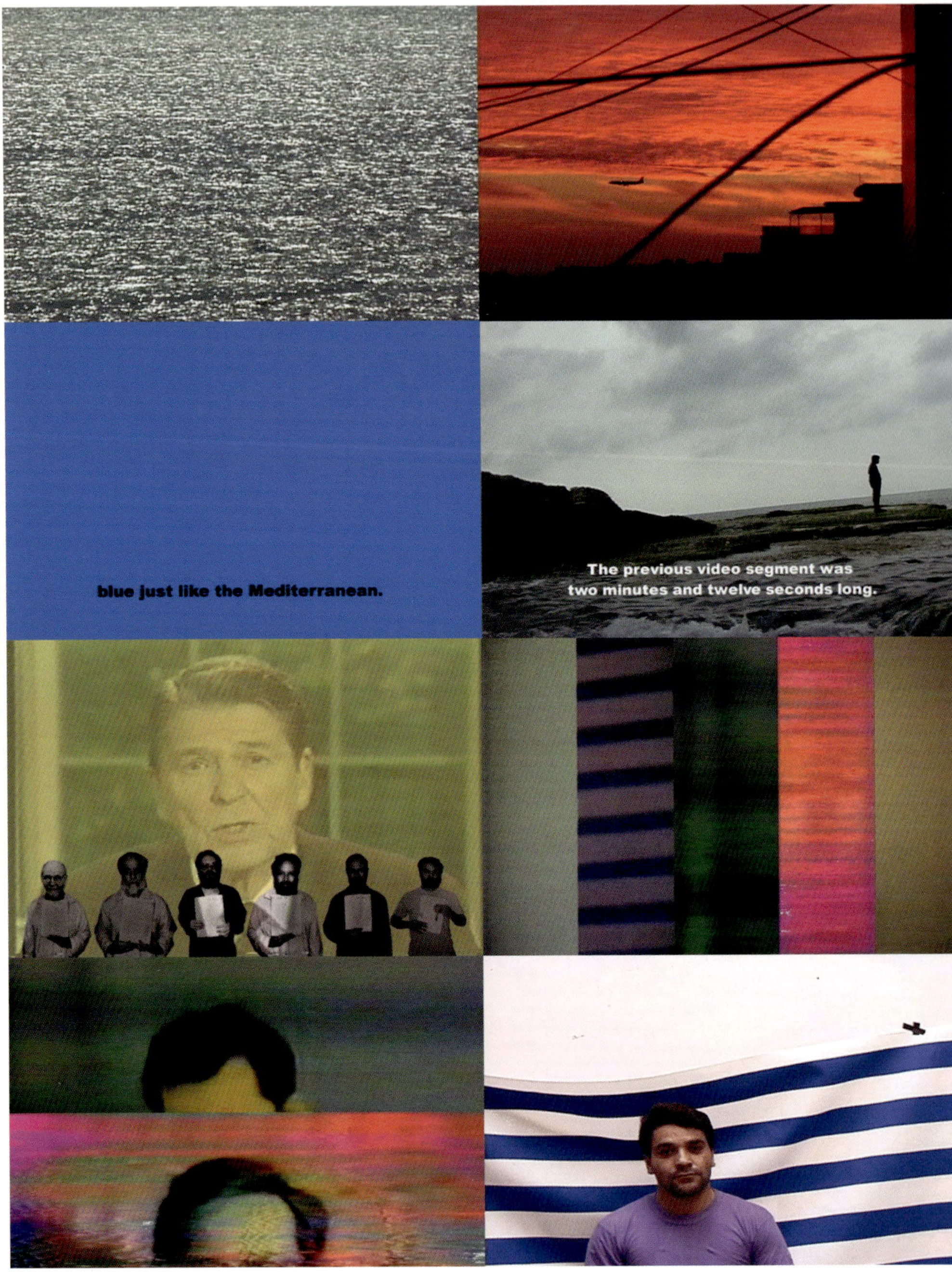

Atlas Group, Stills from *Hostage: The Bachar Tapes (#17 and 31)*. English Version (2001).
Courtesy Walid Raad.

[See p.247]

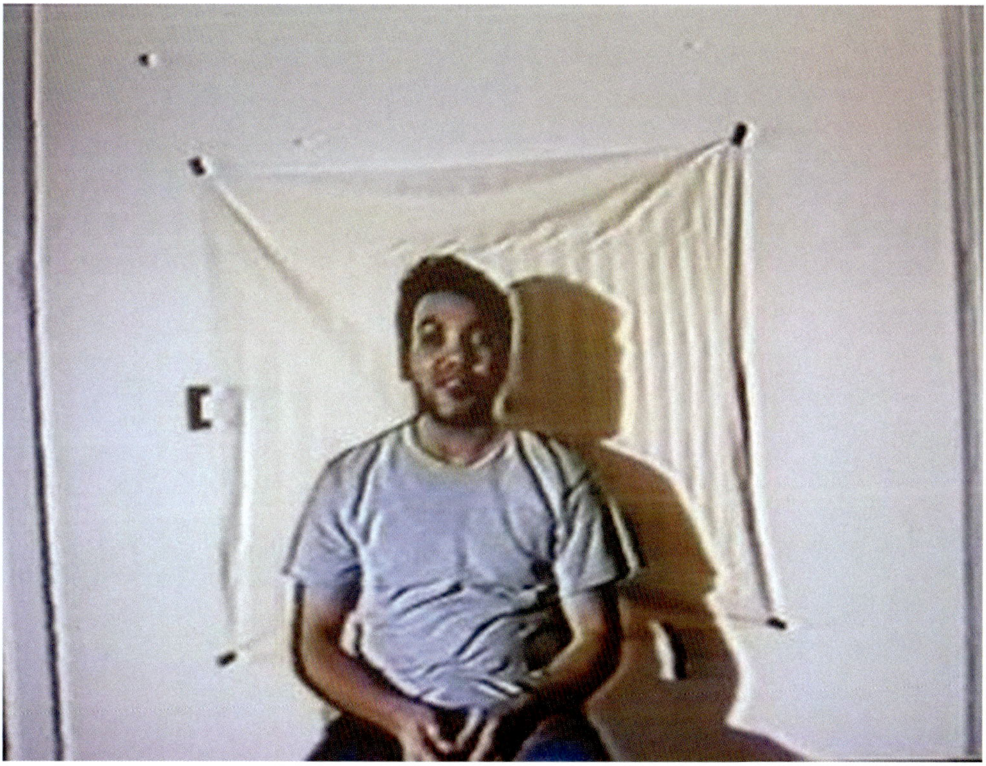

Atlas Group, Still from *Hostage: The Bachar Tapes (#17 and 31)*. English Version (2001).
Courtesy Walid Raad.

[See p.247]

n the following tapes into
y where the tapes are screening.

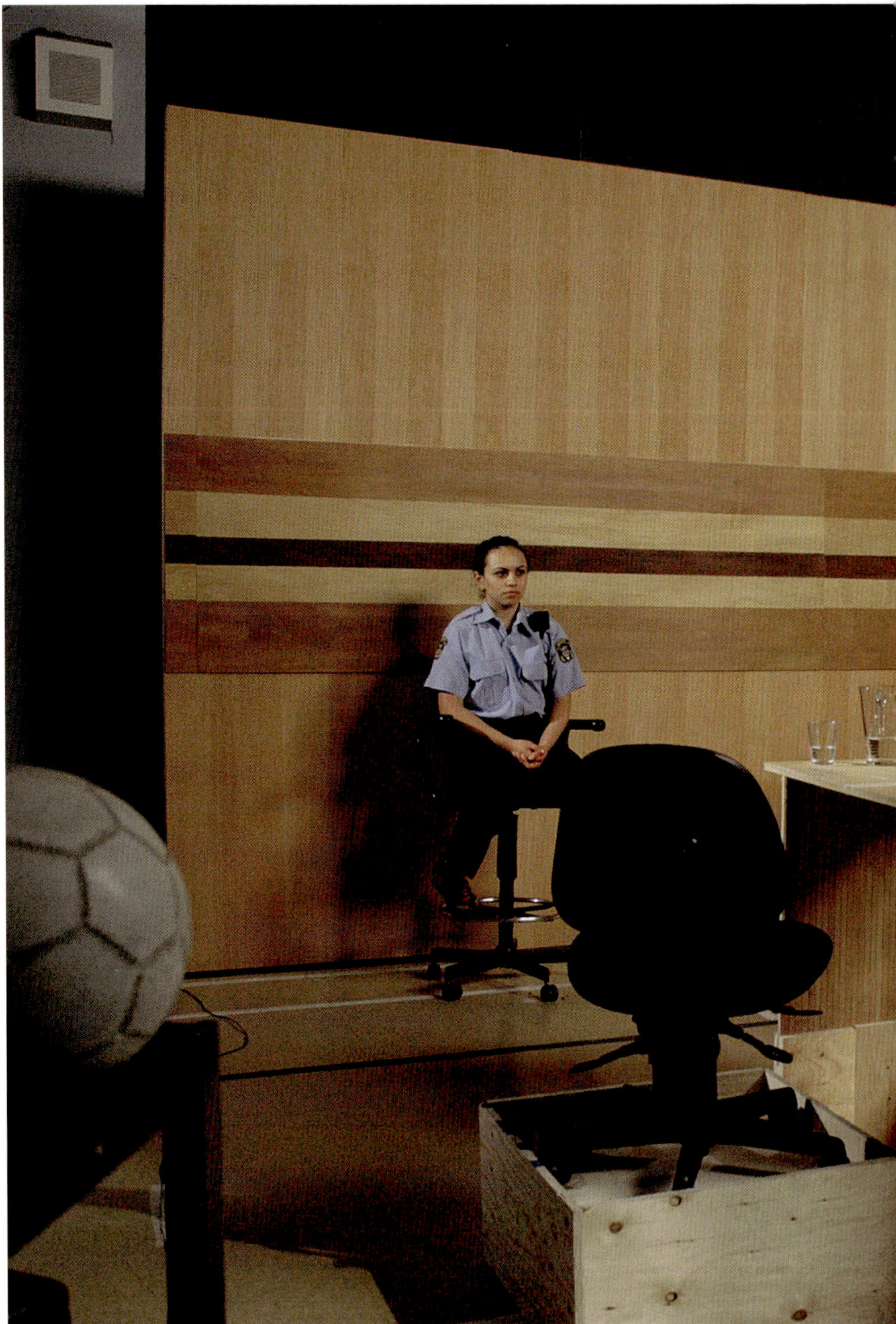

Judy Radul, *World Rehearsal Court* (2009).
Multimedia installation, production still. Courtesy the artist and Catriona Jeffries Gallery.

[See p.247]

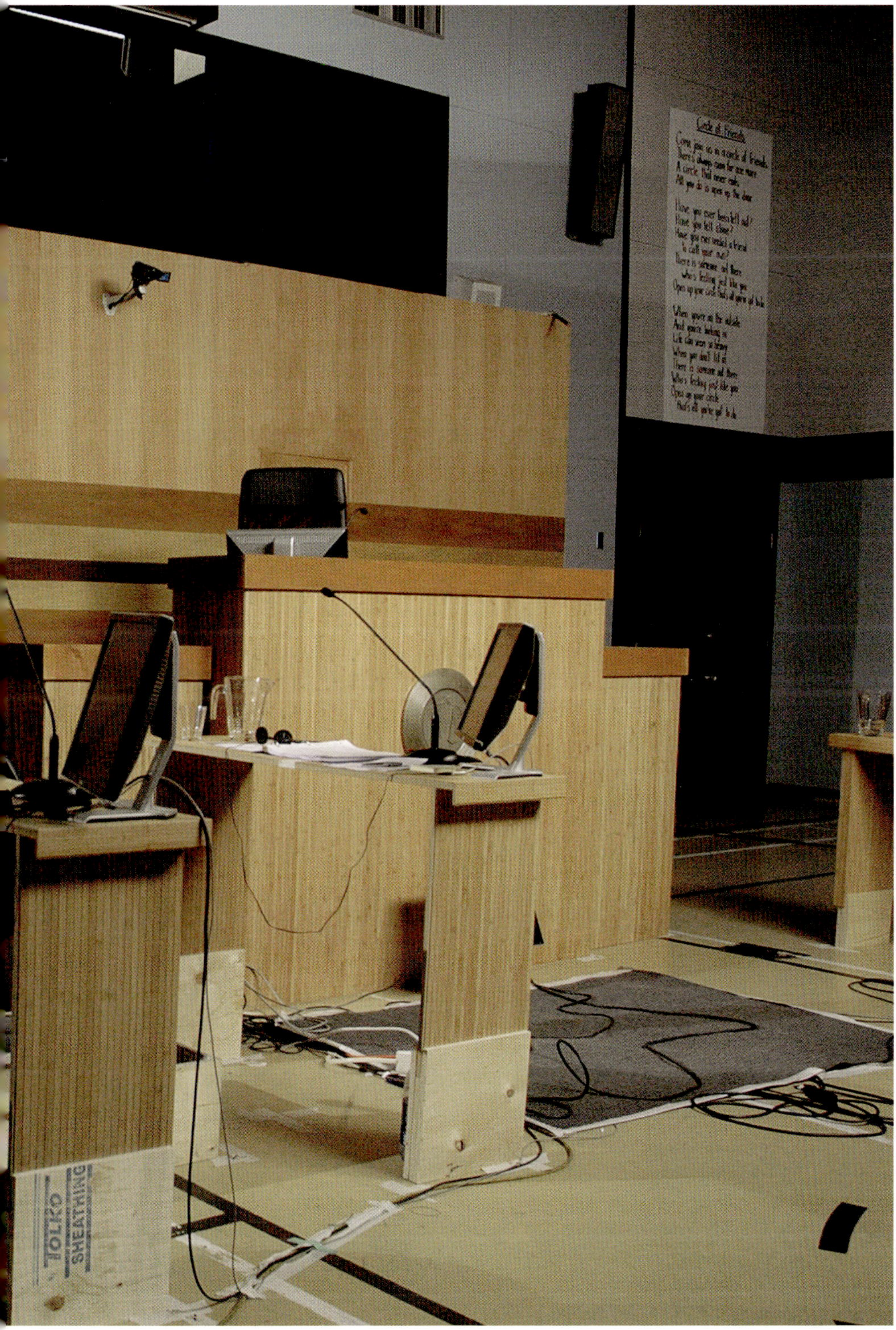
Circle of Friends
TOLKO
SHEATHING

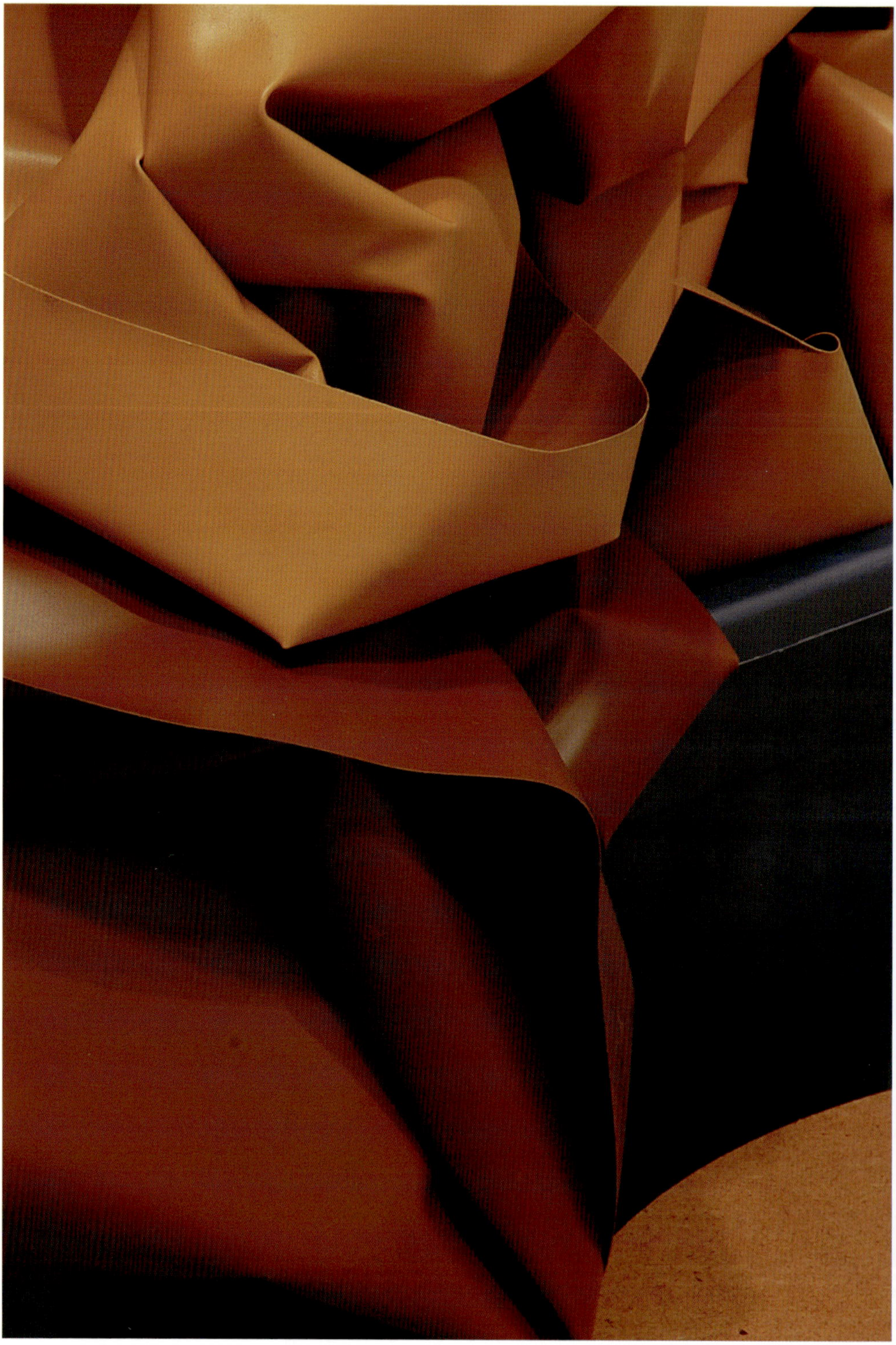

Judy Radul, *World Rehearsal Court* (2009). Multimedia installation, detail.
Courtesy the artist, Morris and Helen Belkin Art Gallery and Catriona Jeffries Gallery.

[See p.247]

A THOUSAND EYES:

MEDIA TECHNOLOGY, LAW AND AESTHETICS

Edited by
Marit Paasche & Judy Radul

Sternberg Press

A Thousand Eyes: Media Technology, Law and Aesthetics
is published on the occasion of the exhibition of Judy Radul's
World Rehearsal Court, curated by Tone Hansen

Henie Onstad Art Centre Oslo, Norway June 19 – October 2, 2011

Editors: Marit Paasche and Judy Radul
Published by Henie Onstad Art Centre and Sternberg Press
Design: Eriksen / Brown, Oslo
Print: Cassochrome, Belgium

ISBN 978-1-934105-66-5

The Henie Onstad Art Center gratefully acknowledges the generous support of the Freedom of Expression Foundation toward the publication of this book.

The Henie Onstad Art Centre is owned by the Sonja Henie and Niels Onstad Foundation. The Art Centre was opened in 1968 and was a gift from Henie and Onstad. They also donated their collection of international contemporary art, and set up a found with which to run the activities. The building was designed by the architects Jon Eikvar and Sven Erik Engebretsen. It was expanded with a new wing in 1994, designed by the architect Stein Halvorsen. An outdoor stage was constructed in 2008.

Sternberg Press, Caroline Schneider, Tatjana Günther
Karl-Marx Allee 78
D-10243 Berlin
www.sternberg-press.com

CONTENTS

ARTWORKS (part 1)

—

TEXTS

—

Quotes on the inside flaps of this book:

1
Jack Spicer, "Letter to Lorca" *The New American Poetry: 1945–1960*, ed. Donald Allen (Berkley: University of California Press, 1999), 413.

2
Gilles Deleuze and Claire Parnet, *Dialogues II*, trans. Hugh Tomlinson, Barbara Habberjam, Eliot Ross Albert (New York: Colombia University Press, 2002), 69–71.

PREFACE

The short answer is: because none of us are outside the law. That is why you have in your hands a book of texts about the law produced by an art centre. Franz Kafka has shown that the very quality of our reality carries a legal dimension. We inculcate the law within as a profound sense of what can and cannot be said, thought and done. Therefore whether there can be an illegitimate approach to the law, in the form of an art-book or any other, is debatable (and of course the debate itself is a legalistic structure).

The shock of recognition has been a guiding principle in bringing together the texts in this book: encounters with the law, and particularly the trial, are, we have found, rife with practices commonly deemed to be within the bounds of art, representation, aesthetics, mass media, theatre, and performance. The court of law is a place where reality only exists through representation and where – traditionally – the spoken word has been the main medium for establishing the facts of the case. As Avital Ronell states in her essay, the ability, or inability of a witness or victim to translate experiences and traumas into words will be imperative for the creation of the court-reality. She writes: "Reality, whether of a historical or more personally cut nature, is not pregiven, and cannot by any means be taken for granted but recurrently foregrounds the contestability of the referent. Reality is 'always potentially in suspense, or in dispute.'"

The medium of film created a new and unmatched analogy to reality at the beginning of the twentieth century. With cinema and photography (and later TV and video) came a growing need to refer to reality and to define what reality is. The German philosopher Martin Heidegger has referred to this moment in time as defining for the modern world. The modern world is, according to him, characterized by the very fact that "the world becomes a picture."[1] One of the first to exploit this world picture with its new and potent technology in the courts was the Stalin regime, staging grotesque show-trials against the opposition, for purely political purposes. Julie A. Cassiday describes these spectacles as illegitimate not because of their reliance on theatricality and melodrama, but rather because of the injustice that "arose from the severe imbalance in access to the dramatic means of representation..."

Martin Jay poses a fundamental question about the status of the visible as it pertains to a notion of justice as impartiality. He traces the development of the figure of blindfolded Justitia and finds that rather than being associated with unmediated truth, the status of the visual in legal history is riddled with iconoclasm. Costas Douzinas' text is concerned with questions of both legal iconophobia and iconophillia. He grounds his enquiry in the case of a dispute concerning the commissioning of an altar for London's St Stephen Walbrook church from modern sculptor Henry Moore. Douzinas articulates the necessity for a critical aesthetics of the law, a "legal iconology," which facilitates the critique of normative systems that police not only beings, but regimes of visibility.

Questions concerning the changing means used to produce images of and in the trial, and particularly the turn to video, run through the essays in this book. Filmmaker Eyal Sivan researched the video documentation of the historic trial of Adolf Eichmann in Israel in 1961. He performs a case study of how recordings, partial witness in their own right, can suppress aspects of the record in becoming official memory. His rather surprising revelation is that there was little interest in the full recordings of the Eichmann trial, held in the Spielberg Archive in Israel. Sivan questions the de-emphasis of these evidentiary images in favor of the re-interviewing of witnesses as part of "history" projects focused on survivors of the Holocaust.

Cornelia Vismann, considers Otto Preminger's 1959 film *Anatomy of a Murder* in the context of the 1954 broadcasting of the hearing of Joseph McCarthy (previously the insatiable head of the Permanent Subcommittee on Investigations, who called 653 people suspected of communist affiliation in front of that committee). McCarthy represented himself against Joseph N. Welch as special counsel to the army. Vismann relates film and television respectively to contrasting types of jurisprudence, the trial and the tribunal. She suggests we continue to witness the dominance of tribunalism (which favors hearings telecast as duels) not only in the current glut of reality-TV trials, but also in the structure of the international court. Richard Mohr takes into account the court's relation to location, and also the history of tensions between the boundedness of the courtroom and the destabilizing necessity to incorporate other sites (sites of crimes, sites of witnesses and constituent audiences) into the court by way of maps, photographs and video.

Piyel Haldar also investigates the particular role images as evidence play in court. He demonstrates that although the tendency in law is to accept technologically reproduced images (such as photographs and composite identity images) as authoritative transmissions of an objective real, in practice the search for proof in an image often atomizes the whole and engages in detailism, finding in the image a multiplicity and polyvalence at odds with the mimetic basis on which legal proof rests. Peter Goodrich charts a change in the forms of visibility by which the law operates, and by which it permits the populace to witness justice being carried out. The move from a theatrical staging to one that often takes place on a monitor or screen has attendant consequences for the discipline of law and literature. Goodrich addresses the specific ways in which "each new medium underpins a new world and a changed form of law." Judy Radul has written a new text for this volume, a consciously peripatetic traversing of examples from art, theory, theatre and cinema to enquire about inside/outside relations and the effects of video on the enclosed nature of the courtroom.

The images and descriptions of artworks included in this book act as a reminder of one of the originating premises of the volume. That is, the intertwinement of aesthetics, and more specifically contemporary art, with issues also germane to legal studies, including: testimony, architecture, the staging of the trial, and objects as evidence. More broadly they also encompass the status of representation and an expanded imagining of "the law" and its effects. This relation of art and law is easily indicated by each discipline's frequent use of the term "representation." The demand to be represented within a system of rights, and the standing in of "advocates" to represent the parties in a trial, are fundamental to jurisprudence. Artistic representations also bring to mind and eye that which is absent. Theorist Claire Colebrook posits representation as a "threshold" of modernity and accounts for two juxtaposed senses, one aligned with self-determination, and the other, dominant in poststructuralist thought, that understands representation as a limit, a continual reminder that the world is not directly available, but limited by the subjects powers of representation.[2]

Art of the early twentieth century, from Picasso, Magritte and Duchamp, took pleasure in dismantling the veracity of the image. Further engagement with the power and politics by which representations transmit cultural norms occupied much of contemporary art in the west in the 1980s and early 1990s. These questions of the truth, legality, or illegitimacy of images continue to resonate in the works in this publication. Several take up the form, substance, or mood of the trial. Works that negotiate between the decision of the artist and the judgment of the viewer provoke questions around the production of narratives. The spatial transmission of power and the force of containment arise in the architectural, sculptural works. Modes of control that rely on the image, and anxiously guard the image are also considered in these works.

However, less literally, artworks engage with the very issue of representation itself as a kind of legal regime, one which recursively reminds the viewer of an absent yet legitimating original source or real world referent from which an image derives. Costas Douzinas touches upon this with his phrase "regime of visuality," which is related to Jacques Rancière's concept of the "distribution of the sensible." Both assert that what is available to perception (what can be seen to exist, what can be spoken of, and the quality of time and space) is a form of politics, and changes from era to era and place to place.

The legal dimensions of the image are preoccupied with the relation of image to referent. However the image can also be a sensation – in the sense that Deleuze and Guattari identify the artwork as a "block of sensations."[3] In this case, rather than referring to an already existing reality, the image brings something into being and therefore the discourse of representation no longer suffices to contain it. This generative potential of the image exists in artworks, and those who attend to legal themes open the door to broader questions of the image: its potential for both legitimation and lawlessness. In fact this door has been set ajar by the increasing use of media in the courtroom. The effects of the image on judgment and judgment on the image are constantly calculated.

The majority of these texts have been published elsewhere and we owe a debt of gratitude to the authors, original editors and publishers for granting us rights and for their role in initiating these discussions. We would also like to express our appreciation toward the artists and galleries that have generously contributed images.

Marit Paasche and Judy Radul

1 Martin Heidegger, *The Question Concerning Technology and Other Essays*, trans. William Lovitt (New York: Harper Perennial 1977), 129.

2 Claire Colebrook, *Philosophy and Post-Structuralist Theory*, (Edinburgh: Edinburgh University Press Ltd, 1999), 2.

3 Gilles Deleuze and Félix Guattari, *What is Philosophy?* trans. Hugh Tomlinson and Graham Burchell (New York: Columbia University Press, 1994), 164.

Marble Columns and Jupiter Lights: Theatrical and Cinematic Modeling of Soviet Show Trials in the 1920s

— Julie A. Cassiday

The explosion of theatrical and theatricalized activity during the first decade of Bolshevik power has received the attention of historians of Soviet drama, culture, and ideology alike (Rudnitsky; Fiilip-Miller; Stites).[1] From amateur theatrical circles, whose spread Viktor Shklovskii described as a cloud of microbes sweeping across the country,[2] to the celebrated mass thousands of scholars have spectacles incorporating participant-spectators, uncovered the avant-garde origins of the theatrical experimentation of the 1920s that would develop into rigid rituals of state conformity in the 1930s.[3] Due to their very name, the show trials, or *pokazatel'nye protsessy*, of Stalin's Great Terror seem likely candidates for this type of examination. However, historians of the purges tend to treat the spectacular nature of show trials exclusively as proof of their coercive illegitimacy and to ignore the tie of these legal melodramas to avant-garde theatricality of the previous decade.[4] The trials of 1936–38 were seamlessly produced displays of the enemy's repentance, confession, and desire to return to the Soviet community, displays whose authenticity depended on disguising their theatrical nature. Yet if we examine the precursors of these legal melodramas from the earlier decade, we see that the institution of the show trial evolved as part of the overall theatricalization of public life during the 1920s. Like other experiments in Revolutionary theatricality, *pokazatel'nye protsessy* put to use the dramatic means of representation available in Soviet society at the time, i.e., the theater and cinema.

Tracing the evolution of public legal spectacles reveals that the illegitimacy of Stalinist show trials arose not merely from their theatricality, a feature shared by public trials as dissimilar as the O. J. Simpson trial, the Nuremberg trials, and the Scopes Monkey trial. Rather, the injustice of the purges arose from the severe imbalance in access to the dramatic means of representation, which figured as an essential part of the Soviet show trial from its earliest instances. Unlike the defendants in the trials mentioned above, those in *pokazatel'nye protsessy* had little or no freedom to use drama in their defense, and as a result, they found themselves the victims of a totalizing script that allowed for no outcome other than guilty as charged. By analyzing the evolution of this imbalance in the two most prominent trials of the 1920s, that of the Socialist Revolutionaries (S.R.s) in 1922 and the Shakhty Affair of 1928, we discover the specific theatrical and cinematic models that merged in the Soviet show trial and helped to formulate the all-encompassing script of the Great Terror.

In discussing the evolution of the Soviet show trial, we must remember the relative novelty of adversarial law in Russia at the time of the Revolution, as well as the Bolsheviks' hostile relationship to the tsarist courts before October 1917. Public trials and representation by legal counsel had entered Russia approximately fifty years before as part of Aleksandr II's legal reforms in 1864. Pre-Revolutionary political trials served as a rite of passage for Russian radicals, such as Vera Zasulich and Sergei Nechaev, who used public courtroom proceedings to disseminate their views in spite of the often fatal outcome of such trials.[5] Like the son in Maksim Gor'kii's novel *Mother* (1906), political prisoners on trial used the courtroom as a platform for denouncing the tsarist government and broadcasting their intent to fight to the death, regardless of the judge's verdict. Initially, the October Revolution did little to change the relatively new practice of publicly trying the ruling regime's political enemies. The events of 1917 simply placed the Bolsheviks on the other side of the gavel, allowing them to suppress opposition to their government as the courts of the tsar had tried to suppress them. The novelty and clear ideological slant of pre-Revolutionary public trials made those in charge of the courts after 1917 particularly aware of the power of the judiciary as a means of propaganda. Lenin himself expounded the need for "the compulsory staging of a number of *model* trials [*obraztsovye protsessy*] (as regards speed and force of repression, and explanation of their significance to the masses of people through the courts and the press)." What he called "the educational role of trials" was just as self-evident and important as the judiciary's function of rendering proletarian justice.[6] In addition, the proletarian court did not profess any objectivity, which legal specialists of the time labeled bourgeois falsification.[7] Hence, those organizing the model trials urged by Lenin generated a variety of legal propaganda, including books, pamphlets, articles, and lectures, that made these spectacles comprehensible and accessible to the masses they hoped to educate.

Alongside these more traditional media, the cinema and theater also helped to disseminate the messages of Soviet show trials. Documentary films recorded the proceedings of the era's most prominent court cases and allowed for their distribution across the entire country. The theater provided the opportunity not only to reenact famous trials of the day but also to create entirely new, albeit fictional trials that provided precisely the message and verdict needed for proletarian justice. This new genre of legal propaganda, called the mock trial or *agitsud*, evolved simultaneously with the Soviet show trial and provided the paradigm of confession and repentance that would later characterize the purges of the 1930s. During the 1920s, both actual and mock trials fell under the rubric of the *pokazatel'nyi protsess* and only the slenderest of lines divided the two types of trials in theory and practice. Although the defendants, judges, and sentences in the *agitsud* were entirely fictional, it attacked the same problems as actual show trials of the time.[8] And in spite of the show trial's indisputable reality, actual court cases of the 1920s increasingly contained traits of Russia's avant-garde theater borrowed by the *agitsud*. As the trial of the S.R.s and the Shakhty Affair show, the incorporation of cinema and theater into legal propaganda during the 1920s resulted in a palpable shift in the paradigm of the Soviet show trial. Although the stage and screen were initially intended to augment the propaganda of actual trials, they ultimately modified the very message they disseminated and made the Stalinist show trial a theatrical spectacle played to a movie audience.

— The Trial of the Socialist Revolutionaries in 1922

The 1922 trial of the S.R.s holds significance for this study not due to its primacy, since it was by no means the first show trial held in Soviet Russia, but rather due to its remarkable visibility both within and outside of the Soviet Union. The celebrity of the defendants, the Central Committee of the Socialist Revolutionary Party, and the timing of their indictment allowed Bolshevik legal experts to make the trial a synthesis of the first five years of Revolutionary justice.[9] The S.R.s had posed a serious threat to the consolidation of Bolshevik support at the time of the Revolution;[10] the 1922 trial gave those who had won the battles of 1917–21 a chance to distinguish themselves from their former allies by labeling them enemies of the new regime. In addition, the trial of the S.R.s took place immediately after the adoption on June 1, 1922 of a new criminal code that instituted the legal foundation of the New Economic Policy (NEP). A lawsuit abiding by the new code's articles would demonstrate to the world the Soviet Union's fundamental legality, as well as the lengths to which the new government would go in suppressing opposition. The massive propaganda campaign surrounding the S.R. Trial broadcast to a worldwide audience, for the first time, the theatrical and cinematic methods of constituting justice that would dominate later trials of the1930s, even if the outcome of the 1922 trial resembled that of its pre-Revolutionary precursors more than its Stalinist successors.[11]

Preparations for this international media spectacle began long before the two months of public hearings that lasted from June 8 to August 7, 1922. The twelve most prominent leaders of the S.R. Party had already been arrested by August of 1921; and as soon as the Soviet government announced its intention to try the incarcerated S.R.s, it became embroiled in negotiations with the three Socialist Internationals, which claimed a right to monitor any legal proceedings conducted against their members. After meeting in Berlin with the Soviet spokesman Karl Radek, representatives of the three Internationals obtained permission to defend the S.R.s and a guarantee from the Soviet government that those on trial would be spared capital punishment.

Two alleged ex-members of the S.R. party, G. I. Semenov and L. V. Konopleva, provided evidence that its Central Committee had conducted an armed struggle against the Soviet state, which included two attempts to assassinate prominent, Soviet statesmen (Volodarskii, who indeed had been murdered, and Lenin), and treasonous contacts with hostile, foreign powers.[12] The S.R.s vehemently denied both their participation in these activities and the allegation that such actions constituted a crime, resting their defense on two points. First, indictments against the S.R.s were based on the new Criminal Code instituted almost a year after the accused were deprived of the liberty to commit any crime; the Bolshevik court violated a basic tenet of Western law by applying its laws retroactively. Second, the Soviet government contradicted the general amnesty it had granted the S.R.s in February of 1919.[13] Nonetheless, the prosecution at the trial disregarded these objections, forcing both the Soviet and then the foreign defenders, including Emile Vandervelde and Arthur Waters of the Belgian Labor Party, and Kurt Rosenfeld and Theodore Liebknecht of the German Independent Socialist Party, to abandon their advocacy of the S.R.s as futile.[14]

A public protest took place in Moscow on June 20, 1922, supporting the proletarian court and demanding the execution of the accused S.R.s. After passionate denunciations of the Soviet court, the ten men and two women on trial were found guilty of membership in an anti-Soviet organization under Article 60 of the new penal code. In spite of Radek's earlier assurances to the contrary, the proletarian court sentenced the defendants to the highest possible measure of punishment, i.e., death. However, under strong pressure from the international socialist movement, the Soviet court commuted the death sentence to life imprisonment that would keep the S.R. Central Committee hostage in Soviet prisons as a guarantee for the good behavior of the few S.R.s still at large within the country. In spite of the international controversy caused by the 1922 trial, the case against the S.R.s demonstrated graphically Nikolai Bukharin's statement that in the Soviet Union, "one party is in power and all the others are in prison."[15]

The S.R. trial publicized this message effectively due to the theatricality of courtroom practice in the 1922 case. The

Revolutionary tribunals instituted immediately after 1917 were both conceived and perceived as Soviet renditions of the highly theatrical public trials of the French Revolution.[16] Although explicit references to a French model would quickly disappear, public trials in the Soviet Union of the 1920s continued to be modeled on their predecessors from approximately 130 years before. The consciousness of the theatricality of public trials suggested by the French Revolutionary model allowed for the incorporation of two key principles of avant-garde drama, i.e., spectator participation and elimination of the boundary between the audience and the stage. Interestingly enough, these prescriptions for the Russian theater originated in the plans of the Symbolist poet/philosopher Viacheslav Ivanov for a Dionysian theater some twenty years earlier. In spite of the Symbolist and indeed mystical origins of his theories, almost every manifesto for the "new theater" published in the intervening years replicated Ivanov's call for participation and removal of the so-called fourth wall on stage, as the writings of Anatolii Lunacharskii, Platon Kerzhentsev, Nikolai Evreinov, and Vsevolod Meyerhold attest.[17] Like their Symbolist predecessor, the various new theaters from the early decades of the twentieth century all called for these two features because they promised to make drama capable of shaping and even revolutionizing the lives of spectators.[18] The legal spectacle in the great, columned chamber of the former Nobles' Club in Moscow replicated these formulae of the avant-garde theater in the hopes of magnifying and propagating the lessons of the trial and with the ultimate aim of bringing Revolution into the lives of the trial's audience.

To achieve these ends, the courtroom of the S.R. Trial was modeled on a theatrical stage. Foreign press correspondents quickly noted the set pieces, props, costumes, and dramatis personae of the trial, calling it "as dramatic an event as ever was staged, even in Russia."[19] Correspondent for The Nation Paxton Hibben gives an eloquent description of the theatrical design of the 1922 courtroom:

> The room is lofty; twenty-eight immense marble pillars surround it, and from a high balcony there hang between these pillars twenty-six enormous chandeliers, with twenty-eight smaller ones hanging from the ceiling to light the balcony, all like conical birdcages of scintillating

> crystal, in strings and pendants, on a framework of wrought bronze, like dull gold. But none of these are lighted – this is no ball of nobles. But in each of four small chandeliers, a businesslike, high candle-power electric light bulb has been thrust between the strings of crystal, and burns there like a glowing bird in its cage.
>
> The court sits on a slightly elevated platform at one end of the great hall, once the concert stage of the Club of the Nobles. Above the heads of the five judges, stretched across four of the pillars, is a band of red bunting, like a banner while from one pillar hangs a poster representing a worker at an anvil, against a red, rising sun, holding a loft in one hand a placard on which is the inevitable "Workers of the world, unite!"[20]

As Hibben's description points out, the stage for the trial visually represented the pre-Revolutionary regime. The addition of red bunting and the ubiquitous icons of Soviet power placed a distinctly Soviet set on the tsarist stage. By replacing the once glittering, candle-lit chandeliers with four stark, electric, light bulbs, the audience of the trial literally saw the opulent, imperial stage in a new light. The high-wattage bulbs shed the glaring light of modern, technological truth on the proceedings of the trial, illuminating the contrast between pre-Revolutionary decadence and proletarian justice.

On such a stage of contrasts, we would expect the *dramatis personae* to costume themselves in typical proletarian or Bolshevik garb, i.e., to place themselves in clothes that complemented the banners and lights of the trial's set. On the contrary, neither court officials nor the accused donned working clothes and leather jackets, as Hibben describes later in the same article:

> Piaterkov [*sic*], the president of the tribunal, in a dark blue blouse with white polka dots, and a black coat over it, occupies the center ... N. Bukharin, in shirt sleeves, his collar unbuttoned, his hair rumpled, his trousers unbelted and constantly slipping down as he darts here and there.... Most of the accused are in their shirt sleeves, though no one else in the court is save Bukharin.... Most of the men are lean-faced, with soft shirts open at the throat and hair brushed back to resemble André Chénier or Lamartine or Shelley.[21]

Rather than copy the Bolshevik soldier or Soviet worker, both the prosecution and the defense at the S.R. Trial took stereotypical images of the romantic revolutionary as the model for their costume. Although the ruling power had changed since the days of pre-Revolutionary political trials, all the participants in the S.R. case used stock images that they had learned from their experience in tsarist courts. By imitating the informality of Chénier, Lamartine, and Shelley, court officials and defendants alike tried to build sympathy in the trial's audience by casting themselves in the role of the romantic revolutionary.

Yet the accused S.R.s found themselves at a clear disadvantage in garnering such sympathy since those organizing the 1922 case chose the trial's audience just as carefully as its set and costumes. Foreign press correspondents who obtained tickets to the trial were scrutinized multiple times before entering the courtroom.[22] Common Soviet citizens interested in attending the trial found it impossible to get tickets if their names did not appear on a predetermined list of audience members.[23] Tickets to public hearings, approximately 1,200 for each day of the trial, were distributed through the workplace, and attendance was compulsory for loyal trade union and party members.[24] The need for the correct expression of audience participation at the trial proved so great that GPU agents even sat among the trial's spectators to provoke appropriate responses to testimony and the final verdict.[25] By carefully assembling spectators, trial organizers hoped to control their reactions and to create an ideal audience that would carry the trial's message from the courtroom into the streets. Accounts of the actual attentiveness and enthusiasm of the hand-picked audience vary widely; nonetheless, the selection of audience members for the S.R. trial amounted to no less than the scripting of the spectators' role in the unfolding legal drama.[26]

The ultimate expression of scripted audience participation in the S.R. trial was the mass demonstration of June 20, 1922 on the fourth anniversary of Volodarskii's death. An estimated 150,000–300,000 people marched through Red Square, led by members of the court.[27] After a prolonged series of speeches by workers and officials, the demonstration burst into the courtroom to voice support for the Proletarian court and demanded the heads of the accused S.R.s. As in the case of ticket distribution, people's genuine participation in the June 20th demonstration has been sharply questioned.[28] The international press strongly censured Soviet authorities for allowing the public to breach the sanctity of the courtroom; nonetheless, the court willingly risked rendering its verdict invalid by encouraging and even simulating (if the accounts cited above are accurate) the interference of the Soviet masses in the S.R. Trial. Following the model of the avant-garde theater, the June 20th demonstration demolished the barrier separating the stage of the court from its audience and allowed the trial's spectators to take part in the legal drama.

In spite of their ability to control the audience of the S.R. Trial, court officials found themselves incapable of scripting the testimony of the men they had indicted. In 1922, the accused S.R.s and the Western socialists defending them could still use the trial as a platform for condemning Soviet excesses and preaching their own brand of socialism. The defendants denied their guilt and even managed to stage a number of their own dramatic moments, such as a hunger strike and the publication in the West of vitriolic letters denouncing the Soviet court, in an attempt to sway public opinion in their favor. The final statements of the accused S.R.s were striking for their refusal to confess and complete lack of repentance; instead, they declared, "If death awaits us, we will accept it without fear, and if we are to remain among the living, then we will conduct our battle with you after our liberation just we have conducted it to this day."[29] Such defiance earned the praise of socialists in the West, but the accused S.R.s grossly miscalculated the potential impact of their actions if they believed that such statements would aid in their acquittal.[30] Although the theatrical means of representation still lay within reach of the S.R. defendants, the Soviet authorities' complete control over the national media, in particular newspapers and the cinema, made their dramatic gestures, as well as those of their foreign defenders, entirely in vain.

As Dziga Vertov's coverage of the trial in *Kinopravda* shows, it proved to be a very simple task of editing to delete the S.R.s' denunciations from newsreels distributed to movie houses across the Soviet Union. Interestingly enough, Vertov's portrayal of the trial in *Kinopravda* and a short documentary that recycled this footage did not focus upon the counter-Revolutionary nature of the accused S.R.s; the massive barrage of propaganda that preceded the trial had already explained at great length that the defendants were enemies of the Soviet state by the time the trial began.[31] Instead, the 1922 newsreels and 1923 film show a semicircle of weather-beaten tables that stand on approximately the same level as the trial's audience and behind which court officials casually shuffle through the heaps of legal documents pertinent to the case. This arrangement gave the courtroom a surprisingly intimate atmosphere, one in which spectators occupied the same space as the members of the court, who dressed, smoked, and even sat in the same circle of chairs as they did. Vertov's films not only cut testimony unflattering to the Soviet government from records of the trial but also communicated to its viewers that those attending the hearings participated in passing judgment.

To intensify the message of spectator participation that created contact between the courtroom and real life, Vertov inserted a short fictional passage into the final edition of *Kinopravda* devoted to the trial (no. 8). Most of the newsreel depicts testimony by the accused, their defenders, and members of the proletarian court. In the final minutes of the film, a legal stenographer transcribes the words of Commissar for Enlightenment Lunacharskii, which are printed on a flier within the hour and distributed to the crowds outside the courtroom. The flier then becomes a newspaper, which those on the street buy and read. One copy of the newspaper is pasted on the wall, a second is handed to a passenger on a moving trolley, and a third is given to the driver of a motorcar, all of whom read and discuss the news with great interest. Curiously enough, Vertov cast himself in the role of the trolley passenger to show how spectator participation propagated the lessons of the 1922 Trial. Even if the S.R. defendants still had access to the theatrical means of representation, the Soviet state monopolized the cinematic means of representation, which allowed for the correction of any shortcomings in the dramatic spectacle of the 1922 trial and the dissemination of the message deemed most appropriate for citizens of the Soviet Union.

During the next six years, enemies of the Soviet state, including Boris Savinkov, the Provocateur Okladskii, and Patriarch Tikhon, were tried in much the same way as the S.R.s. By and large, these trials resembled the 1922 case and copied the theatrical and cinematic modeling that characterized the early paradigm of the Soviet show trial. The defendants in such trials rarely confessed their guilt, and when they did, they showed no signs of remorse for their crimes and no desire to return to Soviet society. Organizers of these early show trials followed a theatrical paradigm that brought the audience of the trials into the legal drama and thereby erased the boundary between the courtroom and real life. The combination of theater and cinema promised to intensify the Revolutionary message of such trials and to broadcast it to the largest number of Soviet citizens possible.

— The Shakhty Affair in 1928

At the end of the NEP, a crucial change occurred in the paradigm of the Soviet show trial, as the 1928 case of fifty-three coal-mining engineers from the Donbass, commonly called the Shakhty Affair, demonstrates. The institution of the first Five-Year Plan in the same year required the mobilization of all of Soviet society toward the plan's ambitious goals, as well as finding a scapegoat when these goals had not been reached.[32] No longer did the enemy of the people follow the model of the S.R.s and proudly state his opposition to the Soviet regime; instead, he was an apparently upstanding member of society who secretly sabotaged the construction of socialism. Modifications in the paradigm of the show trial proved necessary to detect these hidden saboteurs and to force them to confess publicly their responsibility for any shortfalls in meeting the targets of the planned economy. The Central Committee of the Communist Party under the direction of Stalin himself encouraged the Shakhty Affair as the new legal model for routing the hidden enemies of socialism.[33]

An overview of the basic events of the Shakhty Affair shows that the 1928 court case had much in common with the S.R. Trial of 1922, as well as with the trials of the Great Terror for which it would provide the model. Public hearings in the

Shakhty Affair opened on May 18, 1928 in the glare of international media; as was true six years before, preparation for trial began months before with the arrest of the accused and a coordinated media campaign.[34] By the time the Shakhty Affair officially opened in the same columned hall of what had become the House of Trade Unions in Moscow, the Soviet public was thoroughly familiar with the group of German and Russian engineers from the highest echelons of the Soviet coal industry, all accused of coordinating a vast network of sabotage whose roots lay outside the Soviet Union and whose branches reached across Soviet heavy industry.[35]

The inclusion of a few German engineers among the Shakhty defendants created understandable tension in German-Soviet relations, and as a result, a remarkably small amount of time and attention was spent on questioning the German engineers about their alleged crimes.[36] Instead, the prosecution put most of its effort into extracting confessions from the Russian engineers. Nikolai Krylenko headed the prosecution of both the S.R. Trial and the Shakhty Affair, but he successfully extracted confessions from the majority of the men on trial in 1928 and managed to convict forty-nine of the fifty-three Shakhty engineers with these confessions. Nevertheless, the Shakhty Affair did not pass without incident. Foreign press correspondents and their Soviet counterparts were often at a loss to make sense of the murky circumstances of the crimes and the confusing series of confessions, recantations, and repeated confessions that came to light during the course of testimony. The Soviet media relentlessly demanded the death sentence for the Shakhty engineers, just as it had for the accused S.R.s in 1922. After approximately six weeks of public hearings, the court handed down its verdict on July 5, 1928: three engineers were acquitted, eleven were sentenced to death, thirty-eight were given prison sentences of lengths varying from one and a half to ten years, and a single remaining Russian engineer "fell ill ... with a protective conscious reaction," i.e., suffered a mental breakdown during interrogation and was hospitalized.[37] The trial's outcome was taken as proof positive of the existence of sabotage in Russian heavy industry, a fact that initiated a series of wrecking trials that spread ever wider throughout Soviet industry and ever deeper into the Soviet technical intelligentsia.

As in the 1922 trial, the former Moscow Nobles' Club provided the backdrop for the Shakhty Affair. Yet this time, the organizers of the trial constructed a special, elevated platform for court officials, witnesses, and the accused. Foreign press correspondents described a courtroom modeled on the theatrical stage but ready for the movie camera:

> Their presence [of the defending counsel], purely a matter of form, served only to enhance the scenic effects of the specially built and artificially lighted judicial dais, which was large enough to hold the fifty-one defendants, three judges, the prosecutor and his staff, a dozen lawyers, half a dozen stenographers and a large detachment of GPU guards armed with rifles and fixed bayonets.[38]

> Sputtering Jupiter lights played on the scene, photographers and cinema cameramen maneuvered their equipment into position...The gleaming white marble column shad sprouted ugly clusters of loud-speakers. Immense crystal chandelier shimmered in the shifting lights. But the dominant note was a blatant red – red cloths on the tables on the platform, red inscriptions on the walls.[39]

As had been the case six years previously, the tsarist stage was equipped with a Soviet set, replete with red banners and high-wattage lights. The new additions of an elevated platform and hanging loudspeakers made the theatrical action of the courtroom all the more ready for radio transmission and movie cameras.

Although the camera-ready sets of the two trials bore some similarity, the costuming of the actors in the Shakhty Affair differed significantly from that of 1922. If the accused S.R.s had copied the romantic garb of nineteenth-century revolutionaries, the Shakhty engineers donned typical worker's clothing in hopes of eliciting the sympathy of the proletarian court, as the correspondent for *Berliner Tageblatt* noted: "The accused, in jackets, top-boots, and often without collars, look themselves quite proletarian."[40] Given the fact that the engineers on trial came primarily from the upper ranks of the technical intelligentsia, their decision to dress down as workers shows that a small portion of the dramatic means of representation still lay in the hands of the accused in 1928. Nonetheless, comments on the costuming of the defendants were all but drowned out by the particularly strong reaction which head prosecutor Krylenko drew with his choice of clothes, as New York Times correspondent Eugene Lyons noted:

> Throughout the six crowded weeks of the trial [Krylenko] wore sports clothes – riding breeches, puttees, a hunting jacket. We called it a hunting outfit and its fitness for his role added to the drama of the proceedings. Krylenko, the man-hunter.[41]

The emblematic significance of Krylenko's costume pointed to his role as huntsman for the truth and tracker of the class enemy.[42] The six years that separated the Shakhty Affair from the S.R. Trial had taught not only Krylenko but also the defendants a new kind of costuming that symbolically depicted their roles in the legal drama. The Soviet court had refined its set and costuming by 1928, and it correspondingly perfected the procedures for audience selection in the Shakhty Affair. Once again, journalists and the public could gain entrance to the 1928 trial by pass only, and the secret police distributed tickets to transform the audience into "an accusing chorus, mocking the pitiful attempts of some of the prisoners to defend themselves."[43] Moreover, approximately three times the number of spectators in 1922 attended daily sessions of the Shakhty Affair, and the constantly changing, daily audience of 4,000 made for an estimated total of 100,000–150,000 members of the Soviet working class who attended the 1928 trial.[44] By bringing the greatest possible number of Soviet citizens into the trial, organizers hoped to change each individual spectator through participation in the legal drama and to turn these spectators into living conduits of trial propaganda who would carry the lessons they had absorbed from the courtroom into their homes and workplaces.[45]

Sheer size was not the only salient feature of the 1928 trial's audience, and spectator participation in the events of the Shakhty Affair figured just as prominently as it had six years before. Propaganda described the involvement of the working class in all phases of the Shakhty Affair, particularly in raising and lowering the curtain on the intricately constructed legal drama. Common workers had allegedly uncovered the original sabotage that resulted in litigation, demanding that the wreckers be called to account in court.[46] In addition, four engineers sat on the court's raised dais and officially represented the participation of proletarian spectators in judging the defendants. Copying a technique used in the *agitsud*, the court included these four representatives of the trial's immense audience to assure the actual instigators and judges of the trial, i.e., Soviet workers, that the court would carry out their will.[47] Similar to the angry mob at the June 20, 1922 demonstration during the S.R. trial, the audience of the Shakhty Affair even broke through the fourth wall, entered the courtroom, and demanded the death sentence for the accused engineers.[48] Such participation supposedly occurred spontaneously, yet it was actually part of the audience's script that included the roles of police, judge, and jury in the courtroom and beyond.

If we can compare the Shakhty Affair to the Trial of the S.R.s in a discussion of set, costuming, and audience participation, all such comparisons break down once we examine the tightly-cessfully defied the Soviet court and maintained their fierce opposition to the Bolshevik regime, even if they lost their case at the 1922 trial's end. The mere fact that foreign defenders were allowed to enter the courtroom of the earlier trial meant that the accused S.R.s still had a significant amount of control in representing themselves. On the contrary, the Shakhty Affair culminated in the confession of over 90 percent of the accused and took the form of "a modern morality play with Evil personified on the stage. Evil confessing, even insisting on its own evil nature."[49] While a small number of the defendants forgot their lines and others willfully improvised out of turn, the Shakhty Affair seldom deviated from its set script of confession and repentance.[50] Under the strict guidance of prosecutor Krylenko, each defendant methodically revealed first his criminal activities, second his counter-Revolutionary sentiments, third his ultimate goal of overthrowing the Soviet regime, and fourth his desire to return to productive life as a Soviet citizen. The venue had changed and consequently the result of such testimony was imprisonment or death, but those who confessed in the Shakhty Affair were actually repeating the same formula for confession, repentance, and reintegration into society of fictional defendants in the *agitsud*. Just as in mock trials of a few years earlier, this rigid formula for confession compelled spectators of the trial to identify themselves with the defendants. The same "accusing chorus" that condemned the Shakhty engineers' alleged crimes identified with the enemies of the people; and spectators found themselves, like the accused, compelled to undergo the ritual of *samokritika*, i.e., to detect and correct any counter-Revolutionary tendencies that might be lurking in them.[51]

The ability to compel *samokritika* in both defendants and spectators shows that the Soviet court had gained command of all the dramatic means of representation by the time of the Shakhty Affair. Nonetheless, there were noticeable cracks in the theatrical facade of the 1928 trial, missed cues and fumbled props that the court would learn to fix by the time of the Great Terror.[52] Some of the Shakhty defendants confessed too zealously, while others refused to confess at all.[53] The use of props in the trial was so poorly coordinated that foreign press correspondents made fun of "A raincoat, sent from Germany as a 'signal' for sabotage."[54] In one botched performance, the engineer Skorutto first refused to confess in public, then admitted to charges of wrecking. As it happened, his wife attended that day's session, and when she heard her husband's confession, she cried out, "It's a lie! Kolia, why are you doing this!"[55] Skorutto immediately retracted his initial statement and the head prosecutor asked for a court recess. After several days away from the witness stand, Skorutto returned to uphold his original confession, predictably expressing his desire to return to the Soviet work force.[56] By 1928, the Soviet court had learned to monopolize the legal drama by whatever means necessary; but court authorities had yet to perfect the implementation of the dramatic means of representation and to create the seamless spectacles of 1936–38.

The newsreels and short documentary films of the Shakhty Affair reinforce this sense of hierarchy newly introduced in to show trials.[57] Even if the *Sovkino-Zhurnal* newsreels of the Shakhty Affair lack the cinematic polish of Vertov's work and later feature-length trial documentaries from the 1930s, they nonetheless show the rigidly hierarchical organization of the 1928 court as opposed to the relatively egalitarian staging of the S.R. Trial. The newsreels show the raised platform of the

Shakhty Affair supporting an unbroken line of massive, wooden tables with equally massive, wooden chairs, whose backs rise at least a foot above the heads of court officials. Those who watched the newsreels of the 1928 case replicated the gaze of spectators who attended the trial's public hearings: while the defendants were approximately on the same level as the viewer, one had literally to look up through the hierarchy to see the judge, president, and people's representatives at the trial. Although the proletarian spectator had been told that he acted as police, judge, and jury in the Shakhty Affair, the physical separation of the audience from the court visually represented his true place at the bottom of the hierarchical legal drama. The spectacle of the Shakhty Affair indeed maintained the rhetoric of audience participation that had been a feature of show trials since 1922. In spite of this, the hierarchy of the court, as seen in these newsreels, made it unequivocally clear to the spectator that his actual role was closer to the accused, whose position in the courtroom approximated his own.

The *Sovkino-Zhurnal* reports also served to homogenize and discipline the Shakhty Affair's audience, i.e., to reduce the many individual viewers who had their own, personal reactions in Vertov's newsreels from1922 to a single, obedient,

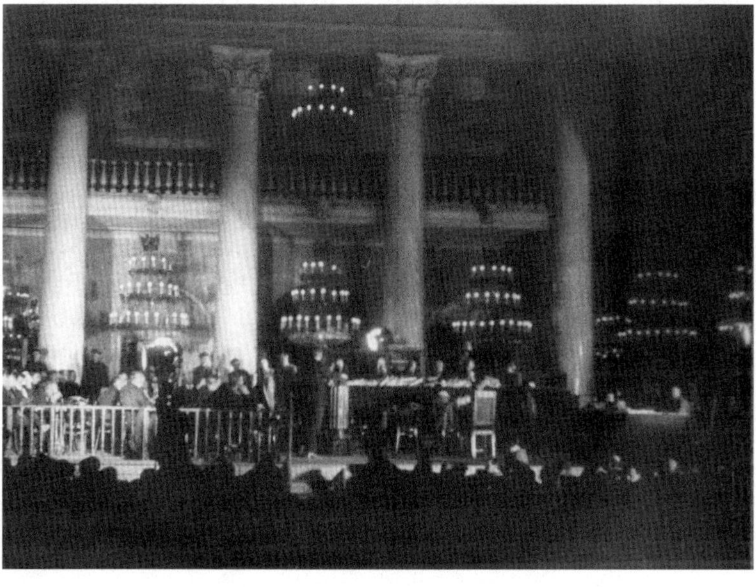

Taken from *Sovkino-Zhurnal* no 23 (1928)
Reproduced with permission from the Russian State Documentary Film and Photo Archive.

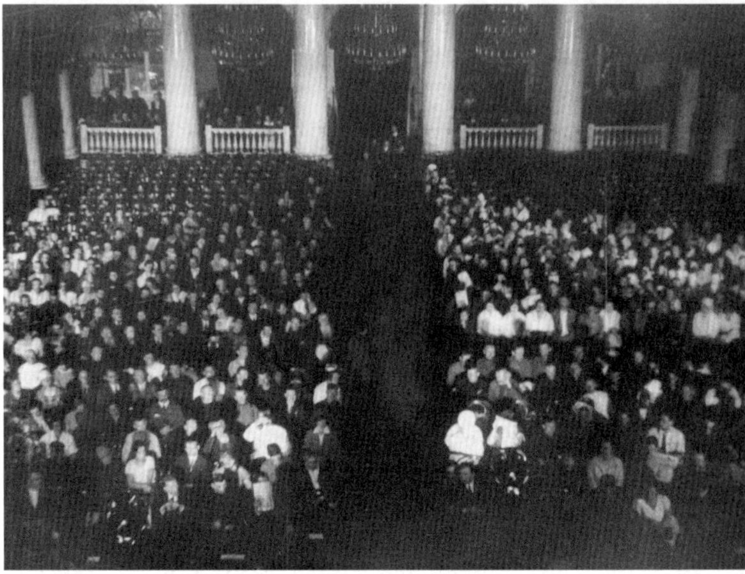

Still showing the audience of the Shakty Affair. Taken from *Sovkino-Zhurnal* no 23 (1928) Reproduced with permission from the

spectating mass. In *Kinopravda*, Vertov depicted viewers at the S.R. Trial primarily through close-ups, often showing them as more interested in their cigarettes and the other people around them than in the testimony of the trial. In the rigidly hierarchical story of *Sovkino-Zhurnal,* the Shakhty Affair's massive audience occupied orderly, parallel rows of chairs, with all eyes fixed on the raised dais at the front of the room. Those who watched the Shakhty Affair's attentive and disciplined audience in these newsreels could have no doubts as to what their own response to this spectacle should be. No degree of distraction, dissent, or humor was allowed in the mass audience of this most serious of legal dramas. The rhetoric of the Shakhty Affair repeated stock phrases brought from the avant-garde theater, such as the need for spectator participation and erasing the boundary between stage and life; nonetheless, the 1928 trial scripted the form that audience participation could take just as strictly as the confessions of the accused engineers.

The hierarchical and totalizing discourse of the Shakhty Affair made the 1928 trial what several historians have called the dress rehearsal for later show trials of the 1930s.[58] During the following decade, each successive show trial built upon the foundation of accusations and confessions of the trial preceding it, honing the theatrical and cinematic techniques of the Stalinist show trial to virtual perfection.[59] What started with an obscure group of mining engineers in the Donbass coal region eventually reached such Revolutionary leaders as Rykov, Tomskii, and Bukharin in the purge trials of 1936–38.[60] Only when the hostility of the capitalist West resulted in open gunfire at the start of the Second World War, did the ever widening circle of sabotage, espionage, and suspicion cease to find its stage in the columned hall of the Moscow House of Trade Unions.

Show trials of the Great Terror downplayed their theatrical and cinematic modeling and even used accusations of melodrama and theatricality against their defendants. Nevertheless, the S.R. Trial of 1922 and the Shakhty Affair of 1928 bare the dramatic devices that made these later *pokazatel'nye protsessy* effective yet unjust legal spectacles. The S.R. Trial brought theater and cinema into the courtroom, while the Shakhty Affair concentrated their power in the hands of the Soviet court. If we doubt the effectiveness of this theatrical paradigm played to a movie audience, we need only to remember the startling successes of collectivization and industrialization that accompanied the show trials of the 1930s, as well as the rapid spread of legal

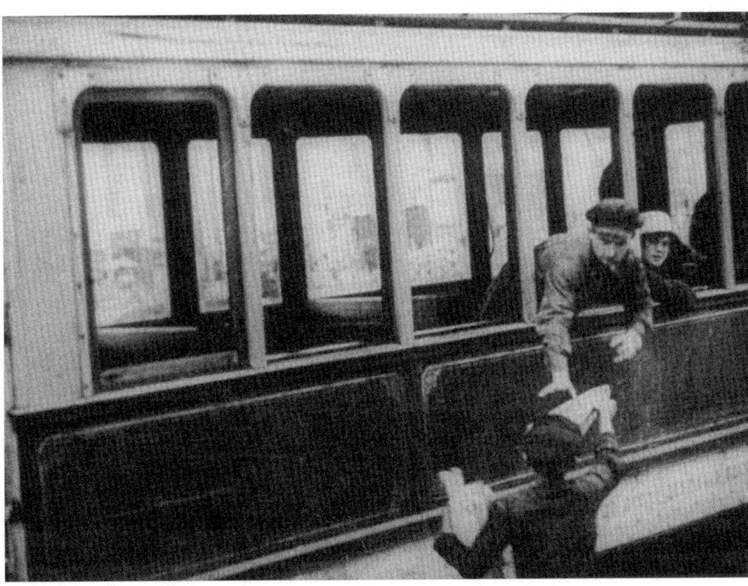

Dziga Vertov receives a newspaper with coverage of the S.R. Trial. Reproduced with permission from the Russian State Documentary Film and Photo Archive.

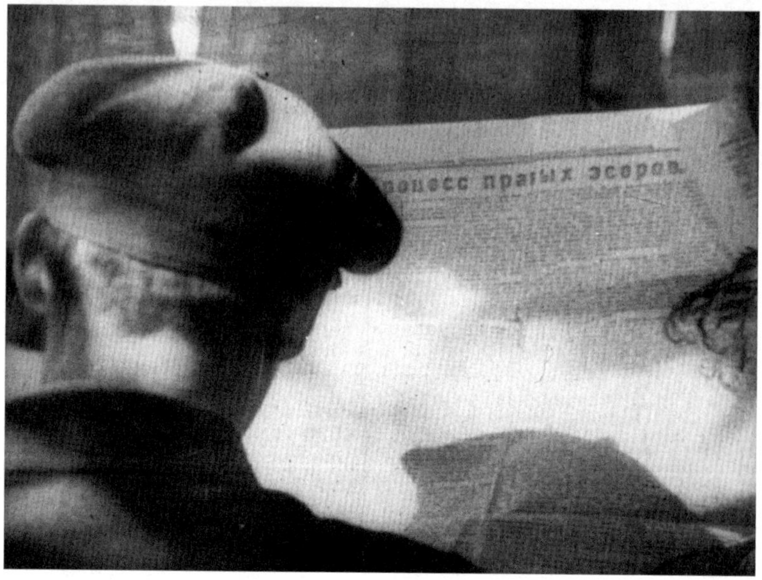

Still from Dviga Vertov's *Kinopravda* no 8 (1922)
Reproduced with permission from the
Russian State Documentary Film and Photo Archive

melodrama back onto the Soviet stage and screen. The fictional crimes of the hidden enemies, saboteurs, and spies exposed by show trials found their expression and justification in works such as Maksim Gor'kii's drama *Somov and Others* (1931, first published 1941), Aleksandr Afinogenov's play *Fear* (1931), and a myriad of documentary and feature films.[61] Ultimately, the Soviet show trial proved capable of fulfilling the extremely ambitious if not utopian goals of the avant-garde theater. Plans for a Dionysian or Revolutionary theater that would spill into everyday life, embrace ever larger groups of people, and transform social life into an aesthetic endeavor never achieved these goals within the theater proper. Yet the Stalinist show trial invaded all of Soviet reality, engulfed an ever larger part of the population, and changed society into a vast arena for fabricated indictment, confession, and contrition. Much as the theatrical experiments of the twenties ended in the dictatorship of the director in the Russian theater, the political experiments of the same time ended in Stalin's dictatorship of the Soviet state. By the end of the 1930s, Soviet statecraft had become Soviet stagecraft: those who wrote, directed, and staged the script controlled the actors as well as the audience.

Julie A. Cassiday "Marble Columns and Jupiter Lights: Theatrical and Cinematic Modeling of Soviet Show Trials in the 1920s" was first published in *The Slavic and East European Journal*, vol. 42, no. 4 (Winter, 1998), 640–660. ©SEEJ

1 See Konstantin Rudnitsky, *Russian and Soviet Theatre: Tradition and the Avant-Garde*, trans. Roxane Permar, ed. Lesley Milne (London: Thames and Hudson, 1988); René Fülöp-Miller, *The Mind and Face of Bolshevism: An Examination of Cultural Life in Soviet Russia*, trans. F.S. Flint and D.F. Tait (London: G.P. Putnam's Sons 1927); Richard Stites, *Revolutionary Dreams: Utopian Vision and Experimental Life in the Russian Revolution* (New York: Oxford University Press, 1989).

2 Viktor Shklovskii, *Khod konia: Sbornik statei* (Moscow/Berlin: Gelikon, 1923), 59.

3 See Katerina Clark, *Petersburg, Crucible of Cultural Revolution* (Cambridge: Harvard University Press, 1995); Boris Groys, *The Total Art of Stalinism: Avant-Garde, Aesthetic Dictatorship, and Beyond*, trans. Charles Rougle (Princeton: Princeton University Press 1992); James von Geldern, *Bolshevik Festivals, 1917–1920* (Berkeley: University of California Press, 1993).

4 The use of a theatrical metaphor to condemn the Great Terror as illegitimate legal practice is so widespread that it occurs in virtually every document on the topic, which I have had the opportunity to examine. Interesting examples include G. S Agabekov, *Ch.K.za rabotoi.* (Berlin: Strela, 1931), 79–86; Anton Antonov-Ovseenko, "Teatr Iosifa Stalina" *Teatr 8* (1988): 118–39; N. P Antsiferov, *Iz dum o bylom: Vospominaniia*, (Moscow: Feniks Kul'turnaia initsiativa, 1992), 354; A. Avtvorkhanov *Tekhnologiia vlasti* (Frankfurt/Main: Posev 1976), 112; Roi Medvedev, *O Staline i stalinizme* (Moscow: Progress, 1990) 247; Aleksandr I. Solzhenitsyn, *The Gulag Archipelago, 1918–1956: An Experiment in Literary Investigation I–II,* trans. Thomas Whitney (New York: Harper & Row, 1973), 362–411; H. Hessell Tiltman, *The Terror in Europe* (New York: Frederick A. Stokes, 1931), 92; Robert C. Tucker, *Stalin in Power: The Revolution from Above, 1928–1941* (New York: W. W. Norton & Company, 1990), 6, 77, 171; Dmitrii Volkogonov, *Triumf i tragediia: Politichesii portret I. V. Stalina v 2-kh knigakh* (Moscow: Agentstva pechati Novosti, 1989) and Bertram D.Wolfe, "Dress Rehearsals for the Great Terror," *Studies in Comparative Communism 2* (1970), 404, 413. For memoirs of show trials in Eastern Europe that also use the theatrical metaphor in this way, see Paul Barton, *Prague d l'heure de Moscou: Analyse d'une democratie populaire* (Paris: Editions Pierre Horay, 1954) 75–89; Eugen Loebl, *My Mind on Trial* (New York: Harcourt Brace Jovanovich, 1976), 189, 202–3; and Artur London, *L'aveu: Dans l'engrenage du Procès de Prage* (Paris: Gallimard, 1968), 255. Unlike most historians, Sheila Fitzpatrick has bared the theatrical devices of provincial show trials in the late 1930s to reveal their function as "participatory political theater," Fitzpatrick, "How the Mice Buried the Cat: Scenes from the Great Purges of 1937 in the Russian Provinces," *The Russian Review 52* (1993): 299–320.

5 V. Soukhomline, *Les Proces Celebres de la Russie* (Paris: Payot, 1937), 5.

6 Trotskii was also firmly convinced of the educational value of public trials, as his interest in a show trial of Nikolai II in 1918 illustrates: "I proposed that we hold an open court trial which would reveal a picture of the whole reign, with its peasant policy, labor policy, national minority and cultural policies, its two wars, etc. The proceedings of the trial would be broadcast throughout the country by radio; in the *volosts*, accounts of the proceedings would be read and commented upon every day. Lenin replied to the effect that it would be very good if it were feasible." See Leon Trotsky, *Trotsky's Diary in Exile: 1935*, trans. Elena Zarudnaya (Cambridge: Harvard University Press, 1958), 80. However, Nikolai II was never brought to trial and Trotskii's plans remained entirely unrealized; see Mark Steinberg and Vladimir M. Khrustaläv, *The Fall of the Romanovs: Political Dreams and Personal Struggles in a Time of Revolution* (New Haven: Yale University Press, 1995), 224–5, 233–4, 287–8. Trotskii repeated his expression of interest in the educational role of public trials in a telegram discussing the organization of the 1919 Trial of Mironov; see V. A. Kovalev, *Raspiatie dukha: Sudebnye protsessy stalinskoi epokhi* (Moscow: NORMA, 1997), 23.

7 See Piers Beirne and Alan Hunt, "Lenin, Crime, and Penal Politics, 1917–1924" *Revolution in Law: Contributions to the Development of Soviet Legal Theory, 1917–1938*, ed. Piers Beirne (Armonk: M. E. Sharpe, 1990), 99; N. V Krylenko, *Za piat' let, 1918–1922 gg.: Obvinitel'nye rechi*

po naibolee krupnym protsessam, zaslushannym v moskovskom i verkhovnom revoliutsionnykh tribunalakh (Moscow-Petrograd: Gos. Izd., 1922), 13–14; and Nurmin, "Protsess es-rov (Zamechaniia i vpechatleniia)," *Krasnaia nov'* no 4 (8) (July–August 1922): 272–3.

8 Julie A. Cassiday, *The Theater of the World and the Theater of State: Drama and the Show Trial in Early Soviet Russia*, Ph.D. dissertation, (Stanford University, 1995) 49–82; and Elizabeth A. Wood, "The Trial of a Prostitute: Theater and Political Culture in Revolutionary Russia, 1920–1930" (by permission of the author).

9 Krylenko, 8.

10 Leonard Schapiro, *The Origin of the Communist Autocracy: Political Opposition in the Soviet State, First Phase, 1917–1922* (Cambridge: Harvard University Press, 1955), 140–52.

11 I have relied primarily on the comprehensive and well–documented work of Jansen in my own reconstruction of the S.R. Trial. See Marc Jansen, *A Show Trial Under Lenin: The Trial of the Socialist Revolutionaries*, *Moscow, 1922,* trans. Jean Sanders (The Hague: Martinus Nijhoff, 1982). Shub also briefly summarizesthe events of 1922, but he neither contradicts nor augments the work of Jansen. See David Shub, "The Trial of the SRs.," *The Russian Review* no. 23 (1964): 362–9. Further, I find Solzhenitsyn's account of the S.R. Trial of little scholarly use due to the author's blatant bias and the limited number of sources and eyewitness accounts upon which it is based (354–67).

12 See Wassiljew G. Ssemjonow, *Die Partei der Sozial-revolutionäre in den Jahren 1917–1918 (Ihre Kampftätigkeit und militärschen Aktionen*) (Hamburg: Kleine Bibliothek der Russischen Korrespondenz, 1922).

13 Jansen 6–9.

14 See Emile Vandervelde and Arthur Waters, *Le Procès des Socialistes Révolutionnaires à Moscou* (Bruxelles: Libraries du Peuple, 1922).

15 See Nikolai Bukharin, "Rech'tov. Bukharina," *Trud* (November 13, 1927): 3.

16 See Bessie Beatty, *The Red Heart of Russia* (New York: The Century Co., 1919), 292–311 and Sergei Kobiakov, "Krasnyi Sud: Vpechatleniia zashchitnika v revoliutsionnykh tribunalakh," *Arkhiv russkoi revoliutsii,* no. 7: 246–75.

17 See Ivanov for a statement of his vision of a Dionysian theater, which adapted Richard Wagner's and Friedrich Nietzsche's ideas for revitalized drama to the Russian scene; Viacheslav Ivanov, "Predchuvstviiai predvestiia: Novaia organicheskaia epokha i teatr budushchego," *Po zvezdam: Stat'i i aforizmy* (St. Petersburg: Ory, 1909). Citations refer to the Letchworth-Herts edition. Repr. Letchworth-Herts, England: Bradda Books Ltd, 1971), 189–219. For examples of theatrical writing from the first two decades of the twentieth century that betrays Ivanov's broad influence, see Anatolii Lunacharskii, "Sotsializm i iskusstvo," *Teatr. Kniga o novom teatre: Sbornik statei* (St.Petersburg: Shipovnik, 1908) 7–40; Platon Kerzhentsev, *Tvorcheskii teatr: Puti sotsialisticheskogo teatra* (Petrograd: Kniga, 1918); Nikolai Evreinov, *Teatr kak takovoi (Obosnovanie teatral'nosti v smysle polozhitel'nogo nachala stsenicheskogo iskusstva i zhizni)* (St. Petersburg: Sklad Izd. Sovremennoe iskusstvo, 1912) and V. E. Meierkhol'd, *O teatre (Sbornik statei). Stat'i, pis'ma, rechi, besedy. Chast' pervaia, 1891–1917* (Moscow: Iskusstvo, 1968), 103–257.

18 Cassiday, 6–49.

19 See F. A. Mackenzie, *Russia Before Dawn* (London: T. Fisher Unwin, 1923), 232.

20 Paxton Hibben, "Moscow's Treason Trial," *The Nation* CXV, no. 2986 (27 September 1922): 299–300.

21 Ibid. 300.

22 Mackenzie, 238.

23 See E. Olitskaia, *Moi vospominaniia* (Frankfurt/Main: Posev, 1971), 154.

24 See *Dvenadtsat' smertnikov: Sud nad sotsialistami-revoliutsionerami v Moskve.* (Berlin: Zagranich-noi delegatsii P.S.R., 1922) 54; Mackenzie, 234; Vandervelde and Waters, 129.

25 Mackenzie, 248.

26 See Walter Duranty, "Defy Soviet Court in Treason Trial," *New York Times*, June 10, 1922):1 [i] and "Goad Communists to Fury in Moscow," *New York Times*, (12 June 1922):3 [ii], section 3.; Hibben 300; Mackenzie 234, 237; and S. P. Mel'gunov, *Vospominaniia i dnevniki. Vypusk II (Chast' tret'ia)* (Paris: Les Editeurs réunis, 1964), 79.

27 See Mackenzie 240–1; Nurmin 272; and V.M. Zlobina, *Bor'ba partii bol-shevikov protiv melkoburzhuaznogo vliianiia na rabochii klass v pervye gody NEPa (1921–1925 gg.)* (Moscow: Moskovskii universitet, 1975), 102.

28 See Walter Duranty, "Soviet Chiefs Stage Anti-Treason Show," *New York Times,* June 22, 1922, [iii], section3; *Dvenadtsat' smertnikov* 75; Boris Dvinov, *Ot legal'nosti k podpol'iu (1921–1922)* (Stanford: The Hoover Institution on War, Revolution and Peace, 1968), 137; G. P. Maximoff, *The Guillotine at Work: Twenty Years of Terror in Russia (Data and Documents)* (Chicago: The Chicago Section of the Alexander Berkman Fund, 1940), 215; P. E. Mel'gunova-Stepanova, *Gde ne slyshno smekha: Tipy, nravy i byt' Ch.K. Otryvki iz vospominanii (1917–1922 gg.)* (Paris: Rapid-imprimerie, 1928); 189–91; Pitirim A. Sorokin, *Leaves from a Russian Diary-and Thirty Years After*, (Boston: The Beacon Press, 1950), 297; and Tiltman, 80.

29 See *Dvenadtsat' smertnikov,* 79.

30 See Mackenzie 239 and Olitskaia 155.

31 Vertov's 1923 feature film on the trial was titled *Protsess pravykh Es-erov s 8-go iiulia po 7-oe avgusta1922 g.* Some of the more bizarre and fascinating instances of propaganda were Petrushka puppet plays that traveled the country depicting the lessons of the trial, political poems by such luminaries as Dem'ian Bednyi and Vladimir Maiakovskii, and popular songs that preached the lessons of the trial. (*Dvenadtsat' smertnikov* 41–2; Dem'ian Bednyi, "Dliaeseraego zhe mera." *Pravda*, (20 June 1922):3, "Gnetuchka Polushutia, poluvser'ez)" *Pravda* (20 July 1922):2; and V. V. Maiakovskii, "Ballada o doblestnom Emile," *Izvestiia*, (28 May 1922):2.

32 See Medvedev 226, 230; Michal Reiman, *The Birth of Stalinism: The USSR on the Eve of the "Second Revolution,"* trans. George Saunders (Bloomington: Indiana UP, 1987), 58; and William Reswick, *I Dreamt Revolution* (Chicago: Henry Regnery, 1952), 246.

33 See Medvedev 229; Reiman 59.

34 See Eugene Lyons, *Assignment in Utopia*, (New York: Harcourt, Brace and Co., 1937), 114; and Reiman 60.

35 This room has a long and illustrious history in Russian culture (Koriakov). Interestingly enough, the building is located on Theater Square (next to the Bol'shoi, the Malyi, and several other famous theaters) in the heart of Moscow. It provided the stage not only for the trial of the S.R.s and the Shakhty Affair but also for the most famous show trials of 1936–38.

36 See Louis Fischer, *The Soviets in World Affairs: A History of Relations between the Soviet Union and the Rest of the World, Vol. II* (London: Jonathan Cape, 1930), 772–4; Reiman 123–2; and Kurt Rosenbaum, "The German Involvement in the Shakhty Trial" *The Russian Review* no. 21 (1962): 238–60.

37 See A. Agranovskii, Iu. Alevich, and G. Ryklin, *Liudi-vrediteli: Shakhtinskoe delo* (Moscow-Leningrad: Gos. Izd., 1928), 17; and Lyons 116–17.

38 See Reswick, 247.

39 See Lyons, 114.

40 See Paul Scheffer, "Das Klassengericht," *Berliner Tageblatt* (30 May 1928): 1.

41 Lyons, 116.

42 See Louis Fischer, *Men and Politics: An Autobiography* (New York: Duell, Sloan and Pearce, 1941), 503; and Scheffer.

43 See Wolfe, 10.

44 See Walter Duranty, *USSR: The Story of Soviet Russia* (Philadelphia: J.B. Lippincott, 1944), 154; Lyons 122; and A. Vyshinskii, *Itogi i uroki shakhtinskogo dela* (Moscow-Leningrad: Gos. Izd., 1928).

45 Duranty (1944), 155.

46 See Agranovskii, 57.

47 Ibid. 21.48 Lyons, 130.

49 Wolfe, 8.

50 Lyons, 131.

51 For a detailed discussion of the ritual of *samokritika* in the Soviet sciences, see Alexei Kojevnikov, "Rituals of Stalinist Culture at Work: Science and the Games of Intraparty Democracy circa 1948," *The Russian Review 57* (1998): 25–52.

52 Fischer 1941, 503; and *The God That Failed*, ed. Richard Crossman (New York: Harper, 1949), 209–10.

53 Agranovskii, 11, 171.

54 See Lyons, 118; Reiman 64; Wolfe, 14.

55 Agranovskii, 301.

56 Agranovskii, 306; Lyons, 124–5; Wolfe, 17.

57 See *An Affair of Counter-Revolutionary Economics in the Donbass; The Shakhty Affair; Sovkino-Zhurnal,* no. 14, 23, 27 (1928); no. 1, (1931).

58 See Wolfe; Koriakov, "Listki iz bloknota," *Novoe russkoe slovo,* (30 May 1963: n.p); and Arkady Vaksberg, *The Persecutor and the Prey: Vyshinsky and the 1930's Moscow Show Trials,* trans. Jan Butler (London: Weidenfeld and Nicolson, 1990), 46.

59 To gain a sense of the ever increasing control over both defendants and the audience of show trials during the 1930s, see the feature-length documentary trial films of the era, such as *The Trial of the Industrial Party (13 Days)* (Ia. Posel'skii, 1931) devoted to the 1930 case of Professor Ramzin, *The International of Interventionists* and *The Blok of Interventionists* (both 1931) from the Menshevik Trial of 1931, and *The Sentence of the Court is the Sentence of the People* (I. Kanalin, 1938) covering the Bukharin and Rykov trial of 1938.

60 Robert Conquest, *The Great Terror: A Reassessment* (New York: Oxford University Press, 1990).

61 According to film historian Peter Kenez, approximately one-sixth of the 308 feature films released in the Soviet Union between1933 and1940 deal with the battle against spies and saboteurs. Prominent examples include *The Road to Life* (N. Ekk, 1931), *Peasants* (F. Ermler, 1935), *The Party Card* (I. Pyr'ev, 1936), *A Great Life* (L. Lukov, 1939), *Engineer Kochin's Mistake* (A. Macheret, 1939), and the second series of *A Great Citizen* (F. Ermler, 1939). Kenez describes the scripts of these films as a continuation and elaboration of the script for the era's purge trials: "The scenarios closely resembled the tales of the most vicious story-teller of them all, Andrei Vyshinsky, the Chief Prosecutor at the purge trials. In the films, as in the confessions at the trials, the enemy perpetrated the most dastardly acts out of an unreasoned hatred for decent socialist society. In fifty-two out of the eighty-five films dealing with contemporary life (i.e. more than half) the hero (for it was usually a man) unmasked hidden enemies who had committed criminal acts. The hero could never be too vigilant. The enemy turned out sometimes to be the hero's best friend, sometimes his wife, and sometimes his father." (Peter Kenez, "Soviet cinema in the age of Stalin," *Stalinism and Soviet Cinema*, ed. Richard Taylor and Derek Spring (London: Routledge, 1993), 54–68. For additional discussion of enemies, traitors, and spies in Soviet feature films of the 1930s, see Liliia Mamatova, "Modelkinomifov 30-kh godov," *Kino: Politika i liudi (30-e gody)* (Moscow: Materik, 1995): 52–78.

FILMS

Blok interventov [film]. 1931.

Delo ob ekonomicheskom kontrrevoliutsii v Donbasse [film]. 1928.

Internatsional interventov [film]. 1931.

Kinopravda [film]. Dir. Dziga Vertov. No. 1–4, 7–8, 1922.

Krestiane [film]. Dir. F. Ermler. 1935.

Oshibka ingenira Kochina [film]. Dir. A. Macheret. 1939.

Partiiny biilet [film]. Dir. I. Pyr'ev. 1936.

Prigovor suda – prigovor naroda [film]. Dir. I. Kanalin. 1938.

Protsess pravykh Es-erov s 8-go iiuliă po 7-oe avgusta 1922 g [film]. Dir. Dziga Vertov. 1923.

Protsess Prompartii (13 dnei) [film]. Dir. Ia. Posel'skii. 1931.

Putevkav zhizn' [film]. Dir. N. Ekk. 1931.

Shakhtinskii protsess [film]. Dir. Eshurin. 1928.

Sovkino-Zhurnal [film] No. 14, 23, 27, 1928; no.1, 1931.

Velikii grazhdanin [film]. Dir. F. Ermler. 1937 and 1939.

Archive Images: Truth or Memory
The Case of Adolf Eichmann's Trial

— Eyal Sivan

I come from Israel, a country where the political use, or the "instrumentalization," of what we call memory is an integral constitutive element of the political culture. As early as the 1930s, David Ben-Gourion – later Israel's first prime minister – theorized "the transformation of Jewish suffering into Zionist redemption."[1] No other country in the world uses the memory of suffering as Israel does, to justify not just its policies but its existence. And obviously no other country dares to pretend to be preserving the legacy of the victims of one of the largest crimes in history.

Zionism (the Jewish nationalist movement) and its political expression (Israel) attained legitimacy through the genocide of the Jews during World War II. The United Nations' General Assembly Resolution 181, calling for the partition of Palestine between Jews and Arabs, was approved by a large majority in 1947, because the memory of the events of the war was still so fresh. Israel's political policies get their morale stature from the commonly accepted idea of that nation as the homeland of the survivors of genocide.

Beyond its relation to historical fact, the importance of this common belief is its place in the Western conscience. It gives Israel a privileged moral position: victims, we know, are generally seen as being on the side of the good. Paradoxically, though, this "untouchable" position also weakens Israel, exposing it to a recurring criticism: how can a people that has suffered so much make others suffer? How can the victims' memory not prevent them from becoming criminals themselves? We hear and read such notions regularly.

To put the problem this way, however, is to ignore the political function of collective memory. "This screen-memory, which shows some of the horrors so as to hide others, is only the chosen weapon to defend all the lying strategies and murderer propaganda," writes Rony Brauman.[2] As a political argument, memory easily becomes an instrument that stimulates, encourages and justifies different types of collective and political violence.

Did the genocide of Tutsis and moderate Hutus in Rwanda prevent the country's new regime from massacring Hutus refugees in Zaire in 1999, or from establishing a rule of terror at home? Did the memory of their persecution by the Nazis and earlier Turks keep Serbs from killing Bosnians? Did the memory of Japanese war crimes keep China from building concentration camps and prosecuting Tibetans? Did the memory of the deportation of the Boers prevent their descendants from deporting black Africans in their return? Did African-American soldiers' ancestry of slavery make them behave better than white soldiers in the Vietnam War? Did participation in the Resistance during the Nazi Occupation of France prevent some men from later becoming torturers in Algeria? The list is of course endless.

"What ethnic cleansing, what forced migration, what pulse vengeance, has not found its inspiration in this linear memory and in the cult of the victim that is associated with it?" asks Brauman.[3] One reason for this, it can be argued, is that the linear vision of collective memory easily creates dichotomous and antagonistic categories. Nations rarely see themselves as criminals or cowardly; in the world of memory, they are either victims or heroes, sometimes both. Tzvetan Todorov writes,

> The world of heroes, and maybe this is its weakness, is a one-dimensional world, which includes only two opposed terms: we and them, friend and enemy, courage and cowardliness, heroes and traitors, black and white.[4]

This is also the case in the representation of the victimhood.

And of course this is also the case in Israel. Memorial vision was imposed on the country in the early 1960s through the trial of Adolf Eichmann, which opened in Jerusalem on April 11, 1961. As a senior officer in the Gestapo, Eichmann had been in charge of the mass deportation of European Jews, Poles, Slovenes, and Gypsies to the concentration and death camps. After his capture by the Israeli secret service, in Buenos Aires 1960, he was tried in Jerusalem. The trial, in a brand-new theater auditorium called Beth Ha´am (house of the people), was an international event – the first big public trial of a Nazi criminal since the Nuremberg trials at the end of World War II. More, it was the first trial dedicated entirely to the crime of the Holocaust.

To ensure that the event would "carry" – it was intended to be a lesson to both Israeli society and the world – the trial was conceived as a show. And what gave it is full spectacular dimension was the fact that millions of people around the world could follow it on television. The U.S. election of John F. Kennedy the year before, with its election campaign fought out on TV, had demonstrated the impact of this new medium. Few realize that the first hearing in the Eichmann trail was held a month before the event's official public opening: on March 10, 1961, the court held a special session to discuss the request of the attorney general, Gideon Hausner, to permit videotape recording in the court "for the purpose of television broadcasts and cinema showings in Israel and abroad."[5]

This was an original request. The proceedings of no earlier court had been recorded in their entirety on video and broadcast on TV; "We know of no relevant statutory provision," the judges said.[6] Hausner's proposal was closely linked to the political purpose behind the Eichmann trial: for the young state of Israel, the exposure of the sufferings of the Jewish holocaust victims was a political and didactic need. As an event, the trial was intended to become a monument in public memory. The guilt of the defendant and the revelation of the truth were secondary. In fact, Hannah Arendt wrote, "it was the trial done by Zionism to Nazism."[7]

The staging and the filming of this trial were supposed to constitute a full representation of Jewish suffering during the war. Through the voice of the attorney general, they were to reflect Israel's position as the unique *owner* of these sufferings. Robert Servatius, Eichmann's defense counsel, strongly opposed the request for a televisation, fearing the risk of "a distorted presentation of the proceedings," and "a desire [of the witnesses] to play-act before a world-wide audience."[8] Alternatively, he asked the court to make its consent conditional upon "an objective presentation of the proceedings."[9] Despite the general mediocrity of his defense of Eichmann, the remark is interesting: we might say that this idea about objectivity of images is a function of the time, the 1960s, but even today we sometimes still hear "objective" visual documentation claimed.

After a short debate, the court concluded, this danger does "not outweigh the favorable aspects of the proposed recording."[10] The judges had mentioned these "favorable aspects" during the debate, quoting the philosopher Jeremy Bentham: "Where there is no publicity, there is no justice ... Publicity is the very soul of justice."[11] The decision, then, addressed the present moment, the time of the trial. Nothing was said of the future, or the fact that the film would become a factual trace, an archive for future generations.

The Eichmann trial was of considerable importance from every point of view. The human and historical value of the evidence presented, and the extraordinary view that it provided of the Nazi death machine, gave it a dimension no earlier trial had attained. The Israeli state charged an American company, under the direction of the filmmaker Leo Hurwitch, with all of the video recording. In return the company commanded exclusive marketing rights to the trial images for a period of a year. About 500 hours of video were recorded for posterity. (A large part of these recordings, however, would eventually turn out to be unusable). The Eichmann trial lasted over five months, and more than 100 victims and witnesses testified. It was the first time that victims of the Nazi persecutions had spoken publicly. The media attended for the testimony, and the world was fascinated and horrified by the stories that emerged.

Two months after the trial began, a unique witness took the stand. Before the court and the survivors, Eichmann responded to fifteen charges concerning the elimination of several million people. The prosecutor presented him as incarnation of evil. In his defense, he cited his obligation to obey orders from his superiors, but he meanwhile described in detail the functioning of a destructive engine of which he had been a chief engineer. Answering questions from the prosecutor, his own counsel, and the judge, he narrated exactly what he had done with the Nazi regime. Denying none of the facts, he gave the court a full view of the Nazi extermination machine.

What is striking, listening to Eichmann, is the fact that there is no contradiction between his own testimony and the victims'. But the perpetrator and his truth were of relatively little relevance to the purpose of the trial. In a filmed interview, Hurwitch would remember,

> I was terribly excited that Eichmann was going to be tried because it had a possibility of exposing why these events happened.... I felt sure that people in Israel would be interested in that ... but it seemed they were not interested in discovering the nature of fascism. They were only interested in dramatizing the terrible events that happened to Jews.[12]

Although Eichmann's trial was filmed, only a few images of the Holocaust victims, and a single image of the defendant declaring "Not guilty," became iconic representations of the trial. Of the hundred of hours of film, only a few canonical icons were left in memory. Eichmann was condemned to death on May 30, 1962. The following day he was hanged, and his ashes were dispersed in the Mediterranean. After the execution, the footage of the trial vanished, buried in an unknown archive. Memory replaced history.

In 1977, on the trial's thirty-fifth anniversary, the film was discovered, in the United States, and was returned to Israel. Shortly afterward the Steven Spielberg Jewish Film Archive was founded in Jerusalem, its mission the conservation of audiovisual material concerning contemporary Judaism. It was housed at the Hebrew University of Jerusalem.

In 1978–1979, the Spielberg Archive decided to prepare a selection of seventy-two hours of the trial footage. The logic of the exercise was hard to understand: these seventy-two hours of images, recorded on poor-quality tape, were presented not as copies but as originals; the rest of the footage was declared inaccessible or nonexistent. Responding to criticism of the archive in the 1990s, its director declared, "All the sensational moments of the trial are available. The essential is safe."[13] A few sequences were regularly sold, becoming standard illustrations of the trial. This trade in a few pieces of memory was obviously more profitable than the long and arduous task of archiving the complete material. The original tapes were stored haphazardly, and without adequate labels, in the only place the archive could find that was cool enough for the purpose of conservation: an unused washroom. It was here they were discovered, in 1991, by the production team of my film *The Specialist*.

A comparison between the catalogue of images and the trial transcript has shown that almost a third of the video archives, essentially evidence from camp survivors, seems to have been lost for good. This is a deep paradox for an archive institution dedicated to preservation. It shows to what extent, and how easily, the display of the *duty* of memory can replace the real *act* of memory.

If the videotapes of the Eichmann trial have turned out to be virtual archives, that is because the trial itself in fact fulfilled its purpose. The pleas of European Jewry, their torture, the

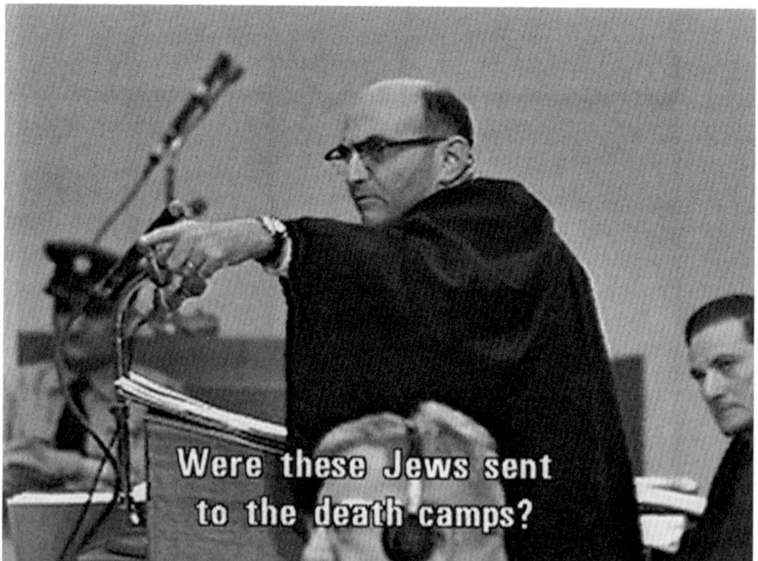

Still from *The Specialist* (1999), a documentary about the Eichmann trial, by Eyal Sivan.

memory of the catastrophe, found a home in Israel, where they became an indisputable source of national legitimacy, symbolized by the icon of Eichmann in the glass booth installed for him in court. The staging of the trial, like the decision to film and record it, was intended to put the viewer in direct and immediate contact with the harsh testimony of the survivors. The origins of this decision lay in the desire to reflect, in the optical sense of the word, the horror experienced both by those who had survived and by those who had died but would live again through the trial testimony's preservation of their trace. The viewers of the video footage were to be exposed to this horror alone; for this purpose, in the eyes of the Israeli state, the few minutes that we know from their many TV broadcasts were probably enough.

Hundreds of books and thousands of shorter studies have been written on the Eichmann case and trial, but not one scholar, scientist or historian has discussed the video archive. Although it constitutes a full record of the trial, it seems to have been ignored as a historical document. Do scholars attach no truth to this material? Or is it only a question of time? One expert on the Eichmann case, Hans Safrian, of the National Holocaust Museum in Washington, D.C., has said that he has no interest in seeing Eichmann

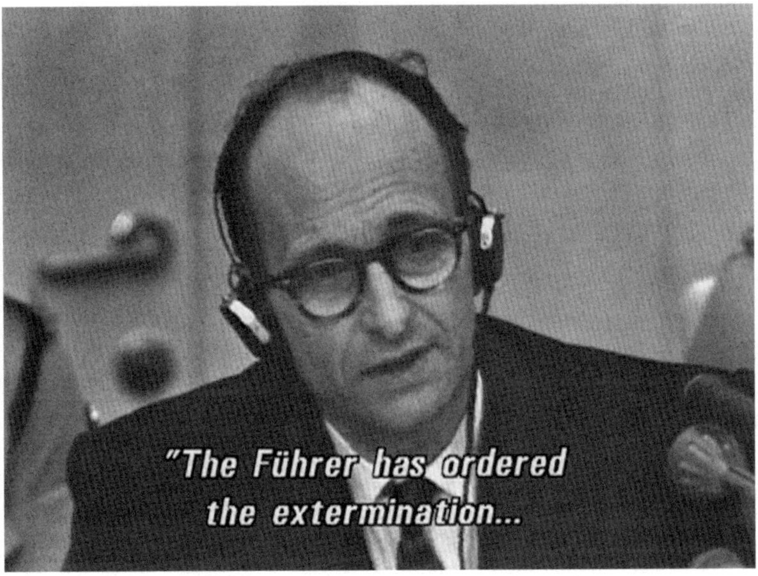

Still from *The Specialist* (1999), a documentary about the Eichmann trial, by Eyal Sivan.

or his trial.[14] In fact, almost no scholar has wanted to hear the perpetrator speak. And what of the victims and the witnesses? The Eichmann trial video footage is one of the biggest filmed archives of their testimonies. It includes a full range of witnesses from all over Europe, from 1933 to 1945, from the rise of Nazism to the camps and the liberation. The women and men who testified in the trial did so just sixteen years after the event, when they were relatively young and their memory still fresh. Yet the archives were forgotten. In 1982, Yale University recuperated the New Haven Holocaust Survivors Film Project, begun in the late 1970s, and transformed it into the Fortunoff Video Archive for Holocaust Testimonies. In 1994, Steven Spielberg began the project of filming the survivors of the Shoah. But no one cared about preserving the images of the witnesses in the Eichmann trial.

What was this footage needed for if the images of neither the perpetrator nor the victims were to be used or even preserved, if historians haven't even looked at the as a document? There is no question of truth here; the beginning of an answer might be the question of the function of collective memory. The act of filming allows an emphasis on the spectacular function of the event; some images, mainly of victims, help to create icons of memory – what we used to call "monuments."

One of the most famous icons of the Eichmann trial is the fainting and the removal of a witness who collapsed under the burden of evoking the horror. Spectacular and moving, this tragic sequence became a symbol of the endless trial. Used in almost all of the films about the event, and in many others about World War II more generally, it clearly illustrates the issue of the archive, truth, and memory.

The witness was Yehiel De-Nur. Forty-five years old in 1962, a native of Poland, he had spent two years in Auschwitz, and was the only member of his family to survive. After the liberation he took the name "Ka-Zetnik," a play on the letters "KZ," for *Konzentrationslager* (concentration camp), and wrote one of the first books on Auschwitz published in Israel. Although he was famous in his country, he was known only by pseudonym and had never appeared in public, even in photographs, before testifying in the Eichmann trial. There he spoke, in few sentences, about the "Planet of Auschwitz" and its inhabitants without names. "I see them, they are staring at me, I see them, I saw them standing in the queue,"[15] he said. Stopped by a question from the attorney general, Ka-Zetnik fainted and collapsed unconscious. In the deeply distressed courtroom, ambulance men ran to his rescue. Today, Ka-Zetnik himself does not recognize the description of Auschwitz he uttered on the stand as his own. Since the Eichmann trial he has taken back his own name and now situates Auschwitz in our own planet, as a specifically human construction rather than some unworldly and alien blight. If he is still afflicted by anxiety, it is now as a man facing the future: he is currently expressing himself as a citizen by struggling against the peril of nuclear weapons. In these circumstances since the trial, perhaps contemporary use of the spectacular scene of Ka-Zetnik's fainting amount to a betrayal of Yehiel De-Nur.

To make this kind of selection of a particular scene – in effect a form of film editing – involves a kind of censoring, since to choose is to eliminate. The truth of every film lies not in an unlimited absorption of reality but in a rebuilding of it, creating a structure and establishing criteria of choice. And strangely, although there is a great tradition of documenting, collecting, and archiving images and stories of victims, documentary cinema and archival work have rarely dealt with representation of perpetrators. This is true of both the Yale and the Spielberg projects; I might also mention recent projects in Rwanda, Bosnia Argentina, and elsewhere.

It seems that images of victims fascinate, and their stories are recurrent subjects of study. This focus often seems to be defended as a *duty of memory.* How strange, though, that this claimed duty should fall on the victims rather than the perpetrators, who are far more commonly the subjects of fiction. And how strange also in the case of the Holocaust, fiction films dealing with the perpetrators so often make use of aesthetic prototypes designed by the Nazis themselves, and more precisely by the Nazi filmmaker Leni Riefenstahl. Except for Ernst Lubitsch and Charlie Chaplin, directors dealing with this period tend to see the SS as they themselves wanted to be seen. Showing and hearing perpetrators like Eichmann would be a starting point for breaking the conventional clichés, if iconic ones, of their representation.

Historians have certainly used documents of the Nazis to describe the process of destruction and to analyze the crime, but they haven't shown the criminals speaking for themselves.

When we discovered the audiovisual material relating to the Eichmann trial, we decided to follow in the spirit of Primo Levi in our film *The Specialist*: in his preface to the memoirs of the Auschwitz commandant Rudolf Hoess, Levi invites the reader to discover a "human itinerary which is, in a way, exemplary" and describes this autobiography as "one of the more instructive books ever published."[16] But writing is not an image; and the image may not be holy, but it has its own logic. So the film shows Eichmann on-screen. Here he is, animated in face and speech. He has a conscience, and speaks of his doubts in a man's voice. More, he is in a position of weakness in his glass booth, facing the judges who keep him under control. Here he is, frail, vulnerable, all in all: human.

Hidden behind fictionalized, quasi-mythic representations, perpetrators become inhuman – they become monsters, beasts, maniacs. The representation of victims, on the other hand, corresponds to the Jewish and Christian idea of redemption, so that their images work similarly to the crucifix on the church wall. It is true that to focus on the perpetrator is to risk making us identify with him; as he explains and justifies himself, tells us about his work, his joy, his sorrows, he looks like a anyone else and we grant him our understanding. The technical problems he has had to resolve, his problems with his conscience, the "duty" that obliges him to follow orders – these are experiences that all of us can recognize. But it is precisely on this familiarity with him that we should count. It is the small space, which involves identification, comprehension, and indulgence that we can choose to evaluate him.

The use of dramatic recurring icons to represent crimes, the daily display of the sufferings of the victims, a thousand times seen, a thousand times commented on, turns them into clichés in the sense described by Roland Barthes:

> Facing these images, we are deprived of our judgment. Somebody has trembled for us, thought for us, judged for us. The photographer has left us nothing, just a simple intellectual acceptance.[17]

When it comes to the images of horror, I prefer to rely on the power of the imagination. I do not share the idea of their clarifying and denunciatory power. We hear that to show a crime against humanity is already to start to fight it. This kind of euphoric cliché eludes the question of political responsibility by substituting the show of horror for the thinking about horror. As Brauman and I have written, "When the political event is reduced to a pathetic current affair, pity paralyzes thinking and the aspiration to justice is reduced to a humanitarian consolation. Here you find the banalization of evil."[18]

After the Eichmann case it became part of the juridical show to film the trails to those who had perpetrated crimes against humanity. So it has been with the Klaus Barbie's trial in 1985 and Maurice Papon's in 1996, both in France, and of course, with the international criminal tribunals for the former Yugoslavia, in the Hague, and for Rwanda, in Arusha. The latter two courts are actually television studios. The trials are fully recorded; most of the images can be seen on the courts' website. Ironically, the faces of the defendants are obscured, hidden. The court respects the dignity of the defendants and maybe even thought that was really important was the testimonies of the victims. Here again we might ask, what will happen to these thousands of hours of images? How and to whom can we guarantee freedom to access to these materials, and the possibility of reconstructing narratives or making artwork out of them?

As an integral part of the process of South Africa's Truth and Reconciliation Commission, it was decided to record and broadcast the full hearings on TV. (This was also done in Argentina). At first the hearings were followed by large audiences all over the country. But they lasted a long time, and as the months passed, interest broke down. Few films were made during the hearings, but the question of the large archive of moving images that the commission generated daily is an open one – as it is in the Hague and Arusha, and as it was at the Eichmann trial. In every case the purpose of the filming is the representation of the victims and the creation of a linear collective memory. Fortunately the images are not considered legal proof; unfortunately they are not considered part of the construction of truth either.

An image is a representation of a segment of reality. The four blacks sides that construct or define the frame hide more than they show, and the truth as it is constructed through images can only be an accumulation of points of view of the same material. This construction depends on the ability to use archival materials, not just to illustrate a single moment, speech, or memory, but to manipulate them freely so as to arrive at a new narrative.

Images can be objects of thought, but icons, as cult objects, cannot. The respect due to the icons cannot be justified for images, which exist only through the work done on and with them. It is strange to remark that the use of images to testify truth, and the creation of audiovisual or cinematic works pretending to be acts against oblivion, are on a growth curve. Memory has become a sort of audiovisual collective experience. Most of the compilations of images dealing with the Holocaust are convenient illustrations of commemorative discourses, and are characterized by the positive cliché "Never again." This memory, or rather this imposed mourning, is possible thanks to the constitution of a visual language. Where a living language is permanently evolving, and can be used for individual, subjective works or points of view, this visual language is constituted more as a code. Like road signs, its images can be read at a glance. Old-looking or deteriorated, they signify the past. Gray silhouettes running through trenches mean World War I. Snow and barbells mean the gulag. The codes are numerous. Together they make up a system of nontransparent images, an empty screen. Like the terms that are used to comment on them, they have become overused. The pile of corpses, the death factories of Auschwitz and Birkenau, the deportees behind the barbed-wired fences, the gray men running in trenches of World War I – like the narratives of the victims, they have lost their *exemplarity.* In their one-dimensional narrative form, these historical images have lost their analogical power to stimulate a point of view and a reflection on the present.

But archival images can be used in a secular, contemporary way to create historical analogies. As Todoro writes,

> Exemplary use of memory ... allows the past to be used in view of the present. Memory can be used as a lesson about injustices acquired in the past and to help fight those taking place at the present, to help us to live our selves and to advance toward the other.[19]

It is the utilization – or the manipulation – of the image that gives it its exemplary dimension. Through the use of all the tools given to us by the contemporary arts, perhaps we can uproot the images of the trials of men like Eichmann, and other perpetrators of crimes against humanity, from their memorial one-dimensional purpose. Bringing these images into our present, we can get a sense of our own environment. We can give these materials a "status of truth" that will allow us to renew the tradition of what can be called political art.

Eyal Sivan "Archive Images: Truth or Memory" was first published in *Experiments With Truth: Transitional Justice and the Processes of Truth and Reconciliation*: documenta 11, Platform 2, ed. Okwui Enwesor [et al.], Hatje Cantz: 2002. Republished with permission of the author.

1 David Ben-Gurion, quoted in Idith Zertal, "Le procès d'Adolf Eichmann, ou la révélation de la Shoah," *L'Histoire*, no. 212 (July–August 1997).

2 Rony Brauman, "Mémoire, savoir, pensée," *Le Débat*, no 96 (September – October 1997).

3 Ibid.

4 Tzvetan Todorov, *Facing the Extreme: Moral Life in the Concentration Camps* (New York: Metropolitan Books, 1996).

5 *The Trial of Adolf Eichmann: Record of Proceedings in the District Court of Jerusalem,* vol.1: March 10, 1961(Jerusalem: Trust for the Publication of the Proceedings of the Eichmann Trial, in co-operation with the Israel State Archives and Yad Vashem, the Holocaust Martyrs' and Heroes' Remembrance Authority, 1992).

6 Ibid. Only about twelve hours of the proceedings of the Nuremberg trials after World War II were filmed.

7 Hannah Arendt, *Eichmann in Jerusalem: A Report on the Banality of Evil* (New York: Viking Press, 1963; rev. and enlarged ed. New York: Penguin Books, 1994).

8 *The Trial of Adolf Eichmann*, vol. 1: March 10, 1961.

9 Ibid.

10 Ibid.

11 Ibid.

12 Leo T. Hurwitz, interviewed by Susan Slyomovics, The Jewish Museum, New York, March 4, 1986.

13 *Ha'aretz Daily*, September 14, 1995.

14 Hans Safrian, at the conference "Il racconto della catastrofe," Verona, Italy, March 1998.

15 *The Trial of Adolf Eichmann*, vol. 3, 1237 (June 7, 1961).

16 Primo Levi, introduction to *Commandant of Auschwitz: The Autobiography of Rudolf Hoess* by Rudolph Hoess, trans. Constantine Fitz Gibbon (London: Phoenix Press, 2000).

17 Roland Barthes, *Mythologies* (Paris: Seuil, 1957).

18 Rony Brauman and Eyal Sivan, *Eloge de la désobéissance* (Paris: Le Pommier, 1999).

19 Tzetan Todorov, *Les Abus de la mémoire* (Paris: Arléa, 1995), 31–32.

Tele-Tribunals: Anatomy of a Medium

— Cornelia Vismann
Translated by Sara Ogger

Today courtrooms are capitulating to television cameras, a tendency not much impeded by legal prohibitions against it. Things were different in America in the 1950s, when the medium of television became popularized. Even though the medium of live broadcast seemed made for covering court trials, instead television concentrated on broadcasting tribunal-like proceedings. Courtroom trials were reserved for another medium, cinema.

Although the court and television have been joined in recent years, it is worth noting that preceding this development were four decades of latency, which the following study seeks to explain through an analysis of Preminger's courtroom drama *Anatomy of a Murder*.

— Hearings

In 1954 the United States Congress set up an investigative committee to examine certain machinations on the part of the military: it was alleged that a member of the army had been unlawfully privileged. Most of the suspicion was directed at a senator from Wisconsin. Had his name not been McCarthy, the army hearing would have received less attention, if any, and perhaps never have been the subject of an investigative committee. But, then again, irregularities within the army may have been a welcome excuse for the newly elected Eisenhower government to put an end to the days of the loyalty oath.

The end of the era for which McCarthy's name had become a synonym was meant to be celebrated in public. Thus the form of an investigative committee was chosen, which, unlike a proper court proceeding, was accessible to all through television. With Joseph McCarthy and Joseph Nye Welch, both nearly the same age, two protagonists arose from the inscrutable mass of those attending the proceedings, each of whom embodied a specific mode of power; the tribunal's symmetrical structure meant that the hearing was styled as a duel between the secret service and democracy. Both Josephs were attorneys, one a circuit lawyer from Wisconsin, the other a trial lawyer from Boston. Both struggled in the name of their nation, and so it is hardly surprising that their meeting should be broadcast nationwide.

When the Investigative Committee vs. the Army convened in 1954, it was, other than the inauguration of President Eisenhower a few months earlier, the first nonsports mass event in the United States to be broadcast on television.[1] At the time, NBC, CBS, Bumont-Station, and ABC made daily broadcasts from the courtroom. During the live broadcasts a drastic reduction in shopping was recorded and there was a rapid increase in the number of television sets purchased. When after a week the two largest TV stations, NBC and CBS, decided to broadcast the daily duel at night, at 11:15p.m., instead of during the day, there was such a vehement protest that NBC went back to broadcasting live, even though it meant losing advertising revenues from canceled shows.[2] A live, directly televised democracy emerged and was tested out on the tube. Since then it is hard to recall any issue in American politics that hasn't been cast in the form of a hearing and telecast as a duel. Indeed, something only really becomes a political issue after having first attained the status of a televised hearing.

Hearings belong to the genre of tribunals, as opposed to the genre of court trial. The difference between the two types of procedure is best demonstrated, in fact, by the army-McCarthy-hearings. When it was Joseph N. Welch's turn to appear in the auditorium as special counsel to the army, he represented an emissary from a realm of law that stood in sharp contrast to the tribunal. It must have been immediately apparent for the spectators in the room that the committee room was not familiar turf for him as a lawyer. According to reports, Welch manifested some annoyance upon entering at the ambiguity of the situation he met: a crowded auditorium with no clear seating assignments or hierarchies, no clear delineations between tribunal members and television crews. With each gesture, Welch indicated that he was used to a courtroom, not a tribunal: "He seemed confused, even immobilized, by the anarchy of the proceedings: the cameras, the bright lights, the crowd, the noise, the whispering of attorneys to witnesses, the inattention of the judges – or were they jurors? – and the endless repetition of testimony." Looking back, this bewildered gentleman describes this experience as a "shock for a lawyer used to the traditionally ordered interiors of courtrooms."[3]

The orderly and hermetic world of the court, with its specifically dedicated architectural environment, stands in contrast to the tribunal, a kind of road show that can be held anywhere. Without the rules and precedent of proper trial procedure, it works not only with cameras, bright lights, and noise, but also with unscrupulous tricks and lies; greedily borrowing procedural forms and strategies from sports as much as from the law. This permeability eats away at the distinction between inside and outside, the very distinction that is most essential to the judicial performance. It is not so much that the cameras transmit the proceedings to the outside, but rather that the great mass audience, glued to the TV-screen, becomes part of the tribunal. In the unmarked tribunal space all positions become an object of contention. The judge's traditional position as moderator is vacated. There is no operator of the proceedings, no one safeguarding the rules of the trial. Procedural anarchy ensues. The winner of a tribunal duel is the one who forces and thereby determines the parameters of the discourse.

Joseph McCarthy was a virtuoso in the arena of the tribunal. His style was antagonistic, aggressive, and no-holds-barred. In the course of the investigative committee hearing, however, the old-fashioned jurist Welch was nevertheless able to achieve mastery over the proceedings. His opponent was well aware that the mood in the auditorium had shifted unfavorably. He fell back on an anti-communist attack against one of Welch's assistants, accusing him of being a member of the leftist National Lawyers Guild. The attack misfired. It even worked against the accuser, as a jurist who followed the scene on TV would later report: "McCarthy wanted to discredit Welch, but he was above suspicion, so he singled out a young lawyer who assisted Welch and accused him, without proof, of communist leanings. Welch turned to McCarthy: 'Have you left no sense of decency, sir?' he asked him."[4] This now legendary retort ended the hearing. It was the final judgment on a man without decency, who would die three years later of causes related to alcoholism.

In an almost old-world European way, Welch refused to engage in a duel whose terms were set by a dishonorable man with contemptible methods, adopting instead the role of sovereign judge. Despite McCarthy's formal acquittal, TV-audiences celebrated Welch as a "hero of American conscience."[5] From then on Welch (whose name sounds to German ears like a pronoun meaning "which") came to stand for decency and dignity in a mercenary and undignified medium. He became a symbol and guarantor of the traditional modes of seeking truth and justice outside the closed system of the courtroom, in the TV studio. By showcasing Welch, TV tacitly endorsed a style that it was in the process of elbowing aside.

— Courtroom Drama

The jurist cited above, who viewed the war of words between Welch and McCarthy on TV, says of himself that "with millions of others [I] had become an ardent admirer of Welch, who was one of the major forces in the defeat of McCarthyism,"[6] but he also saw in it the demise of those very legal forms that were being exploited by television. Five years after the hearing, in 1959, the quoted jurist, who earned his J.D. in Vienna, made a film about law. He had in the meantime become a film director in Hollywood – his name was Otto Preminger.[7] His film *Anatomy of a Murder* depicts a traditional court trial, as if to remind the American public that there is such a thing as proper legal proceedings and not just hearings.

Preminger's film is focused not on the two sides in the trial, as in the adversarial American system, but rather on the judge – who plays no role in a tribunal. This focus lends the film, which was based on a script written by an American judge, its continental European character.[8] It emphasizes a mode of procedure which seems to be overturned by a tribunalized style of investigation.

In order to formulate a filmic argument for the courtroom drama as the antithesis to the tribunal, the person playing the judge became the linchpin of the film. The director first offered the role to Spencer Tracy who turned it down. Then Preminger sought a real judge instead. Joseph Nye Welch was all but born for the job of evoking the realm of justice that the TV hearings threatened to eclipse. With this casting choice, Preminger gave contemporary moviegoers a chance to reacquaint themselves with a public favorite from the days of the tribunal. The figure of the judge in this film, exaggerated almost to the point of caricature, was designed to satisfy what might be construed as a latent American longing for a paternal figure who presides over the trial's search for justice in a way both kindly and strict, and who, despite his inclination for jovial little chats, demands order in the end.

Outside the world of the film this longing for an all-governing *pater justitiae* paved the way for a cult of the great constitutional judges:

> In the USA ... this return of [the image or rather imago of the father] is indicated by the recent rise of a whole literary genre of judges' biographies. Looking back on the 20th century, Supreme Court decisions have been structured according to a series of great personalities in the judgeship who made constitutional history.[9]

Thus it is not accidental that a courtroom film intending to offer a contrast with the tribunal process should approach this task by invoking the spirit of legendary judges. *Anatomy of a Murder* begins with two bachelors getting together to browse through old case opinions. They open a "Selection by Chief Justice Holmes." Here Oliver Wendell Holmes, possibly the most famous jurist in United States history, stands for the idea that justice occurs not just according to logical principles but that the ability to determine and evaluate the truth also depends on the psychological makeup of the judge. In the film, the ideal of the intuitive judge is embodied by Judge Weaver, alias Judge Welch. And this judge is in turn a proxy for another judge. That his name is Maitland, like the name of the famous nineteenth-century English legal historian, may be a hint deliberately inserted by Preminger. Sir Frederic William Maitland is known for his lifelong effort to prove that both justice cultures, the Anglo-American and the continental, had common roots in Roman law. The use of the name Maitland, then, suffices to set aside the ongoing and fruitless comparisons between the two systems of justice and instead to emphasize their structural commonalities. These commonalities come together in the figure of the judge, the mediator, who grants the right to speak and the time to do it, who puts the trial's participants in their place and determines the order in which they may tell their stories.

In the browsing of case opinions scene, Preminger has one of the bachelors, played by James Stewart, bluntly deliver the line: "Powell McCarthy, a good jurist." This casually dropped name is the first nominal connection to the army hearing, thus summoning old ghosts. It is uttered in the same breath as the name of Judge Holmes and calls forth a biographical concordance between these otherwise two very different legal characters.[10] Like Joseph McCarthy, Oliver Wendell Holmes had been a member of the army.[11] When Holmes and McCarthy are named together at the very beginning of the film, the coordinates within which the trial will take place are already determined: judges who were in the war and soldiers who were called before the court. Accused of murder is a "marksman in the army who saw combat in the Korean War." His wife, a divorcée, had formerly been the wife of an old army buddy from the Second World War. Even the murder weapon, a Luger developed by a countryman of Preminger's, comes from that war. The defendant took it from a fallen German soldier and brought it, unchecked, over to America, whose freedom, as is well known, expresses itself in the right to bear arms. The defendant excuses his killings with a classic form of argument in films about military courts: the incompatibility between standards of military and civilian orders.[12] What would be seen as a patriotic act in war is reviled in the civilian world as manslaughter or murder.

Not that this state of contradiction exonerates the defendant. His attorney assumes an entirely different tack. He takes a page from the lay psychologist Oliver Wendell Holmes and pleads the incapacity of the perpetrator, since at the moment of the deed he was in an extraordinary psychological state. The argument carries the jury. Still, this success remains short-lived. Once acquitted, the defendant himself sews the seeds of doubt about the verdict simply by repeating the very words used by his lawyer, "irresistible impulse," in justification of his taking off after the trial without paying his lawyer's fees.

Like a flash of lightning, this laconic misuse of an allegedly legal term exposes how truth in the courtroom is a matter of form that is beholden to legal procedure. It draws our attention to a semantic game with little relevance outside the criminal justice system; ultimately it proves nothing. In the film, the only things revealed are the mechanisms of the search for justice, rather than any substantial truth.

What this filmic autopsy of the court reveals is merely the skeleton of a murder, its anatomy, not the passions and drives that led up to it. Two different motives are suggested to the viewer: jealousy or revenge. Either the defendant avenged the rape of his wife by murdering the rapist, or he killed his wife's lover. Enraged jealousy or cold-blooded revenge – the clues could speak for either version. The welts and bruises on the wife's face may have resulted from the rape or from a jealous, violent husband. Both motives are equally probable; neither is ultimately verified in the film.

This judicial morality play eschews hermeneutic certainty. The camera, which in other court films often shows us the truth that the court is unable to reach, here offers the audience no privileged knowledge. On the contrary, in *Anatomy of a Murder* the camera is strictly limited to the perspective of the court. In this respect it resembles the camera in classic courtroom films. These films had their raison d'être in the fact that the courtroom trial is one of the few, if not the only, real-life situations in which the theatrical unity of time and place can be translated into the cinematic setting with any plausibility. However, if the court and the camera are coextensive – that is, reduced to an equally limited perspective, the viewer is placed in the jury's position and has his or her sense of mystery flattered.

The camera of the former theater director, who wrote plays for the stage based on sensational Viennese trials, does not aim to bring the genre of cinema back to its theatrical roots.[13] True, the camera in *Anatomy of a Murder* is nearly as immobile as the judge in his chair. But by leaving the courtroom at the end of the trial, it affords a glimpse of the outside. That alone suffices to render the edifice of truth-so-carefully constructed from the witness statements, cross-examinations, and expert testimony – as fragile as a deck of cards. The brief dissociation of the camera's position from that of the judge does not install some omniscient point of view above and beyond that of the judge. Its effect is more subversive. It alerts us that the alliance between camera and judge is dissolved and, in doing so, illuminates the machinery of legal justice by cinematic means.

Is it a coincidence that this metacourtroom drama was never shown on television during Preminger's lifetime? Preminger won a successful suit against a broadcaster that, having secured the television rights to the film, wanted to reduce its length to a TV-friendly ninety minutes and to interrupt it with blocks of advertising.[14] Even in such incidental matters the indecency of the television medium became offensive to the film's director, who exercised a judge's sovereignty over his work. Preminger insisted on unlimited control of the process: "It is ... my job as a director, to direct everything – even the writer, just as I direct actors."[15] His biographer characterizes his directing style as a thoroughly rigorous process: "he asserts complete control over everything he does and never relinquishes it until his films are out of distribution. Even then, the pictures remain under his jurisdiction."[16] This power over his own images was endangered the moment pictures were shortened and sequences chopped up for the sake of ratings and commercials – instead of following an autonomous aesthetic code.

— Tribunalization of Trials

These two key scenes from 1950s America – the hearing of 1954 and the courtroom film of 1959 – show a dividing line between the anomie of television and the autonomy of cinema, which sets up its own aesthetic rules, and thus also between the tribunal and the courtroom trial. While court and film achieve a certain complicity in their mediality, the tribunal seeks a greater affinity with television.

Justifiably wary of television, the legal system, which does not belong to the media-saturated world of television, for a long time delayed the invasion of cameras. From the beginning of cinema, when reporters in the new medium sought the right to report on court proceedings via film, the American Federal Court had recognized no such right. Going further back, the 1846 federal rules of criminal procedure were interpreted in such a way that film cameras were prohibited from main trials. The federal courts reaffirmed the prohibition many times, extending it to include television cameras as well. In 1972 the prohibition was expanded to include civil courts. This remains true on a federal level, but many individual states have loosened up their restrictions.

In Germany cameras are likewise prohibited in the courtroom. Section 169 of the Court Constitutional law (*Gerichtsverfassungsgesetz*) decrees that for the duration of the proceedings no sound or film recordings intended for the public are to be permitted.[17] That the law was passed in 1969 is no coincidence, for it was a time when households in the Federal Republic of Germany were becoming fully equipped with TV sets – mostly for the occasion of the televised moon landing – and so for the first time they could receive live reports in their living rooms.

It is easy to write off the media shyness of Germany's judges[18] as a kind of snobbery.[19] But it also revealed a fear that the admission of TV cameras into the courtroom, would make a fair trial impossible. Chief Justice Warren Burger – one of the most vehement opponents of broadcasting Supreme Court cases and, as it happens, a former professor of media-obsessed and tribunal-savvy Special Prosecutor Kenneth Starr – expressed this concern in simple terms when he compared trial reportage in newspapers with live broadcasts on TV: "In a newspaper the words aren't coming right out of the mouth of the judge or attorney. On television you see the person and it's coming right out of his mouth."[20] What comes directly from the mouth of a representative of the justice system should not be duplicated in another medium. This doubling of speech denies the judge's words their exclusivity. Thus the rationale behind the juridical reserve in the matter of cameras must be sought in the medium itself.

The presence of cameras competes with the mediality of the justice system. "What is a trial if not the putting of words in the place of violence, and money in the place of pain?" asks the French jurist Antoine Garapon, thus reformulating the mediatic function of the court.[21] It is supposed to translate the criminal act into a symbolic form. The court trial posits the frame within which a speechless and unrepresentable act is captured in words and in which the immeasurable suffering of the victims is converted into money. Were a camera present, it would only encourage dramatization, as has often been critically suggested. Dramatic rhetoric has been allowed openly in court cases at least since the introduction of attorneys as representatives of the accused. The camera intervenes in even the forensic ritual of coding violence and threatens to topple the media conversion of act to language in favor of another: act to image.

In the courtroom trial, judge and camera occupy the same position. They mediate the process of arriving at justice, they grant permission to speak, remind witnesses to adhere to the question, and ensure that proper procedure is followed. They are monitors in a literal sense; for precisely this reason judges do not want to share their thrones with their technical counterpart. The simultaneous presence of judges and cameras is only conceivable if the camera were to be inconspicuous. Only cameras that do not challenge the judge's authority have any chance of being tolerated. Thus in 1965 the experimental use of film and TV cameras was permitted but relegated behind a soundproof panel.[22] Excluded from the space of representation, they were allowed to exercise their monitoring function only when hidden from view.

When judges and cameras agree upon a division of labor and monitor events each in their own way, then the recording of trials is at least made more palatable. It is therefore hardly surprising that the U.S. prohibition on cameras at the trial itself was made less restrictive precisely at a time when cameras became invisible without the aid of awkward courtroom enclosures. In the 1980s, "as television cameras became smaller, quieter and less noticeable, a few states began to permit TV coverage," and they found a place in the courts more frequently.[23]

Even German constitutional law has reacted to the technical breakthrough of invisible cameras. A camera "accidentally" left running for the verdict in the 1993 "AWACS trial" served as proof that these inconspicuous devices no longer disturbed the proceedings and the Federal Constitutional Court permitted the retroactive broadcast of this recorded passage. On this occasion the justice system cited television's self-definition as a medium of authenticity, arguing that in such proceedings "the most authentic possible reporting is in the public interest" and was to be placed above all other interests.[24] A section subsequently introduced to Federal Constitutional Court law (17 a) has since allowed for the opening and conclusion of trials at the Constitutional Court to be taped for television. In all other trials, such as those of the criminal and civil courts, there is still a general prohibition, which the Federal Constitutional Court confirmed in a January 2001 decision concerning a complaint lodged by a private television network.

In a dissenting opinion some judges of the Constitutional Court formulated their concerns. They felt that a strict prohibition was probably untenable in this day and age, since the media has become an "important companion to nearly every citizen." The reality of the media had to be recognized by the justice system and it was important that certain trials, or segments of trials, were made available to a wider public than that of the courtroom.[25]

What is currently viewed as a dissenting opinion will someday become the prevailing one, if for no other reason than that television as a medium has its own momentum. Greedy for live broadcasts, it long ago discovered the immediacy and dramatic character of court trials and has produced a number of series based on court events. The arguments currently used by the legal system cannot prevent this tendency. The justice system, which seems to have forgotten its own medial character, has seen its final argument against the competing medium being laid to rest with video cameras that operate noiselessly and almost invisibly.

The media-based arming of the courts has been encouraged by a tendency within the justice system itself, a move toward *tribunalization*. Many of the most recent international courts, such as that at The Hague, have their origins in the tribunal. Tribunals occur when the extant justice system is not appropriate; during transitional periods, after a change in government, and so on. Ruti Teitel calls these tribunal processes "transitional justice," processes in which the illegality of an overthrown system is investigated. From their beginnings, these tribunals have shown a tremendous affinity for the medium of television, because they depend on a public audience for their very existence. In the international courts that originate from the tribunal, then, the presence of cameras has already been written into the architecture.[26]

The lines between real court trials and fictional courtroom dramas are additionally blurred when television series recreate courtroom scenes and TV stations report live from the courts. There is also a similar blurring of lines when a district attorney or large legal firms test out a given trial ahead of time by staging and videotaping anticipated scenarios, down to the details of potential witness statements and jury reaction; and then rehearse their appearances on the basis of an evaluation of the video material. Like a classic courtroom drama, the trial that then takes place follows a script full of unexpected plot twists and surprises for the rest of the trial participants.

If even the traditional courts open themselves to television and video, the strict separation between the inside and outside of the courtroom that is constitutive of the legal system will cease to be valid. The legal scholar Peter Goodrich described how the theatrical logic of the justice system, which is based on the difference between the arcane and the public, avoids the video logic of presence:

> The trials of the century evidence the emergence of law in the videosphere.... These inscriptions, the cameras, the monitors, the networks and relays, displace the older distinctions between inside and outside the court and the law. The law has now become manifestly itinerant, but in a new sense – one in which its relays are as much the subject of media constraints, the genres of spectacle or viewing, as they are the obedient servants of the lawyer's message....

> The law became instantaneous, and the public presence of law was taken out of the exclusive and solemn or learned hands of the lawyers and passed down... to waiting reporters who would read and interpret it live on camera.[27]

According to Goodrich, the instantaneous and itinerant *modus operandi* dissolves a justice system that has built its authority on the obscure power of files and a monopoly on truth bound up with the rhetoric of writing and inimical to the image:

> The videosphere suggests a diametrically different relation between law and its past. Under the performative demands of screen acting, the very visibility and immediacy of decision, the impossibility of hiding behind occult writs or invisible prior judgments, make the decision into a frame of embodiment, a staging of images, a self-conscious and transparent rite.[28]

For to Goodrich, video liberates the judiciary from the rigid script of a court trial that operates, despite all calls for transparency, much like a cabinet behind closed doors. It thus opens new possibilities for drama: "The videosphere makes visible the literal inscription of legality: the pain, the fear, the drama and catharsis, tragedy or comedy of rules."[29] The change looks like this when one thinks of it from the point of view of the judiciary: as visualization and exposure of the court's iconophobic legal formality and its violent inscription in the body of the judged.

Theatricality as a possibility for negating the compulsion and violence of the law sounds like a fine idea. The TV medium itself, which is said to manifest these emancipating effects on the closed trials in court, suggests a different evaluation. The transformations of the judiciary in the videosphere, as Goodrich describes them – the varied occupation of different positions in the trial; the institutional, functional, and spatial boundlessness of the proceedings; their sheer presence – all these, in the end, are characteristics of the tribunal. If television cameras are present in court proceedings, elements that have their origins in the disorder of the tribunal will of necessity seep into the court trial. The ritual of the legal search for justice will give way to the logic of the duel. The judge's function as a mediator – like that of a film director – is disordered as soon as a trial is broadcast on television, made to fit into a broadcast format, framed and interrupted by ads. Under the directives of a televisual system of justice, there would not be a better, less ambiguous justice, if only for the reason that the tribunal can ironize the court trial. Under TV directives an equally ambiguous justice would hold sway, one that would adapt itself ever further until it was indistinguishable from the rest of the television shows in tribunal format.

1 According to Cavell, the inauguration of President Eisenhower several months earlier had been the first media-based mass event in the United States. Stanley Cavell, "The Fact of Television," in *Themes Out of School: Effects and Causes* (Chicago: University of Chicago Press, 1988): 248.

2 David M. Oshinsky, *A Conspiracy So Immense: The World of Joe McCarthy* (London: Collier Macmillan, 1983), 416.
3 Ibid. 424.

4 Otto Preminger, *Preminger: An Autobiography* (Garden City, N.Y.: Doubleday, 1977), 154.
5 Ibid.154.
6 Ibid. 154.

7 In Otto Preminger's biography the law, theater, and film are tightly interwoven at the most personal level. As assistant to Max Reinhardt, Preminger would one day take on the case of a baron's daughter with the pseudonym Marion Mill, who filed a complaint against a nightclub owner for breach of contract. Preminger, J.D., won the trial, gave his client a role in the piece he was currently directing, and ultimately married her: "Among the legion of pretty girls hoping to make their name in the theatre and to succeed Unter Reinhardt was an eighteen-year-old from Budapest, daughter of a Baron, who just graduated from the University of Vienna. Her stage name was Marion Mill ... Miss Hoffman, realizing that a lawyer involved in the theatre world would be more sympathetic to her case than one from the 'out- side' world, sent her to a young assistant director in one of Reinhardt's theatres who also happened to be a doctor of law ... His name was Otto Preminger." Gerald Pratley, *The Cinema of Otto Preminger* (New York: Castle Books, 1971), 8.

8 The script was by Robert Traver (a pseudonym for John Voelker, then a retired judge).

9 Ingeborg Maus, "Justiz als gesellschaftliches Uber-Ich. Zur Funktion von Rechtsprechung in der vaterlosen Gesellschaft," in *Sturz der Götter? Vaterbilder im 20. Jahrhundert*, eds., Werner Faulstich and Gunter E. Grimm (Frankfurt am Main: Suhrkamp, 1989), 122.

10 This juxtaposition of the two names may also contain a reference to Alger Hiss, former assistant to Holmes and the first victim of the HUAC.

11 Holmes, who often based his psychologically intuitive judgments on experiences he himself had in the Civil War, was First Lieutenant in the 12th Massachusetts Regiment of Volunteers, the military body that was to become the United States Army.

12 To name one example, *A Few Good Men* (1992–1993) with Tom Cruise and Demi Moore.

13 In Vienna, Preminger had dramatized a trial that had been a popular sensation, and which shortly thereafter enjoyed success as a Broadway production: *Libel! A Courtroom Drama by Edward Wool.*

14 Prately, *The Cinema of Otto Preminger,* 129.
15 Ibid. 69.
16 Ibid. 23.

17 The exceptions to this prohibition, included in the first draft, were excised from the final version because of pressure by various criminal jurists.

18 Previous attempts to moderate the strict prohibition of cameras in the German justice system have been thwarted chiefly by members of the judiciary. See the dissenting opinion to the Decision of the Bundesverfassungsgericht's (Federal Constitutional Court), ruling of January 24, 2001: 1 BvR 2623/95 par. 90, 101. See also, Peer Zumbansen, "Federal Constitutional Court Affirms Ban of TV-Coverage of Court Proceedings," *German Law Journal* 2, no. 3 (February 15, 2001).

19 In a recent decision of the Federal Constitutional Court on the admission of television recordings in the courtroom – which was not even about the trial in session, but just the beginning and end of a courtroom proceeding – the judges in claimed their right to privacy against camera recordings. See the Decision of the Federal Constitutional Court of July 21, 2000: 1 BvQ 2001.

20 Quoted from Tony Mauro, "The Camera-Shy Federal Courts: Why Are Cameras Accepted in State Courts but Are Dreaded in Federal Courts?" *Media Studies Journal* 12 (1998): 62.

21 Antoine Garapon, "Justice Out of

Court: The Dangers of Trial by Media," in *Law as Communication*, ed. David Nelken (Aldershot, U.K.: Ashgate Publishing Limited, 1992), 236.

22 See *Estes v. Texas*, 381 U.S. 532 (1965). In this 1965 lawsuit with a special vote by Chief Justice Warren the issue was whether the case against Billy Sol Estes could be considered a fair trial once the courtroom was reconstructed for the hidden cameras.

23 Fred Graham, "Doing Justice with Cameras in the Courts: How Important Is the Public Operation of the Judicial System?" *Media Studies Journal* 12 (1998): 33. The Supreme Court mentions this technical development explicitly in a decision from 1981. See *Chandler v. Florida* 101 U.S. 802 (1981), 813: "It is urged ... that many of the negative factors found in Estes – cumbersome equipment, cables, distracting lighting, numerous camera technicians – are less substantial factors today than they were at that time," quoted in Ralph Alexander Lorz, "Gerichtsberichterstattung und Informationsanspruch der Offentlichkeit aus der Sicht deutscher und amerikanischer Verfassungsrechtsprechung," in *Herausforderungen an das Recht der Informationsgesellschaft*, ed. A. Haratsch, D. Kugelmann, and U. Repkewitz (Stuttgart: Mainz et al.: Boorberg Verlag, 1996): 75, n. 88.

24 Decision of the Federal Constitutional Court, 1 BvQ 17/00, printed in *Neue Juristische Wochenschrift* 2000, 2890.

25 See the Decision of the Federal Constitutional Court of July 21, 2000: 1 BvQ 2001.

26 See Laura Kurgan, "Residues: ICTY Courtroom No. 1 and the Architecture of Justice," *Alphabet City 7: Social Insecurity* (2001): 112–129.

27 Peter Goodrich, "Europe in America: Grammatology, Legal Studies, and the Politics of Transmission," *Columbia Law Review* 101 (2001): 2075.

28 Goodrich, 2076.

29 Ibid.

In Between: Power and Procedure Where the Court Meets the Public Sphere

— Richard Mohr

— The Court as a Bounded Place

Dating back to Ancient Greece, courts have been held in special places. Homer described the "polished stones in a sacred circle" which defined the place where the elders decided disputes.[1] In the twentieth century, it is still possible to consider courts as a sacred circle, though different signs now distinguish them from the profane world outside.[2] Robert Jacob has described the evolution of the modern European court, from the place of justice signified by a tree and an enclosure of hazel branches, to the timber paneling characteristic of more recent courtrooms.[3] Legal doctrine itself demands the court be fixed in place, from the Magna Carta's dictum that "Ordinary lawsuits shall not follow the royal court around, but shall be held in a fixed place," to the modern requirement that courts sit at a "proclaimed place."[4]

This paper explores the implications of the courts' fixed place and its borders with the world outside its walls. Major tensions arise, in courthouse architecture and in law, between the place of the court and the other places of which the court must take account: the sites of crimes or injuries, places where witnesses are, and places accessible to the public. Courts are still at pains to patrol their own boundaries, in order to regulate media coverage, to exclude inadmissible evidence, or to control the exercise of judicial power. And yet each of these boundaries must be permeable under the right circumstances: the public must have access to the courts and to their proceedings; admissible evidence must enter the court; and judicial power must not only be manifest in court, but it must be felt far beyond the walls of the court, in compliance with and enforcement of judgment.

— Testing the Limits: Legal Architecture in Four Trials

We may begin the investigation by sketching a few contemporary courtroom scenarios. These are four different examples of courtroom architecture, but not because of the place of the walls or the height of the bench. I have selected them because they each mediated the relationship of the court to the public and the outside world of forensic facts in a distinctive way. We have had an opportunity to see and to discuss a number of examples of built courts throughout this conference. Those courts are examples of court architecture designed by architects, whatever the involvement of judges and court managers in the process. In the following examples, the focus is on the individual trial. In these cases, the judge is the designer of the legal architecture, making use of technology and space to process evidence and communicate within and beyond the immediate courtroom. Before introducing more challenging and nuanced examples, I will contrast the fixity and closure of the conventional courtroom with the world-as-courtroom that we saw in the O. J. Simpson criminal trial.

— The Court as Closed Space: a Conventional Civil Torts Court

In researching the spatial and material aspects of the New South Wales District Court (civil jurisdiction) I was struck by the efforts to which lawyers must go to adduce evidence from other times and places. In scouring the courts for material signs of their role, I one day found a photograph in a corridor. This photograph had presumably fallen from the file of a lawyer in a motor accident damages case. On the marble tiled floor of Sydney's original Supreme Court building (then used by the District Court) was a picture of a country road. There were no cars, no people, just the curving centre lines, paddocks, fences and a few trees on either side. It had found its way to the heart of Sydney's legal precinct, into the

Francis Greenway building which first defined that precinct from the 1820s.

The scene when such a photograph enters the court proceedings is familiar: it is tendered as evidence, passed to a court officer, viewed by the other party, handed to the judge, and recorded as an exhibit. Photographs, maps or other representations of places are then subject to examination and debate. They are shown to witnesses. A barrister asks permission to approach the witness; a map is spread out across the witness stand, and its microphone, while the court monitor wrenches off the headphones in pain. The judge cranes over to see the points in space that are being indicated on the map, while the other barrister tries to gain a vantage point. Without a map or plan it is even more tortuous. Where was the can of petrol when you last saw it? Which part of the veranda? How far from the steps? How high off the ground was the verandah at that point? Again, the scene is familiar. It is the way in which other places, at other times, are reproduced in words through legal questioning so that they may enter the court as evidence.

There is usually no jury, and few members of the public, in court for cases like these. Yet there is a public gallery and an unlocked door: the guarantee of public scrutiny of the judicial process. If the case is of any broader interest to the public there may be a journalist or two, with pens and pads. If there is a television crew, they will be at the bottom of the courthouse steps. The public at home may see one of the parties and a huddle of lawyers, one of whom may even say a few words. The public presence in the court itself is usually more obvious as an absence.

— Court without Limits: The O. J. Simpson Trial

At the other extreme is the televised media trial, of which O. J. Simpson's murder trial is the most notorious example. A US audience could follow every word of the trial, with commentary, on the cable channel Court TV. Images from the trial, interspersed with various interviews, commentary and other images, of course found their way into news, current affairs and infotainment programs across North America and the world. This spatial coverage differs from the conventional space of the courtroom in numerous ways. For the public, the trial is no longer "placed" in a courtroom, with its careful situation of each of the players: judge, defence, prosecution, defendant, witness. It is rather "delocalized"[5] so that the action takes place in cyberspace, as a collage of courtroom, crime scene, television studio and freeway. Not only does the place of the courtroom blend into an undifferentiated and incoherent space, but also the time sequence of the trial is cut in and out of real time, flashbacks, and predictions about the verdict. The trial has no more internal structure, once it is predigested and redigested, than the repeated image from the helicopter of Simpson's car driving interminably around the Los Angeles freeways before his arrest.

Clearly, these two views are at extremes of the manifestations of the place of the courtroom and its legal and architectural boundaries. Although they illustrate a crossroads at which court architecture finds itself, the architectural elements of the court and its procedures are hard to discern in the great gulf between the two. In order to discover what makes up the finer grain of a legal architecture of the courtroom, we may turn to two other trials, as case studies in which courts carefully addressed many of the issues raised in the first two cases. Both these next two trials made extensive and intelligent use of state-of-the-art technology to achieve their results, but the technology is not the focus of this analysis. Instead, they illustrate the ways in which the place of the court can be recreated and the trial's evidence reprocessed in ways, which enhance the flow of information without breaching the legal boundaries of the court. In one instance, a court was able to "sit" in two different United States cities simultaneously. In the other, a court, which sat sequentially in Sydney and Newcastle was able to reproduce, as if in virtual reality inside the court, the site of the accident that it was investigating. In both instances, the needs of a concerned public were given a high priority.

— One Court in Two Places Simultaneously: The Oklahoma Bombing Trial

Judge Richard Matsch, presiding in the Oklahoma City bombing trial of Timothy McVeigh, was determined to avoid the media circus to which the Simpson trial degenerated. Yet he had a problem. The trial was to be held in Denver, to avoid the difficulty of finding an unbiased jury in Oklahoma, but the victims and their families in Oklahoma were exerting great political pressure to gain access to the proceedings. Declining an offer by Court TV to convey the trial to the concerned victims in Oklahoma, the Federal Court took control of all technical and legal aspects of the transmission. An aircraft hanger in Oklahoma was converted into an auditorium, in which a retired judge presided. The security of the closed circuit signal between Denver and Oklahoma was checked by the National Security Agency, the top-secret electronic-eavesdropping agency in the USA. This signal went both ways. Not only did the audience in Oklahoma see the trial, but Judge Matsch had a camera set up in Oklahoma monitoring the audience from the bench in Denver, on which was also displayed the image which was being transmitted to Oklahoma.[6] By effectively making the Oklahoma auditorium an annex to the public gallery of his court in Denver, in which all the same conditions applied, the court was effectively sitting in two places at once. Yet it achieved this with scrupulous attention to the legal boundaries of the court, so that the jury was impartial and protected, just as witnesses would not see inappropriate evidence.

— Place Reproduced in a Mobile Court: The Gretley Mine Inquiry

In mid to late 1997, the Court of Coal Mines Regulation held an inquiry into an accident that occurred the previous year, which led to four deaths at Gretley mine, in the Hunter Valley in New South Wales in Australia. Documents including plans, maps, daily transcripts, legislation and photographs were either keyed or scanned to electronic storage. There was also a videotape of the mine site. All documents were available on a server (accessible to the parties by modem with their own password); transcripts were provided to parties daily by e-mail and hard copy. CD-ROMs were available to the parties monthly, which included all documents and images (e.g. maps), which would be unwieldy to download via modem. In addition to the usual documents (transcripts, acts, subpoenaed documents), the court was dealing with complex three-dimensional spatial relationships. The miners apparently drowned when they tunnelled into disused workings full of water and gas. The error occurred as a result of mistaking the level of the new workings relative to the old, so the spatial aspects of the mine, and its representation in various maps, were crucial evidence.

All up-to-date information was also stored on a hard disk in the court. The computer linked to this hard disk was operated by the judge's associate and networked to a number of screens as well as to computers used by counsel in court. The screens (of various appropriate sizes) showed whatever appeared on the associate's computer and were clearly visible from the bench, the witness box, the bar table and the public gallery. The associate could select the relevant portion of maps or documents to be seen, and scale them up or down as necessary. Counsel could download data directly from the court's hard disk to their computers.

All representations of the mine in question, or of other relevant sites or documents, could be called up on the in-court screens as required by counsel. All of those present in the courtroom were able to view clearly, by means of the on-screen plans, video or photographs of the site, whatever aspect of the mine or its representations were the subject of discussion or evidence. As in the Oklahoma case, there were many families and workers affected by the accident, and providing them with access to all aspects of the proceedings was among the court's top priorities.

Courts of this nature customarily take a view of the site of the accident. By improving the representation of the site in the courtroom, this hearing did not require a view, while sitting in specially prepared and equipped courtrooms in Newcastle and Sydney. The court became more mobile, to the extent that the data on which court and counsel relied was available in cyberspace, whether in Newcastle or in Sydney. On the other hand the court, only sitting in a courtroom, became even more rooted in its traditional, proclaimed, place.

— Jurisprudential and Political Requirements

This legal architecture, which articulates the courtroom into zones and links it to remote sites and to a mass audience, is formed of a curious interplay among a number of cross cutting rationales or requirements. The diverse and competing sources of these requirements lead to indeterminacy of any particular problem, whether it be media access to the courtroom, or the admissibility of electronic and remote evidence. I would like to canvass a number of sources, without endorsing or evaluating them, in the manner more of a history of ideas than a legal or political analysis. Having sketched these in overview, I hope to indicate two broad areas of tension which judges, architects and court managers face in designing courts or, for that matter, in "designing" the spatial arrangements of particular trials.

We could attempt to locate the demands for the spatial integrity of the courtroom in purely legal terms, such as the law of evidence, and laws applying to prejudice of jurors or potential jurors. Yet this would tell a very small part of the story. Within a wider frame, the demands of law are meshed in with the political demands of today and of earlier times, and with changing views in jurisprudence.

— Boundaries: Evidence and privilege

In the broadest terms of jurisprudence, the court protects its borders in order to ensure that only that which is legal enters the courtroom. The "frame" of architecture, Haldar has noted, serves to maintain those "rigid oppositional categories of truth and falsity, reason and madness, logic and emotion, evidence and hearsay, self and other."[7] This is most clearly seen in evidence law, where the borders of the law are patrolled by the requirements that evidence be admissible, introduced by (or at least with the right to challenge by) the parties, marked and stored by the court. Once admitted, evidence crosses from its transient life in the temporal world to a new existence in the law. Gamble and I have previously identified the barriers to and significance of the introduction of important aspects of social reality into the realm of law, where they may take on a new life as precedent or as data for the further elaboration of legislation and policy.[8]

In this way the boundaries of the courtroom protect proceedings from the entry of inadmissible evidence. They form another protective barrier, protecting witnesses from any prejudicial action as a result of their evidence. The proceedings are thus protected from the intrusion of other legal action. Neither the actor inside the court nor a reporter fairly reporting those proceedings may be sued. The proceedings and the actors in court are inviolable within the boundaries of this "sacred circle."

— Judicial Power

Courts are also seen by the law as the seat of judicial power, with the boundaries of the court serving to mark out the limits within which that power may be exercised. The decisions of Australian and United States courts in constitutional cases touching on the role of the judiciary are rich in architectural metaphors:

> Most critically, public confidence in the judiciary is indispensable to the operation of the rule of law; yet this quality is placed in risk whenever judges step *outside the courtroom* into the vortex of political activity.[9]

> For a Judge to descend from his judgment seat to the floor of the Court as a suitor against the man with whom he dealt or could have dealt judicially, seems to be a denial of the majesty of the law, a forgetfulness of his high representative character, an abasement of the dignity of his Court and his prestige as a Judge.[10]

I have considered elsewhere the role played by the physical limits of the courthouse in determining whether a judge is acting as a judge or as a *persona designata*.[11] Recent decisions of the High Court suggest that many factors other than the physical location of the judge (inside or outside a courthouse when making a decision) defines the role as judicial or personal.[12] However, concern with the location of the judge's work indicates the central importance of the physical setting in delimiting the exercise of judicial power.[13] The role of the courthouse in containing and regulating the use of judicial power is summed up by Haldar: "Architecture marks off and signifies that authority-to-judge which can only be found inside a court of law and nowhere else, it assigns legal discourse to a proper place."[14]

— Publicity and Equality

I have already referred to the special importance given to the fixed place of the courts, from Homer's "sacred circle" to the "fixed place" of the Magna Carta. The religious, political and legal rationales for those spatial doctrines would present fascinating objects of study in themselves. I would like to start this brief overview with the early colony of New South Wales, and the jurisprudence of the early nineteenth century.[15] The ad hoc and moveable courts of the early colony were formally fixed in space by the *Summary Offences Act (1832),* which required sittings to be held "in public at designated places." The conjunction of these two concepts, publicity and place, roots the fixity of the colonial courts in the political demands of the era. The political significance of the public sphere, which developed throughout the bourgeois period from the eighteenth to the nineteenth century, was given explicit jurisprudential content in the era that followed the French Revolution. Both Hegel and Bentham founded their theories of law on the principle of publicity as the guarantee of justice in the 1820s, a decade or so after Mirabeau's statement to the Constituent Assembly: "Donnez-moi le juge que vous voudrez, partial, corrupt, mon ennemi même, si vous voulez: peu m'importe pourvu qu'il ne puisse rien faire qu'à la face du public."[16]

By 1832 the young colony of New South Wales was to rely on this principle as the shield against the arbitrary law imposed by the colonial lay magistrate who carried with him "the inherent privilege of making a court when and wherever he liked, so that if only he had his ink-horne and goosequill, his constable and flogger, he could open his law shop anywhere ... according as his whim or duty dictated."[17]

By the mid twentieth century, theorists based the importance of the place of the court upon its power to abolish distinctions of privilege or power between the parties, or the jurors, "equalized by the task and the place."[18]

> Every place from which justice is pronounced is a veritable temenos, a sacred spot cut off and hedged in from the "ordinary" world ... [W]hether square or round it is still a magic circle, a play-ground where the customary differences of rank are abolished. Whoever steps inside it is sacrosanct for the time being.[19]

— Situated Discourse

More recently, philosophers and jurists have remarked upon the connection between the ideal form of fair deliberation upon a disputed issue, which should characterize a trial, and the physical zones and layout of the courtroom.[20] The specific place (in space and time), which is allocated to each participant (prosecution, defense, witness, judge), promotes the coherence of that "complex and very sophisticated unity" which is the trial. For Garapon this "situated discourse" is integral to the deliberation of the court.[21] An appreciation of the position from which the trial participant is speaking is crucial to an understanding of the trial, inside or outside the courtroom. The importance of publicity urges the judge to respond to the demands of the new media to ensure that the public has access to the proceedings, outcomes and deliberations of the trial. Whether this is to involve the fragmented and displaced discourse of an O. J. Simpson trial, or the extended public gallery of the Oklahoma bombing trial, must be determined by the court having regard to the technology available to build the appropriate legal architecture. Even the conditions on the televising of verdicts, such as those of the Supreme Court of Victoria and the Federal Court in Melbourne, constitute elements of the legal architecture by which courts become accessible, and by which the trial becomes comprehensible to the public.

— Essential Tensions

In "designing" the legal architecture of the courthouse or of the individual trial, the judge, architect or court manager must work within a framework which recognizes the jurisprudential demands which I outlined above primarily in terms of the law of evidence and the location of judicial power. This is a complex task, which must also be carried out within the social context of requirements for a public perception of justice that takes account of the need for equality among the parties (including the rights of victims and of defendants) and public scrutiny of the trial. Both the procedure and the architecture of the trial may enhance or detract from the processes of deliberation and active comprehension of the judge, jury, participants and the public (who are more likely to be seated in front of the television than in the public gallery). These legal and social demands, requirements or opportunities may be understood in terms of two essential tensions or paradoxes which are inherent in the very nature of the court as a defined place of justice.

— Places: the Trial, the Place-as-Evidence and the Public Space

If a trial must take place in a courtroom, the places outside the court present problems to the designer in the broad sense, whether architect or judge. While the trial is contained architecturally and delimited in space and time, it must comprehend those places which are to be introduced as evidence. This comprehension must be filtered through the requirements of evidence, taking account of the various legal and technological devices, which are available. This is not unlike a mapmaking exercise whereby a space must be represented in another space. The space in which the evidence must be represented is the space of law, its place the courtroom. A cartographic map is not a legal map. The map may enter the law as evidence, but the legal map whereby an outside place enters the law through a trial may consist of many such maps, as well as photographs, descriptions and re-examinations of descriptions.

Having entered the court, the place-as-evidence must still

work as part of a process of deliberation and understanding. To the extent that a public outside the court and outside the law may need to participate in this process then the representations of place must be capable of emerging again from the court in the form of public information. If we accept Garapon's strictures against trial by media,[22] then this public information should re-emerge, or be amenable to re-constitution as part of a situated discourse. How is the spatial structure of the trial to be retained within the place-as-evidence once it leaves the courtroom? Whether or not the evidence involves representations of places, can it be reconstructed in the public space outside the court? The possibilities of architecture, technology and the media reach their limits in these questions.

— Power: Containment and Diffusion

The court is protected as a locus of judicial power by its containment of that power. This is signified in the court's exclusive authority as the place of judgment, as well as by its elevation, celebration and shielding of the judge. With a few ceremonial exceptions, the judge does not appear as a judge (that is, in a gown) nor does she or he act as a judge (that is, judging) outside the court. As we saw by reference to the language of court decisions, the private capacity of the judge is insulated from the official role by the courthouse walls, and in this way the authority of the official capacity is conserved and enhanced.

The tension in this case arises from the expectation that judicial power will act beyond the courthouse walls. While judicial power is spatially concentrated by courthouses, its impact is to be felt throughout society. This may be seen simply in the need to enforce or to have the community comply with judgments. It should not be seen so simply, of course, that we would expect the judge to emerge from the courthouse to enforce judgment. On the contrary, the very aloofness of the judge, the concentration of authority behind the courthouse walls seems intended to enhance that authority, and hence compliance. In certain cases, and notably in criminal matters, judicial authority is backed by the power of the state. Yet this power is itself only legitimate to the extent that it is accepted as such by the citizens, and deemed to be lawful by the courts. Without that authority a brute, illegitimate strength of the state would not only be unacceptable but it ultimately could not survive.

Here again we must return to the spatial limits of the court. It is not judicial power which emanates from the courthouse, but judicial authority. The court, like the state, rules by consent, which it earns by its legitimacy and public acceptance. That acceptance still derives in part from the institutional reinforcement of ideas of law and respect for tradition and status. The symbolic power and the representations of the authority of the court and the judge continue to play a role in the calculus of consent. But in a democratic age public legitimacy ultimately derives from the knowledge and understanding that people have of the courts and their processes. The courts, while containing judicial power, must also diffuse information. Whether we see this in nineteenth century terms as the presence of the public, or in late twentieth century terms as an appreciation of the situated discourse of the trial, the courts' position rests upon their capacity to communicate.

— Between Outside and Inside: The Architecture of the Trial and of the Court

Architecture is the medium of this communication. That is to say, the courts communicate through the architecture of both the courthouse and the trial. Courthouse architecture includes the foyers and corridors, video links, remote witness rooms and media facilities. The architecture of each trial includes the legal architecture of the situated discourse of the trial, the location of witnesses, the processing of evidence and the accommodation of the public and the media. Architecture gives us walls and doors, closed and open communication channels. This is the architecture which mediates between inside and outside, between the place of the trial and the place-as-evidence, between containment and projection of judicial power, between law and not-law. These boundaries of the law are defined by judges, architects, and court managers. In this paper I have tried to suggest some of the ways in which the boundaries and openings may include as well as exclude the public. In particular, by proposing a court architecture, which takes seriously both the political and jurisprudential requirements, I hope to open a debate about the courts and their relationships with the non-legal world which goes beyond simple assumptions about the role of the media vis-à-vis the courts.

As the case studies of a number of trials illustrated, the relationships between the courts – the places in which trials are held – and the public sphere are potentially redesigned in each case. The architecture of each of those trials was distinctive, whatever courthouse they were held in. The Denver court's Oklahoma annex to its public gallery, the virtual reconstruction of a coal mine in the Gretley inquiry, the undifferentiated flood of public information and commentary in the O. J. Simpson trial, and the impenetrable boundaries of the conventional civil claims court each express a different version of justice, and a view of the court's relation to the public. Judges design the architecture of a trial just as architects design the courthouse. There are variations between the media used by each, but the conceptual building blocks are shared.

This paper was written for the Representing Justice Conference (Wollongong, Australia 1998) and reflects the law and technology at that date. Republished with permission of the author.

1 Homer quoted in P. Goodrich, *Reading the Law. A Critical Introduction to Legal Method and Techniques* (Oxford: Basil Blackwell, 1986,), 168.

2 J. Huizinga, foreword (1932) in *Homo Ludens: A Study of the Play Element in Culture* (Boston: Beacon Press, 1955), 77.

3 R. Jacob, "The Historical Development of Courthouse Architecture / La formazione storica dell'architettura giudiziaria," *Zodiac*, no. 14 (1995/1996): 30–43.

4 e.g. *District Court Act 1973* (NSW) 5, 18F.

5 A. Garapon, "Justice out of Court: The Dangers of Trial by Media," in *Law as Communication,* ed. D. Nelken, (Aldershot: Dartmouth 1996); see also A. Garapon, "Il Rituale Giudiziario," in *I Diritti Nascosti: Approccio Antropologico e Prospettiva Sociologica,* eds., A. Giasanti, & G. Maggioni, (Milan: Raffaello Cortina Editore, 1995).

6 J. Toobin, "Victim Power," *The New Yorker,* 24 March, 1997.

7 P. Haldar, "In and Out of Court: On Topographies of Law and the Architecture of Court Buildings (A Study of the Supreme Court of the State of Israel)," *International Journal for the Semiotics of Law,* vol. 7, no. 20, (1994):185–200, 191.

8 H. Gamble & R. Mohr, "Court and community: tensions and accommodation," in *Delivering with Diversity,* eds., R Mohr and S. Lloyd (Wollongong: Centre for Court Policy and Administration, University of Wollongong, 1996).

9 *Hobson v Hansen (1967)* 265 F Supp 902 at 923 citing JS Wright J, quoted by Gummow J, *Kable v DPP (NSW)* (1996) 189 CLR 51: 132–3 (emphasis added).

10 Troughton v McIntosh (1896) 17 NSWR(L) 334 at 340, quoted by J. McHugh *Mann v O'Neill* (1997) 191 CLR 204: 217.

11 R. Mohr, "Separation of Powers: the Mind and Body of the Judge" (paper presented at Shifting Structures, Shifting Sociology – The Australian Sociological Association Conference, University of Wollongong, NSW, 9–12 December, 1997).

12 Compare *Grollo v Commissioner of Australian Federal Police* (1995) 184 CLR 348 with *Wilson v Minister for Aboriginal and Torres Strait Islander Affairs* (1996) 189 CLR 1.

13 Mason, commenting from retirement, accepted that a judge could act in a personal capacity outside the court without infringing the doctrine of the separation of powers, but regarded as "more dubious [the] proposition that a judge may be entrusted in virtue of his qualification as a judge with a non-judicial function, such as the issue of a warrant authorizing interception of a telephonic communication, as a designated individual on the footing that he is not acting as a member of the court, notwithstanding that he is appointed because he is a judge and that he deals with the application in a court or his chambers, availing himself of his judicial staff and court facilities." A. Mason, "A New Perspective on Separation of Powers," in *Canberra Bulletin of Public Administration* (1996) 82:1–9: 1–2 (emphasis added).

14 Haldar, "In and Out of Court," 169.

15 J. Habermas, *The Structural Transformation of the Public Sphere: an inquiry into a category of bourgeois society,* trans. Thomas Burger (1st German ed. 1962;Cambridge, Mass.: MIT Press, 1991).

16 "Give me any judge you like, biased, corrupt, my enemy even, if you like: it matters little to me as long as he can do nothing outside the public view." Mirabeau, quoted in Robert W. Millar, "The Formative Principles of Civil Procedure," *Illinois Law Review* (1923–24), 18:1–36; 94–117; 150–168: 156.

17 'Garryowen' (E. Finn) quoted in D Neal, *The Rule of Law in a Penal Colony: Law and Power in Early New South Wales* (Cambridge: Cambridge University Press, 1991), 55.

18 Hannah Arendt, "Public rights and private interests," in *Small Comforts for Hard Times*, eds. M. Mooney, and D. Stuber, (New York: Columbia University Press 1977), 105.

19 Huizinga, *Homo Ludens*, 77.

20 Stuart Hampshire, for example, builds a model of decision-making processes upon the institutional arrangements of councils, courts, and negotiating tables. "Often the very

physical setting itself, with an equal number of delegates on each side of the table, expresses the norm of fairness which is to govern the negotiation." S. Hampshire, *Innocence and Experience* (Cambridge, Mass.: Harvard University Press, 1989), 54.

21 Garapon, "Justice out of Court," 298.
22 Ibid.

Video Chamber

— Judy Radul

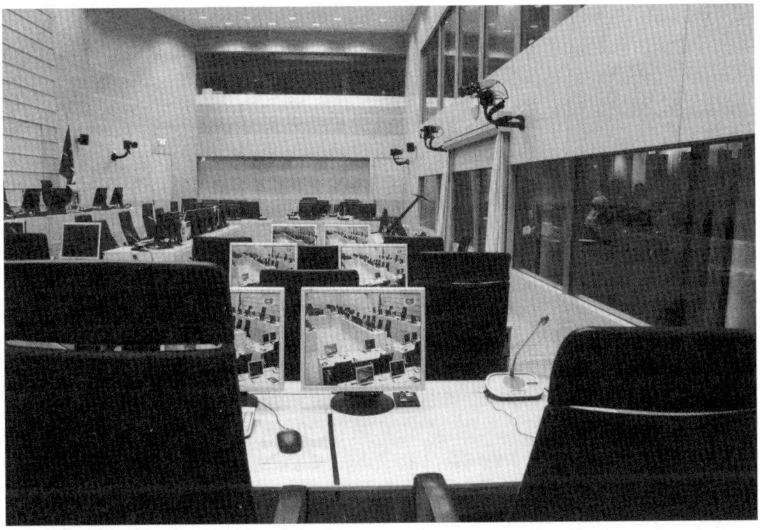

International Criminal Court, the Hague, Netherlands. View from defense side of the court, live feed from court cameras appearing on all monitors. Photo: Judy Radul.

Is it not astounding that the video camera has infiltrated the court of law – a space whose very definition is enclosure? Video cameras appear to extend the effect of glass and mirrors considered by Walter Benjamin in the *Arcades Project*: "The increasing transparency of glass in colourless glazing draws the outer world into the interior space, while covering the walls with mirrors projects the image of the interior space into the outer world. In either case the 'wall', as a container of space, is deprived of its significance."[1] But video cameras are a different type of glazing, they allow a bunker to appear permeable. They necessitate our engagement with questions concerning spatial enclosures, visual fictions, reflections, and phantoms.

This text travels by paroxysms of attention between ideas and instances whose correspondence therefore becomes topologically worn. However, once inscribed, these contiguous neighbour ideas must be complicated by a second story, an effigy level, an airspace comprised of through-the-lens-views-from-everywhere(s) connecting pathless intervals. In cutting and joining ideas, their inextricability increases and an assemblage reveals itself.

— Court theatre

If, for the purposes of argument, one categorically differentiates between theatre and video, one can say that before the incursion of video, the court was a theatrical space. That definition of theatricality would have to encompass the literary, as jurisprudence has long recognized the reiterative, text based foundations of the law, and the theatrical aspects of the trial. The growing acceptance by the 1980s of the field of study devoted to "law and literature" attests to this recognition. But the relation of law and theatre was already addressed hundreds of years earlier. Legal theorist and historian of rhetoric, Peter Goodrich, points out that in Justinian's *Digest of Roman Law* (seventh century A.D.) there existed "The prohibition against acting on stage ... on pain of *infamia* (loss of citizenship or civil death)."[2] In a recent essay Subha Mukherji comments that this relation was and remains a "paradoxical combination of proximity and rivalry between law and rhetoric."[3] Likewise, Goodrich's entry outlines,

> Both practices were determined by forms and conditions of representation. Rhetoric, a discipline that originated in the legal context of persuasion – often called *theatrum veritatis et iustitiae* (the theatre of truth and justice) – was 'the medium through which the drama of law was ... played out'; it focused on the performative and argumentative aspects of legal procedure. But the legal tradition itself developed a resistance to acknowledging the fundamentally rhetorical character of legality, going back to Plato's distinction between performance and law, or rather, between verbal performance and the theatre of justice, which was meant to persuade to a truth beyond artifice.[4]

— Theatre and court as spatial arts

In addition to the theatrical aspects of the legal trial[5] (evidenced by an emphasis on rhetorical argument, dramatic re-telling and ceremonial staging) more salient to our current discussion is the court's alignment with theatre as an art, dependant on spatial arrangement and division. The primary spatial division characteristic of the traditional theatre is that between the players and audience. From there one can discuss the history of theatre in terms of architectures and proxemics, which arrange and rearrange audience and players and frame or disavow the "stage picture" as distinct from the audience behind the "4th (fourth) wall." Richard Mohr writes in relation to the court of law that historically the court too is bound to a site; its location is fundamental:

> Dating back to Ancient Greece, courts have been held in special places. Homer described the 'polished stones in a sacred circle' which defined the place where the elders decided disputes.... Legal doctrine itself demands the court be fixed in place ... Major tensions arise, in courthouse architecture and in law between the place of the court and the other places of which the court must take account: the sites of crimes or injuries, places where witnesses are, and places accessible to the public.[6]

Not only are the courts themselves fixed in space, but also the players in the court drama are assigned a physical location from which they don't deviate.

The metonymies "the bench" and "the bar," are used respectively to refer to the judiciary and the lawyers, and give to each the name of the aspect of the built environment by which they assume and maintain their position. This alignment of subject position with physical location concretizes a rigidity of roles and writes the court *mise en scene* in stone, wood, and carpet (and now Cat-5 cable, screens, microphones, etc). In court, *where* you are, is *who* you are.

So the court is fixed in location, and the players are fixed in a location in the court. However, the introduction of technology such as CCT (closed circuit television) cameras, and presentation television monitors, breaks up this real time-real place

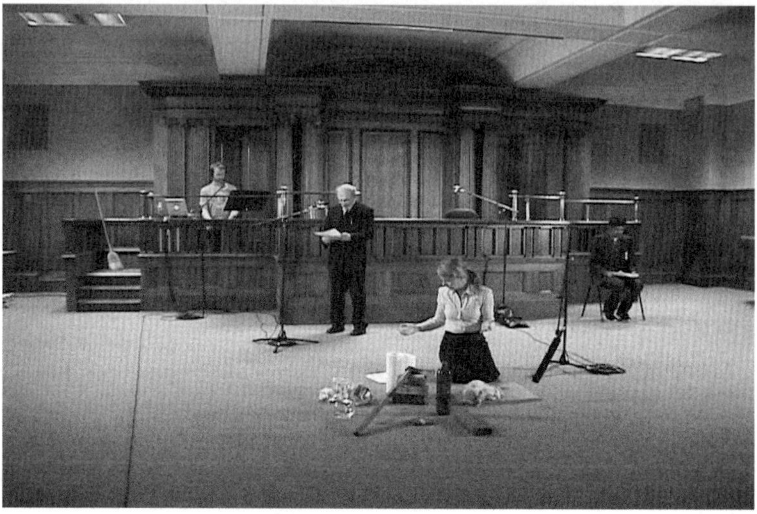

Judy Radul and Geoffrey Farmer, *Room 302*, (2005).
Video installation, video still.
Courtesy the artist and Catriona Jeffries Gallery

of the court theatre while, paradoxically, reinforcing it. Mohr writes about maps and photographs as the first incursion of "other spaces" into the court. However, this ability to bring all images and relevant materials into the court eliminates the necessity for the court to venture off site (a tour of a mining disaster is the example Mohr gives). Thereby the court becomes more anchored in a specific place, incorporating signs and signifiers of other places and times, but becoming monolithic and unmovable. Legal theorist Kirsten Anker documents an instance of a court coping with requirements to conduct activities off site. During the land claims of Australian Aboriginal people there arose a revealing conflict between two different cultural conceptions of space. The supposed neutrality of the courthouse as a place to speak one's claim is in sharp contrast to the law of many of the aboriginal peoples who recognize traditional "legal" obligations concerning provenance or rights to stories, songs, and particularly to speaking of the land. In essence their laws and ways forbade them from speaking of land unless they were on the land; the land is not an abstract object. This being-in-place is referred to as being "on country" and it became necessary for the court itself to become mobile and conduct proceedings at a number of sites related to the land claims. As a related part of the process a giant painting) was made and people who couldn't testify directly on their land, testified while standing on this painting as a manifestation of the land.

The painting is referred to as the Ngurrara Canvas and was presented at the National Native Title Tribunal in 1997. Anker writes about it thus:

> In evidence, the painting illustrates the rights (such as those indicated by boundaries), the origin of those rights in a system of law (such as Dreaming stories) and facilitates the oral evidence of the witnesses. The very production of the painting tends to the proof, following *Yorta Yorta*, that these people not only hold the requisite knowledge about their country, but continue to practice it *as* law. The painting succeeds in proving this in large part because, according to the painters' ways of seeing things, the designs are so intricately bound up in the land that 'they are the same thing', that walking on the painting 'brings [the] country up closer'.[7]

Anker also offers a description of the set up of the court of law when it established itself "on country":

> Even in a desert setting the idiom of order familiar in courtroom architecture (Haldar, 1994) is apparent: during the Miriuwung-Gajerrong hearing, a picnic table was transformed into a judges' bench with a red cloth; maps and stacks of legal papers reinforced the value of the written word; the judge and the lawyers sat on raised chairs and heard from witnesses while they, too were sitting in chairs rather than on the ground; microphones designated who the court would listen to; the whole arrangement enhanced the position of the judge – the performance was for him, who sat in objective distance from it all.[8]

The exception proves the rule, and the continued presence of the court in a stable physical location is underway (for instance) in the building of a permanent International Criminal Court in the Hague. Cases are pursued by this new court (founded on the Rome statute of 1998), when it is deemed too dangerous or destabilizing to hold the trial in the country of the crimes. This purpose-built building has yet to break ground, however its functions will no doubt be based on experiences gained in the recent manifestations of other "state of the art," CCT equipped, fully electronic, security conscious courtrooms. These sites include the building used since 1997 for the International Criminal Tribunal for the Former Yugoslavia, (retrofitted into a former insurance building) and the courtrooms and many floors of administrative offices at the interim location of the International Criminal Court in the Voorburg neighborhood of the Hague.

— Geometry of theatre and cinema

With the assertion that the court, again, like theatre, is an art relying on spatial arrangement, I want to further specify this space as "geometric" and to consider this geometry as a point from which to observe how video functions *in* and *of* the court. It is Roland Barthes who plainly calls theatre a geometric art, writing on Diderot and the idea of theatrical tableau in "Diderot, Brecht, Eisenstein" from 1973. Here, Barthes asserts this relationship between geometry and theatre:

> The theatre is precisely that practice which calculates the place of things *as they are observed*: if I set the spectacle here, the spectator will see this; if I put it elsewhere, he will not, and I can avail myself of this masking effect and play on the illusion it provides. The stage is the line which stands across the path of the optic pencil, tracing at once the point at which it is brought to a stop and, as it were, the threshold of its ramification. Thus is founded – against music (against the text) – *representation*.[9]

The statement above is in the first paragraph of the short essay, which concludes with the confirmation below regarding the geometric and thereby legal (concerned with meaning) nature of theatrical and cinematic representation. Barthes finds these forms *representational*, relating to already existing structures of meaning and not "open" to expansive interpretation in the ways of music and text,

> In the theatre, in the cinema, in traditional literature, things are always seen *from somewhere*. Here we have the geometrical foundation of representation: a fetishist subject is required to cut out the tableau. This point of meaning is always the Law: law of society, law of struggle, law of meaning. Thus all militant art cannot be but representational, legal.[10]

The contemporary court of law is a literal demonstration of a legal-theatrical geometry. It is (most often) laid out with strict rules and acute awareness of sightlines of the participants and the audience.[11] One perhaps surprising rendition of this geometry is courts in which the demand that the witness face the judge directly, results in witnesses sitting with their back to the audience. In the case of the International Criminal Court in the Hague, the attending audience can see the proceedings quite clearly through the glass wall, which divides the court from the viewers. However they are only able, due to the layout described above, to see the witness' face through the closed circuit multi camera system, the feeds from which are cut to a monitor mounted in the viewing gallery.

Barthes visualizes these geometries as necessarily anchored by the viewer's cone of vision – a single point of identification which "frames, focuses, enunciates" and thereby, authors. It seems the theatrical tableau can be epic, politically engaged, and militant, but it can't be "open." In the same paragraph Barthes slips without much comment from the geometry of theatre to the geometry of cinema, and here he finds an instance whereby an authoring point of view can be superseded by a non-human or supernatural gaze.

> In order for representation to be really bereft of origin and exceed its geometrical nature without ceasing to be representation, the price that must be paid is enormous – no less than death. In Dreyer's *Vampyr* ... the camera moves from house to cemetery recording *what the dead man sees*: such is the extreme limit at which representation is outplayed; the spectator can no longer take up any position, for he cannot identify his eye with the closed eyes of the dead man; the tableau has no point of departure, no support, it gapes open. Everything that goes on before this limit is reached (and this is the case of the work of Brecht and Eisenstein) can only be legal; in the long run, it is the Law of the Party which cuts out the epic scene, the filmic shot, it is this law which looks, frames, focuses, enunciates ..."[12]

The theatre and the camera both instantiate a "legal" gaze aligned with a subject who experiences (it)self as the author of the image. However, contra to Barthes, there is a reading

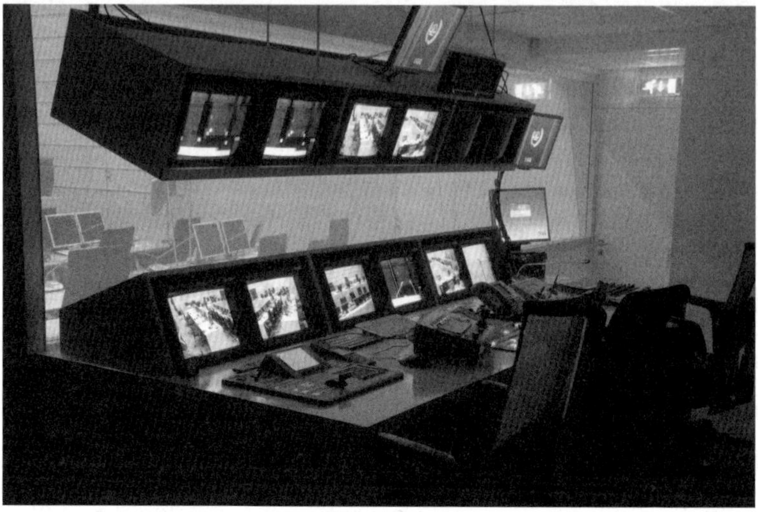

From the International Criminal Court, the Hague, Netherlands. Audiovideo control booth. Photo: Judy Radul.

whereby the dead eye of the protagonist in *Vampyr* isn't at *odds* with the camera eye, but rather *acts out* its blind, non-aligned, illegal, *machinic* gaze. In his 1973 text above, Barthes assumes the identification of eye and camera, but the increasing presence of automated cameras, such as that in your laptop or phone, eliminates the need to bring the camera to your eye and align their vision. This kind of beside-human view separates the geometry of the camera from that of the theatre. In his consideration of "machine vision" American theorist John Johnston takes up Deleuze's liberation of the eye (and the camera) from its role as a "fixed organ" to "an indeterminate, polyvalent, organ."[13] To extend the idea of "machinic vision" Johnston finds it essential to return to Deleuze's concept of a deterritorialized consciousness whose inside-outside permeability shifts notions of what constitutes perception. He validates Deleuze's almost prophetic concepts by cross-reference with developments in cognitive neuroscience, which reconsider previous centralized and top down models of perception.

> When Deleuze turns to the cinema of the brain ... a more complex topology becomes necessary, one in which inside and outside communicate, and circuits of information exchange allow the brain, following the eye, to be in turn deterritorialized....[14]

Perception is tracked in relation to a range of distributed cognitive functions, which Johnston says "brings cognitive science into alignment with Deleuze (and Guattari)'s concept of the assemblage."[15]

In *Cinema 1*, Deleuze writes about Soviet Film maker Dziga Vertov's "kino eye" and (a) montage that "is the pure vision of a non-human eye, of an eye which would be in things ... any point whatsoever in space itself perceives all the points on which it acts, or which act on it.... That is the definition of objectivity, 'to see without boundaries or distances'."[16] It is this tension between a potential radical objectivity of the camera – an objectivity not based on a metaphor of critical distance but a multiplicity of points of view and the asserted objectivity of the Judge that are in tension. The *status* of distributed perception and machinic vision, in relation to the witness (who may now be a camera), the judge (who may now be a camera), and the perpetrator (who may be the dead camera eye of a range of "smart" bombs and war machines) is impossible to definitively recon here. However acknowledging these new distributed, refracted, geometries of vision helps contextualize the current state of the court cameras, anxiously mandated it seems to remain inside the mid-twentieth century visual codes of television (talking heads, static cameras, wide, medium, close shots intercutting at regular rhythms).

In my art work, particularly recent work with moving cameras, I have made use of a lens geometry, which I think of as the architecture of the lens – a space not delineated by walls, but demarcated by the continuous, shifting potential of the lens view. However, unlike a theatrical stage frame machine, animated (pan tilt zoom) lens space is not fixed, but moving and virtual. This space doesn't surround the subject as much as traverse it.

The expanded cinema works of Anthony McCall offer an example of a transition between theatrical cinema and a more architectonic conception of lens and light. Art historian and theorist George Baker writes insightfully on these and other issues in his extended essay "Film Beyond Its Limits" in which he focuses on McCall's period of "solid light films." From 1973 to 1975, McCall made such works as the famous

Line Describing a Cone. These works play with a material manifestation of film as light. They are distinctly geometric, reinforcing the cone of light from the projector by converting it into the "image" and substituting it for the cinematic "drama." Baker opens with a quote from Gilles Deleuze which applies to the both/and (rather than either/or) insistence on sculpture and cinema in McCalls' work, but Deleuze's words also evoke the border traced by the vectors of light issuing from the projector lens,

> Multiplicity is precisely in the "and" which is different in nature from elementary components and collections of them ... AND is neither one thing nor the other, it's always in-between, between two things; it's the borderline, there's always a border, a line of flight or flow, only we don't see it, because it's the least perceptible of things. And yet it's along this line of flight that things come to pass, becomings evolve, revolutions take shape.[17]

The idea of "multiplicity" has become familiar, while the geometry of *potentia* described by Deleuze's "line of flight" purposely resists symbolization – it moves from somewhere to somewhere, a trajectory, not a boundary, infinitely more open than the cut out which frames stage and cinema tableau (as) described by Barthes. To put it simply McCall's films are an instance in which we shift focus from the frame (of the viewfinder/screen) to the impossible "focus" on the pathway of light and sight itself.

In omitting the camera (or at least any indexical gaze) from the production process the identification in Baker's solid light films is not between a camera eye and the viewer's eye. Viewers can bathe together in an expansive middle space; a path of illumination between the projector – that with its centered projective beam becomes a proxy subject – and the delimitated rectangle of light, which is its objective result.[18] However, in McCalls next works, the "long films," the projections are less seductive and have more of a relation to architecture than sculpture, coinciding with architectural planes, and "pushing" people against walls and the floor. In these works Baker discerns a more "disciplinary" dimension:

> In *Long Film for Four Projectors*, the lessons of the form of the plane – its physical embodiment of a barrier or a limit – and the incorporative form of the cone came together in that paradoxical wedding of distance and continuity which since the outset of McCall's work seems to have been his formal (and political) goal.... While pushing the spectator's interaction with the field and the form of film to a new extreme, *Four Projected Movements* becomes, however, rather unlike the other solid light films. In its solidity it seems to take on what Michel Foucault would call a "disciplinary" dimension, as if film had been infected by its crossing of the limits of architecture, only to allow us to feel in an achingly corporeal way the limiting core of architecture itself.... As film takes on the shape and parameters of architecture only to display the limitations of the form it has inhabited, we understand anew what it means for a form to transgress the limits of its form to "correspond" to the limits of another.[19]

The presence of the "disciplinary dimension" exists when architecture (perhaps every upright wall) and video (perhaps every frame) are designed to correspond. Baker describes McCall's transgression of the limits of one form (cinema) to take up those of another (first sculpture then architecture) as a "double movement." Similarly in the work with computer controlled cameras I locate this double movement in the way the cameras seem to function between cinema and

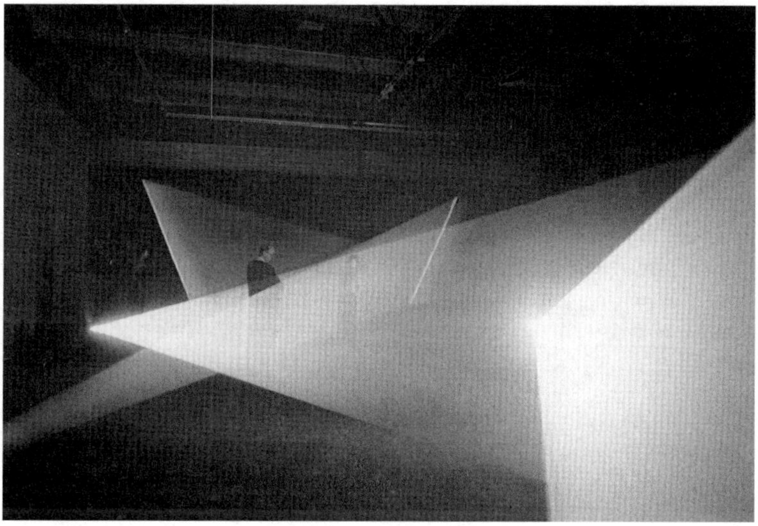

Anthony McCall, *Long Film for Four Projectors* (1974). Installation view (2003). Courtesy the artist. Photograph: Hank Graber.

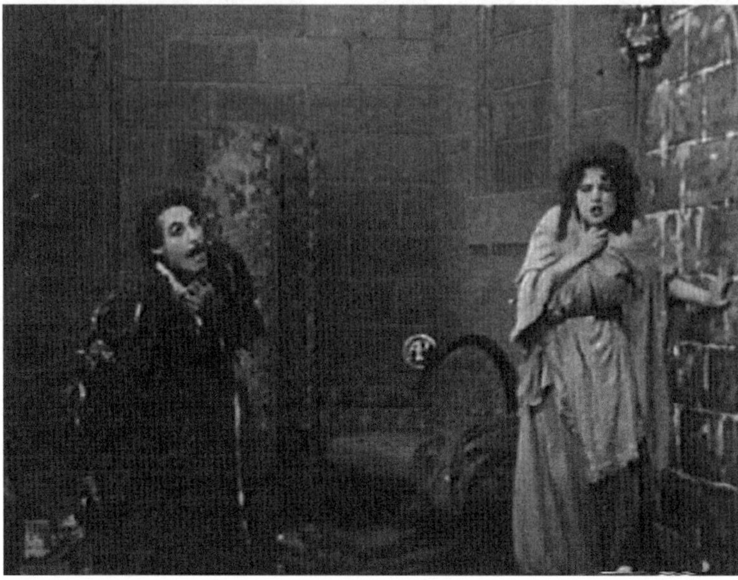

Still from *The Sealed Room* (1909) by D.W. Griffiths.

surveillance. The work doesn't suggest that cinema and surveillance are the same, but that they form a double dimension, coexisting in the same images, or more precisely in the inquisitorial camera movements that produce the images. (The recent emergence of a viable 3D cinema offers a deeper depth, anchoring reality not in the narratives – which necessitate fantastic settings – but through the binocular perceptual apparatus on the viewer. However the camera(s) double vision is revealed when viewed with "glasses off," and non-aligned perspectives ghost the image.)

— Out of frame and sealed rooms

In pondering the superimposition of built space and lens space it may be worth remarking that built space, although it may partition an environment, is fundamentally part of a contiguity, one room leads to the next, the door opens to a street and the street to a field. The lens delimits space in a different way finding its terminus in the videographic frame which selects from contiguous space and therefore continuously refers to an "out of frame" just beyond the cone of vision of the camera.[20]

An instance of the out of frame which can be easily overlooked – as it is neither to the left or right above or below the frame – is the space between the camera and the picture plane of the scene. This space can be activated by objects in the foreground and within the cone of view of the camera, however when it is left blank it reinforces the sense of the camera as seeing in cuboid, rather than an expanding cone, a projection. D.W. Griffith's 1909 short *The Sealed Room* imagines the plane of the film as synonymous with the fourth wall. This recognition of film's concretization of the fourth wall (that boundary between the actors and audience, which is only imaginary in theatre) allows him to produce the effect of two people suffocating in a room. As the subjects gasp for air in their walled up room, it is the apparatus that produces their suffocation. Their gasping for air, although highly theatrical, would never have made sense on the proscenium stage, but rather relies on the camera's frame to seal the fourth wall, which it simultaneously appears to look "through."

The court is also a sealed room – whose very function depends on being formally separated (by space, language, procedure) from an exterior scene, which it is set up to judge. What happens to this sealed room as cameras and screens are increasingly built in? The inside world of the court and the outside world of "evidence" intermingle on these screens. Formally opposite to the centrally radiating views of a panopticon, in new courtrooms the cameras are mounted on the walls and face inward producing a total coverage of the interior. The trial chamber is a core, reinforced with lead and concrete, around which runs a careful frame of separate spaces and passageways. Inside this chamber the lens geometry exerts a further pressure (lets call it a visual pressure, or image pressure) on the interior. Perhaps this camera-covered courtroom is an interior, which can no longer be represented as a void; the space is inverted by camera origami, which unfolds the cube. Perhaps it is not a space at all, as it could be argued that it is continuously experienced on LCD flat screen rather than in three dimensions. This unfolding is a direct result of the court's aspiration to a kind of openness, however, like so many of the dialectical potentials triggered by official forays into representation, this openness produces a new mode of containment.

— Uncanny entrance breaks the seal

Imagining an "interior" relates to, and is related differently by, theatre and video. To imagine oneself theatrically involves the desire to be seen on stage, to be encompassed by an architectonic environment, to play to the rafters and the back row of the auditorium. One imagines oneself as a subject centered by the space and the many eyes on just one. The desire to be seen by a video camera is quite different, it is a desire to appear at a distance from oneself. Video couples the desire to be seen with the desire to see from the point of view of the camera, in the absence of any "encompassing" space that brings myself and my audience together. As Franz Kafka and Louis Althusser have shown, the law also functions as an entity one imagines oneself in front of, or *con*fronted by. In the new technological court of law (as well as other cultural spaces) one finds oneself within both a theatrical and a videographic play subject of these divergent apparatuses. I imagine myself testifying "to" the judge. She looks down at me, and I up at her. However, video evidence (even redirected to the judge through witness testimony) can function to disturb this intersubjective power geometry. Another slight shift would occur if I speak to the judge by video link from the prison. She will likely appear on a monitor, and I will naturally face the monitor, as the camera is not near the center of the monitor, the impression will not be that I am looking directly at her.

— Video in the court; 'Rejouer les Crimes'

Legal theorist Cornelia Vismann in her 2001 essay "Rejouer les Crimes: Theater vs. Video," considers the introduction of video, surveillance tapes, for instance, as evidence. She suggests that the linguistic and theatrical "play" of the court is turned into a "replay" through the presence of video. Video evidence also threatens to displace the judge as the author of the court performance. She writes:

> Under the guidance of a judge, the medium [of video playback] loses its autonomy, so that video pictures appear merely to assist the hermeneutic task of a judge, and not so as to help in the reconstruction of the facts. The delegation of truth finding to the institutional interpreter

> elegantly allows the law to forget that the surveillance camera, and its counterpart in court, the monitor, is in the structural position of the institutional third. Judges merely share the throne with the medium.... Despite these strategies of legal domination, the emergence of a video does impact on the effectiveness and the propriety of the theatrical staging of justice. Above all, it inserts words into the mouth of the inquisitor who can hence only repeat what is displayed on the monitor – a consequence that seems to radicalize what the metaphor of theater invoked from the beginning.[21] The emergence of video assumes the functional place of the script for the theater or play of justice. If this conclusion seems far-fetched, one must at least acknowledge that the emergence of videotapes in trials disturb the classical alliance between stage and court. Certainly it renders the mediating strategies of the theater of justice visible, even if it does not implement them fully in the techniques actually used.[22]

As Vismann suggests the video acting as a script reinforces the existing "citational" aspect of court, where speech is based on previous testimony. However, she suggests that the "classical" alliance, one in which the mediating strategies – the control of utterances that the court institutes through its rules of testimony and evidence – have become part of its more visible or audible articulation. When the judge requests that something should be "rewound" or played back a second time, these requests also enter the record. More to Vismann's point is that the judge or lawyers are in effect given a script by the images that exist on the monitor. To some extent this will be a visual script, and the hermeneutic task will become deciphering what is seen. This is in distinction to testimony, which opens itself to reason whereby further inquiry can be made into the set of previously articulated statements and written records.

— The need to connect to the "outside"

When I attended the Charles Taylor Trail (at the Special Court for Sierra Leone, a precursor to ICC trials and done in the same courtrooms) I could observe the live feed of at least six live cameras on the court walls mixed to a single channel montage on the court monitors. The same feed is (web)streamed. The court has adopted a television aesthetic, primarily the camera is focused on a head and shoulders shot of the speaker (as would be solely the case in courts where the camera is automated by voice activation) but the switching between cameras maintains a rhythm and regularly cuts to wide shots and reaction shots and sometimes when not much is happening, a close-up of a pensive court clerk, may fill the screen, in a kind of moody "cut away."

Through the same cameras and screens that the court employs to solve its problem of constituency – the fact that its audience may be in Sierra Leone, or Serbia – the outside leaves and enters this sealed environment as document and evidence. What seems notable to me is not only that the court controls its image, but that this image then reappears as documentary or news footage, seamlessly interlaced with footage gathered by news cameras. All these images will be montaged together and underscored with a typical informational voiceover. And, not coincidentally, that footage, perhaps of the streets of Freetown, or the jungle of Sierra Leone, may be the same footage called as evidence. When the footage shot in court is supplied to news agencies and re-cut into a story, the segment may begin with a news announcer, cut to a clip of Charles Taylor and his lawyers in court, cut to a shot "on the ground" of militia with guns in the jungle of what appears to be Sierra Leone, then a wide shot of the court, a close-up of the judge, and so on.

What is stunning to me is that this montage between the inside and the outside of the court, seems to bring together what it actually holds apart; the incommensurate inside and outside. This cut between the court and the jungle of Africa may function on a semiotic level, it may make sense as a story, but on the level of spatial politics it represents an impossibility. The trial must not take place "in" the jungle or in Africa. That is why the Hague court exits: to function at a spatial (nation) remove. The court can only relate to what is brought within its bounds. It bears no relation to what is exterior. One could argue, that this confluence of images is just the effect of the inherent possibilities of editing and video. But this is to elide the images produced by the court, *as* the trial, with images recorded for a range of other interests, primarily news reportage. This is to accept that these are "cameras in court" rather than "cameras as court" or at least to skip this difference. Perhaps "news" stands between cinema and the court – each becoming its own visual system. The building of the court, now with cameras as an integral aspect of its structure, becomes a system of recording and transmission. The chamber of the court, reasserts its etymological relation to the camera, and becomes the apparatus. In this case, the court is a camera. Rather than reproducing the feed from the court cameras real "reportage" of the court would show the cameras looking at the court and the court players, looking at an image of the African jungle on banks of monitors inside the court – frames within frames, no outside.

— And yet perhaps no outside or inside, only phantoms?

Not only does video broadcast the court beyond its walls but also the video monitor is naturalized as a window by way of which what is "outside" can enter the court as evidence.[23] Paul Virilio has theorized that since the 70s the television screen functions as a window and takes on an architectonic aspect in North American homes. But what enters through this screen, as framed images, is more coded than life or "the outside" seen through a window. On the other hand, these framed images, entering the court through the video window, are of a very different order than spoken or written testimony. The articulation of visual (as opposed to linguistic) codes stretched the feasibility of semiotics in the seventies and eighties. What Barthes calls the "analogical plentitude" – the overabundance of information and relation that every frame of an image imparts – presents possibly insurmountable challenges for producing laws of interpretation of a visual code.

Suffice to say here that the implications and destabilizations produced by visual technologies in the court are being grappled with by new contortions of legal action and ritual. In this situation, examining other moments of unstable spatial boundaries may be illuminating. Historian and theorist of cinema, Tom Gunning, writes about the early nineteenth-century, when the uncanny shock of the outside (break and) entering the bourgeois interior registers across a number of cultural forms. New uncertain limits of inside and outside can be read in novel architectural use of mirrors and windows, in detective fiction through crimes involving visual complexities, and particularly in Walter Benjamin's writing on the arcades.

Gunning addresses this constellation in his essay "The Exterior as Intérieur: Benjamin's Optical Detective." Not entirely unlike the video screens in court, instances in the nineteenth and early twentieth-century detective fiction poignantly incorporate what Gunning calls "scenes in which complex *optical situations reveal the entrance of the criminal into the midst of apparent bourgeois order.*"[24] He goes on to detail a scene from Green's novel *The Woman in the Alcove* where the particular arrangement of mirrors and windows in a "supper room" allows the detective, who is also a witness in the story, to see an apparition of the killer through a chance-alignment of surfaces, which bounce the reflection from one to the next. Gunning historicizes the "common theme of uncanny vision, or the sudden appearance of another scene within this one."[25] The anxiety that the rational order and homely details of the bourgeois interior are in fact a thin mask for an uncanny torture chamber, continues to pervade the horror genres. However, instead of imagining a scenic space through which a geometry of vision ricochets, the *entire* middle American scene is presented as a brightly colored surface or veil, as epitomized in the work of David Lynch.

I have already mentioned an essay by Cornelia Vismann, and the case from the 1980's at the center of her text likewise attests to the uncanny appearance of one scene within another but now, not by way of mirrors, but by way of a video recording shown in court. It is the case of Corporal Lortie, a disgruntled member of the Canadian forces. In 1984, Lortie stormed into the National Assembly of Quebec building and killed three Quebec government employees. He intended to kill Rene Levesque, the premier of the province, and apparently shouted: "The Quebec Assembly has the face of my father."[26] The exceptional element, which enables Vismann's thesis vis-à-vis video re-scripting the theatre of the court, is that the whole scene is registered on surveillance videotape. During the trial the tape is played repeatedly, but Lortie is unable to associate himself with the image. Like the characters in the novel Gunning mentions, when the scene appears before Lortie on video playback, he is confused by the exteriority and unable to speak from the first person position required by the law. Vismann quotes Lortie and offers an analysis:

> ... I cannot say this was not me, this was I. What more can I say?' His internal struggle gives an idea of the violence of the concept of identity: 'Physically it is my appearance, but I have no recollection of my being in this situation. Nevertheless, I see I am supposed to see me.' The images with which the accused was confronted were arranged within a specific setting so that they assume the quality of mirror images – they are *reduced* to mirror images. The dimension of time, the asynchronicity between acting and watching the action, which characterizes the medium of video in contrast to a mirror, is simply erased from the trial-setting. The accused is expected to integrate the impersonal, restored images into his recollection.[27]

In all these instances of the exterior projected inwards by mirrors and video, is not the simple contiguous extension of the interior, but something foreign and difficult to integrate. Gunning elaborates on Benjamin's thinking on the relationship between the ideologically charged bourgeois interior of the nineteenth-century and the street, in his writing on the Paris arcades, whose style and function produced both anxiety and pleasure in their comingling of street and interior. Gunning writes:

> Performing an essential and canny transformation of Freud's method, Benjamin explains such experiences in terms of the conflict between individual and collective psychologies that capitalism engenders. The unconscious that operates in Benjamin's arcades, while certainly not unrelated to Freud's analysis of dreams and parapraxis opens itself up to the invasion of social history. This invasion operates via the optical unconscious that Benjamin describes in "The Work of Art" essay, a perceptual mechanism that takes in more than it can consciously account for.... These optical experiences of a sudden invasion of the interior by the exterior, and visa versa, undermine maintaining any absolute separation between the realms.[28]

It is clear that the power of lawlessness is strong and the setting into which it may be released has to be stage managed by way of careful control of entrance, appearance, spatial organization and utterance. Video (its entrance into the trial paved by maps and photographs) has the potential to play havoc with these codes as it introduces a visual and durational bias into this theatre whose absolute rule remains the careful transduction of experience into language. Testimony advances by the back and forth of detailed question and answer, the restriction of physical gesture and idiomatic speech risks neutralizing content to suspend judgment, to glean information rather than impressions from witness accounts. One of the most uncanny aspects of attending trials is being subject to narratives of murder, torture, the minutia of expert testimony on weapons, etc. all of which are asked to assume the same impassive tone. The rational, procedural, abstract mode of the trial constitutes a force, which must be in contradistinction to the physical violence of the acts it judges. What kind of force is constituted by video seems yet to be articulated, however from Benjamin to Deleuze there is a positing of moving images and montage as a more affective, molecular, order sometimes closer to the fermentation of raw properties of thought than the sign system of language.

– The middle (surface of the reflection)

Sometimes the former king or the indicted president does not identify with the court's power. Sometimes no one recognizes him/herself when the court holds up a mirror. Sometimes the right hand doesn't know what the left hand is doing. I was investigating mirrors and I came upon this box: the Ramachandran mirror box for healing phantom limb pain.[29] It stuck with me because it reminded me of something – a theatre, or a work by the artist Dan Graham. Simultaneously, I came upon the text by Jack Spicer quoted on the front inside flap of this book. A text against representation, or more to the point; a text enthusiastic about non-literal, literary resemblances, about *correspondences*. Correspondences as Spicer describes them seem like one variant of the assemblage described by Gilles Deleuze (a quote pertaining to the assemblage is found on the back inside flap of this book). For Spicer being open to the resonance by which one thing can conjure another, perhaps quite different, thing, is how we get something *real* into a poem. Correspondences are how we cross paths with the dead – Spicer is writing to Frederico Garcia Lorca, dead some twenty-one years in 1957 when the piece is written. Incidentally, to side step some of the baggage of being an originator, Spicer referred to his later work as a poetry of dictation, externalizing the creative source as if from a radio broadcast, or outside voices. (Actually, phantom voices may not be so incidental. Where as in an anecdote in Gunning's text, Freud doesn't recognize himself in a mirror and Corporal Lortie doesn't recognize his video image, Jack Spicer sees himself reflected through correspondence with the dead.)

How do phantom hands and mirror boxes relate to the law? Phantom limbs correspond with phantom heads. Floating sovereign heads, which we imagine are still attached to power appear on coins, crests, portrait busts, they are heads of state that can become heads on platters. Their insistence on semblance makes them vulnerable to being toppled, to disembodiment. These doubles resonate with the medieval legal theological practice of "the king's two bodies" as related by Ernst Kantorowitcz in his 1957 book of the same name. Here Kantorowitcz describes in detail all the medieval precedents for the fourteenth to seventeenth century practice of royal funeral effigies, which he finds rooted in British tradition. (At Berkley Kantorowitcz was also an influential teacher of Jack Spicer and the Berkley Renaissance Poets informing their commitment to history).

In this book Kantorowitz traces the legal, philosophical and material contortions required to maintain the belief that the king had a "natural body" and a "body politic." Supplementing the physical body of the king was the body politic that was "immutable through time" and constituted the "Dignitas" – the real continuity of royal being and power. Kantorowitcz writes; "The King's Two Bodies thus form one unit indivisible, each being fully contained in the other. However, doubt cannot arise concerning the superiority of the body politic over the body natural."[30] It was at the time of death that illusion and representation were most needed to shore up the notion of the immutability of the sovereign power. The somewhat bizarre practice of displaying a physical effigy made of leather, wood and plaster was introduced in 1327 with the funeral of Edward II.[31] By the sixteenth-century the effigy was eclipsing the body of the mortal king in the funerary rites.[32] The parading of both the immortal body (as an effigy) and the real body (below in a coffin), demonstrated, according to Kantorowitcz "the concurrence of two heterogeneous ideas: the triumph of Death and the triumph over Death." Manifesting this heterogeneity with conviction resulted in some peculiar prohibitions.

> When, for example, Francis I's successor, King Henry II of France, came to asperse the body of his father, it was not the body in effigy but the real corpse which finally replaced again the effigy lying in state. It seems that the new king could not come to visit the image because the image was treated as the live king in his Dignity. Apparently one of the two kings, either the demised or the living one (though *one* only), had to represent that immortal Dignity.[33]

What correspondences arise from bringing the King's Two Bodies and Ramachandran mirror box for healing phantom limb pain into an assemblage? Of course I don't mean to suggest that there is anything hard-wired in our brains that produces our rulers in double form. But we do seem to be better at considering entities that at least *appear* to exist.

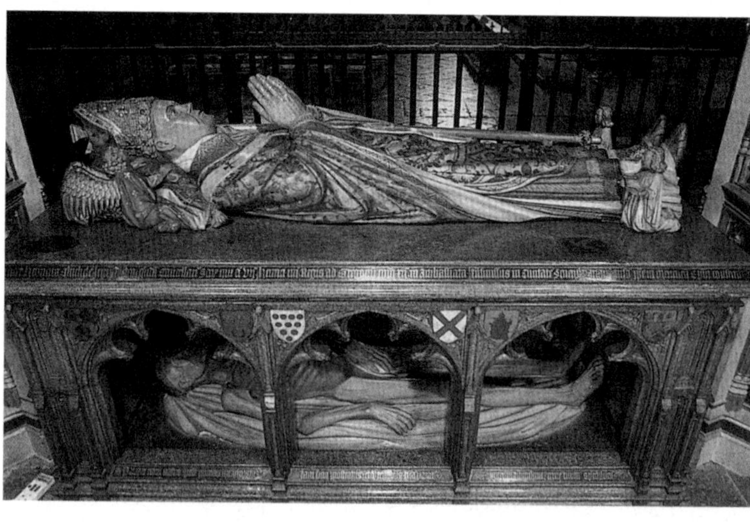

Tomb of Henry Chichele, Archbishop of Canterbury. It shows an effigy on top and a representation of the mortal body below (1424–26).

An abstract entity such as a phantom arm or a phantom king appears operative only when we encounter it in physical effigy. Effigies of a dispersed continuity of power of "the people" are more difficult to concoct, and often result in the de facto veneration of singular form or figure. The International Criminal Court similarly requires a single figure(s) to be held accountable at the top of a systemic wrong. The process of the court works to "reincorporate" the guilty actions with the will of the accused – often a former head of state. (The assignation of blame to the body politic, who permitted or committed crimes under the accused's authority, is

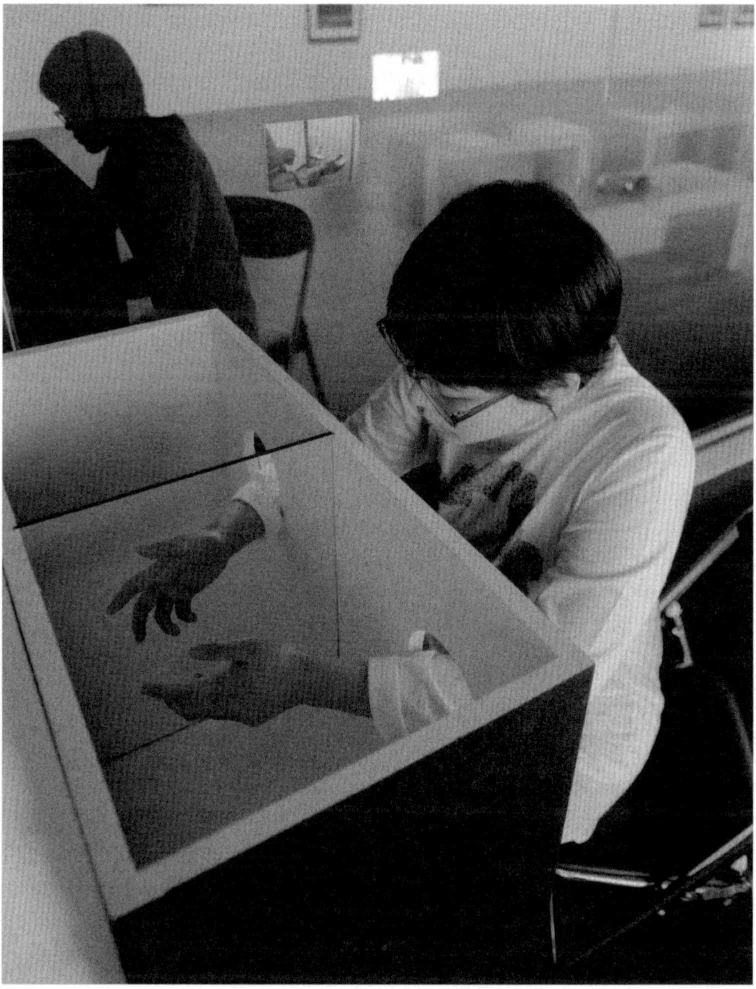

Judy Radul, *World Rehearsal Court* (2009).
Multimedia installation, installation view 2010, detail: mirror box.
Courtesy the artist and Media City Seoul.

more complicated). The arcane contortions medieval jurists needed to preserve the dual nature or "body natural" and *dignitas* remind us that this playing with mirrors and effigies risks revealing that what is fictional is not the effigy but the divide between fiction, representation and the real.

Perhaps then, there is a wider range of phantoms, many more than the king's two bodies, which we continue to invent. The phantom need not be a mimetic construction coercing us to fragile identifications with a real that must be continually shored up with violence and law. As Ramachandran says in his jocular bestseller style:

> [T]here is a deeper message here: *Your own body* is a phantom, one that your brain has temporarily constructed purely for convenience. For your entire life, you've been walking around assuming that your "self" is anchored to a single body that remains stable and permanent at least until death.... Yet these experiments suggest the exact opposite – that your body image, despite all its appearance of durability, is an entirely transitory internal construct that can be profoundly modified with just a few simple tricks.[34]

One wonders about the engineering of the reverse mirror box – the theatre, or video architecture – which performs the opposite of the "Christological" preservation of kingly power through effigy production. "Using one illusion to erase another doesn't seem very surprising after all," as Ramachandran states.[35] How might we imaginatively assemble and operate current and future apparatus, mirror boxes, black boxes, cameras, simulators, and the like, to uncramp or disassociate "illusion" itself.

1 Benjamin, Walter, *The Arcades Project*, ed. Rolf Tiedemann (Cambridge, Mass.: Belknap Press, 1999), 541. Walter Benjamin is quoting A.G. Meyer on the Crystal Palace of 1851.

2 Peter Goodrich, "Law" in *Encyclopedia of Rhetoric*, ed. Thomas O. Sloane (Oxford: Oxford University Press, 2001), 418.

3 Subha Mukherji, "Law and Representation in Early Modern Drama," excerpt (Cambridge: Cambrigde University Press, 2006), *http://assets.cambridge.org/052185/0355/excerpt/0521850355_excerpt.htm.*

4 Peter Goodrich, "Law," in *Encyclopedia of Rhetoric*, ed. Thomas O. Sloane (Oxford: Oxford University Press, 2001), 418.

5 I am referring very generally to practices of law that emphasize trials in open court, primarily stemming from the Babylon/Roman/British traditions. In my own work, the new International Criminal Court, based on the Rome Statute of 1998, and its precursors such as the International Criminal Tribunal for the Former Yugoslavia and the Special Court for Sierra Leone, are exemplary.

6 Richard Mohr, "In Between: Power and Procedure Where the Court Meets the Public Sphere," included in this volume.

7 Kristin Anker, "The Truth in Painting: Cultural artifacts as proof of native title," *Law Text Culture*, vol 9, (2005): 100

8 Ibid. 113, 114.

9 Roland Barthes, "Diderot, Brecht, Eisenstein" in *Image-Music-Text,* trans. Stephen Heath (New York: Hill and Wang, 1977), 69. Barthes goes on to define representation: "Representation is not defined directly by imitation: even if one gets rid of notions of the "real", or the "vraisemblable" of the "copy" there will still be representation for so long as a subject (author, reader, spectator, voyeur) casts his *gaze* toward a horizon on which he cuts out the base of a triangle, his eye (or his mind) forming the apex."

10 This "fetishist" subject is one who "cuts out the scene" and must attach meaning, perhaps disproportionate meaning to a fragment, or proxy, and who also may identify a point of view as his/her own. Barthes, "Diderot, Brecht, Eisenstein," 72, 76.

11 For instance, legal scholar Linda Mulcahy discusses the 813 page British Court Standards and Design Guide detailing extensive rules for courtroom layout in "Architects of Justice: the Politics of Courtroom Design," *Social & Legal Studies*, vol. 16 (2007): 383

12 Barthes, Ibid. 76.

13 John Johnston, "Machinic Vision," *Critical Inquiry* 26 (Autumn 1999): 33. Johnston quotes Deleuze in *Francis Bacon: Logique de la sensation* (Paris: Editiones de la Différence 1981), 37.

14 Ibid. 47.

15 Ibid. 43

16 Gilles Deleuze, *Cinema 1, The Movement Image*, trans. Hugh Tomlinson, Barbara Habberjam (Minneapolis: University of Minnesota Press, 1986), 81.

17 George Baker, "Film Beyond Its Limits," *Grey Room*, no. 25 (fall 2006): 92-125.

18 Baker states, "Cinema ... had always been involved in a kind of false captivation of the social body; McCall countered this capture not by simply dissecting the logic of cinematic identification and incorporation – by countering puritanically the false pleasures of cinematic illusion – but by collectivizing the process, by sexualizing it, by making it excessive, physical and quite literally real." Ibid. 110.

19 Ibid. 112

20 Of course, built spaces can also be characterized by their relation to the out of frame. In the theatre these are enacted by the "wings," the backstage, and the audience area.

21 Vismann, Cornelia. "'Rejouer Les Crimes. 'Theater vs. Video,'" *Cardozo Studies in Law and Literature,* vol. 13, no.1 (2001): 132–133. Vismann continues: "As in every play the drama in the courtroom follows a text. Every word spoken by the accused is already a quotation."

22 Ibid. 133

23 See "The Third Window: An Interview with Paul Virilio," in *Global Television* (Cambridge, MA: MIT Press, 1988), 185–197.

24 Tom Gunning, "The Exterior as Intérieur: Benjamin's Optical Detective." *Boundary 2,* vol. 30, no. 1, *Benjamin Now: Critical Encounters with The Arcades Projec*t (2003): 121

25 Ibid. 125

26 Vismann compares the study of this case by historian of law and psychoanalysis, Pierre Legendre, to Foucault's writing on the case of Pierre Rivière in "Theatre and Video Rejouer Les Crimes."

27 Ibid. 130.

28 Tom Gunning, "The Exterior as Intérieur: Benjamin's Optical Detective," *boundary 2,* vol. 30, no. 1 (Spring 2003): 121

29 The mirror box is a therapeutic tool devised by neuroscientist V. S. Ramachandran. The principle is that an amputee suffering from a phantom limb, uses a mirror, positioned so that the existing hand is reflected in place of the missing hand. By moving the existing hand, and looking at the real hand and the reflection, thus seeing "both" hands moving, the sensation that the missing hand is moving is created. Through repeated use this device has apparently given relief to those suffering from phantom limb pain. The effect for those with two limbs is also eerie, if after moving both hands for some time, one stops moving the hand that isn't seen, but keeps moving the reflected hand, the sensation remains that both hands are moving.

30 Ernst Hartwig Kantorowicz, *The King's Two Bodies: A Study of Medieval Political Theology* (Princeton, N. J.: Princeton University Press, 1997), 9.

31 Ibid. 420.

32 Ibid. 423.

33 Ibid. 429.

34 V. S. Ramachandran and Sandra Blakeslee, *Phantoms in the Brain: Probing the Mysteries of the Human Mind* (New York: Harper Collins, 1998), 61–62.

35 Ibid. 58.

Screening Law

— Peter Goodrich

Twenty years since the founding of the Journal *Law and Literature*, one name change on, and an insistent question haunts the sub-discipline. Two decades have passed, the context has changed, and we have to ask, in the face of new and proliferating videospheres, in the wake of increasingly virtual textual and visual forms, is literature really the horse to be backing, the best use of our money, worthy of our institutional vote? The sages of postmodern interdisciplinarity seem to concur in the view that it is not. Suffering perhaps from the nemesis complex or simply an over-fondness for the end of things, we are told variously that the movement is dead, that law and literature has nothing to offer, that it is an interdisciplinary illusion, that jurists would do best to stick to their discipline and change the world, or in this case do literature, politics or cultural criticism on their own time.[1]

There is much that makes sense, amuses, informs and persuades in the argument against law and literature. The Republic of letters is undoubtedly shrinking. Rome is burning. Students don't read, they watch or they view. Law and literature has aged prematurely, and if it isn't being born, then it is busy dying. Not so much a case of burn after reading as burn before reading. Yet in every conflagration there is an opportunity and to this we must add that burning now means downloading from the screen, writing to DVD, not destroying text but encoding *html* – hypertext markup language – onto disc. Burning makes reading possible. So the question emerges, insistently, as to what this means, if not for literature as such, at least for law as a genre of rhetoric and as a form of literature. Can it still bear the same name? Is its future dimmed, its dogma to be jettisoned, its reality a vanishing sign?

I will take, perhaps unfairly, the allusion to illusion that one of the most articulate and engaging of the critics of law and literature makes. Julie Stone Peters, but a few years back, posted an essay in the PMLA's official journal arguing that law and literature is "an interdisciplinary illusion." It represents what others have termed "weak thought," and is more an expression of inadequacy, an existential scream for help from within the prison house of law or the funhouse of literature, than a coherent method or a plausible project. I will argue here that her thesis is elegant and her conclusion correct. Law and literature must now be viewed as an illusion. This does not mean, however, that its time is at an end, nor that nemesis is near. To the contrary, being an illusion and focusing upon illusions, and we can note here that the Latin root of the word lies in *ludere*, to play, is the only hope that the inter-sub-discipline can claim. Literature is, after all and amongst other things, the study of illusion, of fiction and play, and it makes sense that in addressing these imaginary bases of society, the invention of social institutions and the fictions that support them, the literary and the legal respectively take on the illusions, the play and the figures of social theater they describe.

My argument will proceed in two and half stages and in many respects will track and mirror not only the trajectory of the stone casting Peters' article, but also the order and remit of her publications, the path and pattern of her career. No harm is done here in mixing the *ad feminam* with the *argumentum ad hominem* that she has made. First, there is the birth of law and literature in the context of critical legal studies and the sociologically driven radicalism of the post sixties generation in the legal academy. Here I will argue that the law and literature movement was a rebirth, a branching out or *prise de position* that has much older roots and must be understood not as an *ex nihilo* creation but rather in the perspective of the *longue dureé* and specifically in the context of drama and law. Note also the gentle irony that this will lead us past the theater of the book that Peters has so elegantly recuperated, portrayed and relayed.[2] Law and literature, from a long term historical perspective, looked at now, twenty years, or better thirty years on, is frequently a distraction, a precious and precarious, often tedious divagation into poorly chosen canonic texts and the beard and sandal protocols of their interpreters.

Step two is to argue that law and literature was never enough, a missed opportunity, too narrow and, being frank about it, uptight and frontal in focus. What is interesting in the literary effusions of law, in the fictions and figures of legal doctrine, in the *dicta* and other disseminations of judgment and legislation is precisely what escapes the text, what gets under the skin, what is incorporated as law for us. Here the driving question is the limit instance or exception, the changing form of law and literature, what escapes from it as well as what lingers within. Here, in looking at the affective structures and appeals of law, in addressing the juridical as a strange object of love, as an obscure yet persistent desire, we approach the ethical substrate of the norm. The better-executed forays into law and literature have worked hard to address the question of justice, the image of the good that law borrows, reformulates, and sells.[3] Here we address the conjunction of the populist tradition, the spectacle of law's enactment as well as the legal books of emblems and the plastic forms of law as the expression and product of literary drives. As the Chinese proverb has it, "when the wise man points at the moon, the foolish man looks at his finger."

Finally, *envoi*, last stage, but only half a move because this argument relates to something in becoming, not yet vested, illusion, chimera or future play. The theatrical and emblematic dimensions of legality place the text of law in the critical context of its performance. It stages and disseminates, it reasons and transmits, it is legal and literary. Literature then was never an adequate or full description of the political spectacle of legality nor was it anything approaching a complete definition of the transmission of law as keeper of the social imaginary, as purveyor of subjective identity and communal bond. These were and are mixed forms and depend upon mixed media. The classical trinity of *ordo, lex, medium* holds true for the contemporary world. Each new medium underpins a new world and a changed form of law. Thus the current move from text to screen because the new mode of humanist letter is in the form of the scroll page, the new emblems of legality are Court TV, Judge Judy, Boston Legal, CSI, the screens that range from real time news, cameras in court, to planet Hollywood and IMAX. Netflix and Youtube are the new pre-law or more prosaically law as social bond, as imagined community, gets screened much more than it is written and is most likely to be viewed before it is ever read, indeed if it is ever read.

— The Theater of Justice and Truth

The lapidary Peters, fittingly enough, begins her argument as to the "interdisciplinary illusion" of law and literature by presenting her own illusion, or more exactly a little play. She starts with an imagined symposium and offers a short treatment, replete with graphic description of the *dramatis personae*, professors of law and of literature come together to lucubrate upon the political state and disciplinary future of their relationship. She follows this with a brief illustration of their dialogue and adds comments that could well be taken as stage directions. The imagined scene ends with the organizer of the symposium storming out of the room – *exeunt omnes* or literature departs with Peters in its disciplinary trail. The humanities, the old time arts, *literarum studium*, divorces the law.

Already there is a certain mixing of genres. The figure of the trial, of law judging literature, of literature arraigning law, is a familiar one. The courts of reason, literature, conscience and majesty all involve a moment of the suspension of reality, of acting 'as if', in the hypothetical, as the visual drama of evidence, of seeing the recreation of what was done, is played out before the eyes of the various courts. To this, we can add the use of dialogue, a familiar legal and literary form, which in conjunction signals a question of jurisdiction, of who has the power to speak, is generally a mode of challenging or shoring up foundations. Where the question is one of founding, of institution or demise in the sense of chaos and fall, then dialogue has traditionally been the preferred form because the theatrical makes visible and accessible what legal prose, with its hieroglyphs, argot and prolixity will tend to obscure.

My point is that it is no accident that the foundational question of genre and of mixing genres receives a dialogic and theatrical presentation. In fact it is a rhetorical necessity. The figure of *topographia* or description of an imaginary place is the rhetorically proper form by, which to introduce an evaluation of law in a court of love or before the critics and sages, the practitioners and commentators of literature. The play's the thing, illusion the most visible reality. The illusion, be it legal fiction, the "as if" of jurisprudence, the semiotic of courtroom and trial, or the literary mode and scope of juridical doctrine is intrinsic to law as a practice, and specifically to its modes of instituting the structures and parameters of social life. Here, first point, law developed historically in conjunction with rhetoric, later philology and hermeneutics. Forensic rhetoric, recollect, was the first systematized rhetorical genre and was concerned precisely and explicitly with the enactment of justice and truth.

The lawyers, the early *actores* as Cicero calls them, were trained in the art of persuasion that of appearing successfully before the judges and juries of locality, city, sovereign and state. No need for a history lesson, but we can briefly ask what rhetoric taught. The answer, in whatever handbook and changing little over time was that the art of eloquence – of speaking justly in civil matters – was concerned primarily with acting out the narrative of a legal cause and in doing so sufficiently persuasively to move an audience to action. Eloquence meant appropriateness to the audience and aptness in persuading it. To this end the study of the tropes and figures was dominated by the requirements of the juristic drama but it remained for all that no less a dramatic form, or morality play. Law and theater, in the form of a strictly coded rhetoric of legal causes, was all about conjuring the illusions, the *phantasma*, of earlier deeds or transactions and conveying a sense of their justice or iniquity, their innocence or guilt.

The figures of rhetoric are visible forms. Originally trophies or carved images on buildings, tropes and then figures of speech refer to the engraved and monumental, to forms that strike auditor and viewer, that bring the past to life and give movement to texts and laws. The figure of speech is a surprising usage, a play based upon likeness or sleight of mind and carries the audience by dint of a sense of identity with, compassion for or fear of the end proposed. The legal rhetorician dressed up, put on a costume and went on stage. Consider then the remarkable proximity of theater to law, a closeness that was geographical and architectural, as well as being artistic, institutional and existential. I am tempted to ask, rhetorically of course as you are reading this, what could be more theatrical than the Socratic classroom? But I will not travel that path just here. The broader point is that a training in legal rhetoric was an inculcation in all of the artistic tools necessary for acting, or more prosaically for successfully staging a cause of action.

Take the example of the early modern Inns of Court. They were housed in a complex built in the shape of an ear and situated amongst the flourishing theaters of what is now London's West End.[4] The lawyers spent a large amount of time in the playhouses, learned from the actors, drew their concerns and techniques from watching the stage. One time Attorney General Sir John Davies offers the following epigram:

> Publius student of common law,
> Oft leaves his bookes, and for his recreacion:
> To Paris Garden doth himselfe Withdrawe[5]

So too, within the Inns of Court theater, revels and plays were emblematic and constant forms of entertainment and instruction. *Otium* but also *negotium* if one considers the modes of legal training, the dinners, the moots, the bolts, the readings before benchers, the rituals in which a senior judge would hide in a cupboard and more. Drama persisted throughout the training process, as well as being an essential feature of the life of the Inns of Court understood as an emblematic community and sovereign body.[6] Law spoke, was enacted, from within a ceremonial space, from a solemnized stage as a profoundly theatrical symbolization of the gravity of majesty and social rule. This was the theater of the real, a point that can be briefly enhanced by considering the rivalry between theater and law.

First case in point, the Roman prohibition upon any citizen taking to the stage. The *Digest* records this enigmatic injunction: "the following incur *infamia*: ... anyone who has appeared on stage to act or to recite, anyone who has kept a brothel ..." A citizen who joined the theatrical troops was subject to the penalty of civil death, in the immediate and necessarily significant textual company of dishonorably discharged soldiers and brothel keepers. Why this draconian ban, which lasted for at least two centuries and then was repeated in later eras at various points, though most notably in the banning of the French law clerks, *the basoche* who used to stage satirical legal causes, *causes grasses* as they were called? The answer lies ineluctably in the competition between theater and law, their rivalrous similarity, their commonality of form and function. It is precisely the proximity of the genres that generates their cloying hostility, their long-term uneasy co-existence, their barbed interdependence.

There are of course other reasons, local and specific, for the ban on engaging in theatrical pursuits. Florence Dupont lengthily and brilliantly elucidates these in relation to the Roman theater.[7] Her thesis can be summarized for our purposes in terms of three features. First, theater, at least the banned form of theater, was associated with Greek culture and as such was viewed as foreign and threatening. With respect to Greek tragedy one could also surmise that it came too close in content to the substance of legal drama and was thus a threat in terms of form and subject matter. Second, the ban was primarily triggered by and directed toward that class of actor termed *histrionae*, actors noted for dance and gesture, for physical enactment, erotic choreography and imagistic seduction. These vamps were too persuasive, too close, too likely to perform upon the flesh, too prone to getting under the skin. Thus, finally, the theatrical threatened the legal actors by making their art too visible, their symbols, vestments and bodies too evident and hence their dramatic or ritual role had to be protected so that their *gravitas* could be preserved.

Move then from the negative argument, the thesis that the legal profession, trained in rhetoric, in the art of dramatic performance and eloquent persuasion, existed in a relation of denial with respect to theater, and look to the simultaneous embrace of drama by law. Here, in addition to the pervasive presence of spectacle and stage, enactment and pronouncement, rhetoric and gesture, in sum the histrionic and the tragic, there is also the explicit invocation of drama in the now resurgent argument as to jurisdiction.[8] Understood as the power of enunciating law, the essentially oral and dramatic pronouncement of legal power, jurisdiction refers to the grounding of legality in a visible legitimacy, its symbolic validation and present authority as defined through its staging and enactment. Law has to be differentiated and separated from other social discourses and jurisdiction is the discourse of that separation and authorization. Arguments as to jurisdiction create spaces of law, protected and authorized sites of enunciation of legal speech, stages for the performance of law that need their own distinctive and solemnized props, their own juridically formulated scenery uncluttered by or ferociously free of the accoutrements of other genres of stage and play.

The theater of justice and truth, my subtitle, is taken from an early modern treatise on ecclesiastical law by Jean Baptiste de Luca.[9] The theater in question is that of the Roman ecclesiastical jurisdiction viewed both internally as a hierarchy of Church courts, and externally in relation to the various jurisdictions of civil law. It is a massive treatise, as befits a collation of judgments, principles and doctrines that essentially map the entire world according to the dictates of spiritual law. What is at issue is the staging of all things pertaining to the spiritual world – *quae ad regimen animarum pertinet*. What was crucial to the jurisdiction was the proper ordering and circumscription of the sites of decision and enunciation of the relevant law. Jurisdiction here means putting on stage, the *mise-en-scène*, of rule, and hence the enactment of law, its coming to life in its proper social space and accompanied by its appropriate figures and tropes, its designated modes of manifestation.

Common law inherits or better it annexed the spiritual jurisdiction and so whatever Cardinal Luca attributed to jurisdiction is incorporated, internalized in the common law tradition. We can see this early on in the relaying of Latin tags in the work of Coke and other sages. Here is Coke at his most succinct: *judicium semper pro veritate accipitur* – a judgment is always to be taken for the truth and to this he adds elsewhere that *juris dicta*, the sayings or maxims of law are to be received as truth.[10] The verdict, again simply making the etymological argument, is the statement of the truth and comes from the space of authority and judgment, of the pronouncement of law. So here, following Bradin Cormack's excellent elaboration, jurisdiction is the theater – and we can note that he discusses mainly plays and maps, visible insignia – of legal presence, the means of solemnizing and creating a social reality: structure, form and visible words. These are the epiphanies of legality one could say, meaning that the coming to presence of law, its embodiment in the social, requires precisely an emergence in physical form, appearance, phantasm and theater one and all.[11]

— The graphic and the visual

The theme of legal theater, of the jurisdictional staging of law as the institution of authority, reason and rule can take us to a second point. The drama and enactment of law competes with the theatrical staging of public life, and the passage over time to death. Even if theater is banned, trivialized or dismissed it still needs its dramatic techniques, its modes of publicity, its stage directions, and indeed it ornaments and flowers of rhetoric, however these may be concealed. Law has to be rendered visible and while the drive to publicity, the requirement that "just not only be done, but be seen to be done" remains constant, the forms of visibility change over time. True enough, in the Christian tradition image and word have always traveled together but their conjunction, the specific trinity of *ordo, lex, medium* is subject to repeated reformation and reformulation. Theater has declined dramatically but the theatrical has proliferated exponentially. Law again is in the thick of this transformation, carried along and shouting out as the concept of jurisdiction and the authority of law take dramatically different forms.

Consider first the long-term trajectory of modern law and the structural traits of a disciplinary method that emerged with the printing presses and the war against images. The text ruled, the law was in the books or it was not law as Coke puts it, and in this manner the *sola scriptum* of the Reformers translated into a version of scriptural method in the development of the system of institutes, case reports, works of authority and then hierarchy of precedent and rule. On the continent, as I mentioned, there was Justinian and the *Corpus iuris*, in England there was Littleton and his somewhat creative commentator Sir Edward Coke. Littleton, as Coke mentions in the lengthy eulogy that forms the preface to his *Commentary on Littleton*, is not the name of a person, but rather a direct reference to the law. More than that, his tomb is his tome, his book of *Tenures*, in which work, on whose pages, one can, if diligent and perseverant enough, perceive his face.[12] In Coke's hands, according to his very rhetoric, Littleton's text, the book, the portrait of his mind that lingers between the lines, these all become his body, his sempiternity, his living on as the letter of the law.

I will not here rehash – time is short, it is Wednesday already – the various well rehearsed debates over the passage to a common law system of precedent. Let others venerate the reason of case law. The significant feature of the new printed form of legality, law's emergence in what Debray coins as the graphosphere, is that the theatrical dimension of the juridical is now transferred in large measure to the book.[13] It is the reported and published text that becomes the prime forum of law's dissemination. There are different ways to read this and of course the context changes but a few general observations as to the figurative status to the book merit recuperation. The manuscript tradition was self-evidently esoteric, and the plea rolls, tables, writs, fines, and lists of early common were subjects of special offices and skills. With print, the text became available and was frequently translated but even in such conditions of apparent openness it was and remains the case that visibility is not necessarily the equivalent of accessibility. The texts of law remained opaque and enigmatic. The words of law were, as the jurists are fond of saying, *sileni Alcibiadis*, meaning they were the signs of an obscure and most importantly absent source and authority.[14] Legal symbols were expressly hieroglyphs and should those unlearned in the law attempt to take their causes into their own hands, then ruin would ensue. In short, the law book was a symbol, a figure of record and truth, an object of reverence as well as being an enunciation of substantive judgments, principles, or rules of law for those sufficiently trained and semiotically skilled enough to unveil their meanings. It is this symbolic status of the text, the rhetorical dimension of all legal writing that needs to be retraced. Every piece of written law has to find its place in the *theatrum juridicum*.[15] Indeed in medieval Latin *pictura* meant writing.

Start with the book as a picture or figure of truth. It is a metaphor for God's will, for the moving hand that writes all things, and nature is like scripture, a text that hides a divine intent.

Everything, as Derrida argued in *Of Grammatolgy*, is written. Writing precedes speech and that means that if something is written, a writ for example, this is a sign, a hieroglyph or shadow of what is ultimately a sacral author and cause.[16] It is within this tradition we need to place the texts of law as also being printed images, visible forms, figures of sovereign and sacral intent. Presently, however, it is the theater of print – *theatre imprimatur* – that is most suggestive. Books were not simply complex signs – *verba visibilia* one might say in the Christian idiom – they were images in the sense of spectacular presentations, props in the rites of law, part of the scenery of judicial and professional appearance. I have already mentioned Coke on Littleton, and have elsewhere discussed the emblem, portrait and tree of consanguinity that appear as imagistic supports in the text.[17] Here I want to turn to a different point, namely the express theater of legal print, and specifically the popularizing use of images within the texts of law.

The starting point is necessarily the invention of the emblem book by Italian humanist and lawyer Andrea Alciato. Like most great discoveries this particular invention was something of an accident, a chance conjunction of the jurist's moralizing epigrams and a printer's visual imagination.[18] It was the publisher who suggested to Alciato that the maxims and brief didactic discourses would benefit from woodcut illustrations. Here and to considerable consequence, law and humanism collided in the development of what is later termed a pedagogic *sensualium* or didactic publication of pictures of the world, "of all things visible" to which "things invisible are reduced after their fashion" (in their likeness).[19] I mention this not to show that I have read more than Professor J. S. Peters, which I have not, but so as to make a more general link to a concept and practice of textual transmission that far exceeds the purportedly rational positive content of the book or letter being delivered.

Word and image travel together. We can frequently see this quite literally in both externally in the housing of manuscripts and books, in public readings and ritual performances conducted with book in hand, as well as internally, so to speak, in illuminations, woodcuts, frontispiece icons, tables, figures, emblems, covers, portraits and illustrations in manuscripts and in printed books. More than that, the internal figures of language, the strange usages and surprising connections that rhetoric elicits all further conjure phantasmata in the candleless theater of the skull. The emblem book, a legal invention, relays a variety of juridical norms, cautionary tales and exhortative narratives to the social theater of civic duty and public life. As Menestrier, one of the most prolific of systematizers puts it in his synoptic treatise on the philosophy of images: "Jurisprudence is the Image of the public good."[20] The text is also an image and both uses and conjures images visible and unseen, express and implied. The lawyers in particular, hugely unpopular as they were during the radical growth of the profession in the sixteenth century, needed the protection and comfort, the affect and effect of images. Their books needed protection and popular presence and it was to this amongst other ends that the emblem books proliferated alongside the breviaries, collections of statutes and volumes of reports in their ornate and foreign languages.

According to his letter to his publisher, Alciato's little book of emblems was written for the festival. This coincidence should be enjoyed and elaborated. The festival is a *dies non*, a non law day. At common law this meant that the King's courts did not sit but another law took hold and took precedence during the festival, the *saturnalia*. The festival, in honor of Saturn, the Deity of law and melancholy, is in essence a theatrical and spectacular popular occasion. Hierarchies were reversed, the everyday inverted, and comedy rather than tragedy held sway. The festival was an illusion, a moment of laughter and play, of social dialogue in Bakhtin's formulation, and spelled out the norms of community, of friendship and justice upon, which law depends. It is into this moment of theatrical, indeed histrionic social bonding, of incorporation and release that Alciato chose to throw the first book of emblems.

The figures of law, the images that persuade, disseminate and transmit are proposed and displayed explicitly in the emblem books. They offer a law of law, a conspectus of forms of good and evil, which gain a much more coded and esoteric representation in the later prosaic figures, the *aenigmata* of the legal treatises and reports. Take this reference to the festival and theater one step further and we can conclude this excursus on the emblem by noting a little remarked feature of the legal emblem book, namely the frontispiece or title page or pages designed in the form of a stage, monument or public placard. Oratory, as Cicero belabors, depends upon delivery and he goes on to observe, and I am sure I have no need to remind you that the orators, the lawyers in particular, "are the players that act real life." But this role, he laments has now been taken over by the *histriones*, actors, "who only mimic reality."[21] If the legal emblem book is to enact the real then it needs the proper props of such a solemnized ritual, of such serious illusions.

If we turn then to the emblem of the emblem book, the title page, the frontispiece, we can clearly see the solemnized inscription of their ritual role. We can start a little way back with the frontispiece to an English work of armory, published by a member of the Inns of Court, Gerard Legh. The discipline of armory, which predates the emblem books, is that of the visual representation of genealogy, meaning honor, social place, dignity, office and role according to a coded visual lexicon of colors, stones, figures and mottos. The title page from the 1576 edition of *The Accedens of Armory*, in vivid and intricate detail, shows the hierarchical staging of sociality and law.

Top center of the image is Moses, passing a sword with his right hand to the crowned sovereign, and the tables of the law are delivered with his left hand to the Chancellor or chief judge, the figure that represents the church and the law to the populace. Below Moses is a shield with four places and symbols engraved. First a glass or mirror without image, representing prudence, and more expressly fear of a faceless and invisible God. The second image is of the scales of justice. The third, a broken column represents fortitude, and resistance to idols. Last, a cup and wine, shows temperance and faith. Below the sovereign and chancellor is an arched and raised stage, the image of the social, with a scholar, surrounded by books and a laborer standing next to a plough. Between them a mirror or plaque upon, which is inscribed PIFT, standing for the four virtues described: prudence, justice, fortitude and temperance.

The title page of the book shows in properly theatrical form the content that will follow. It stages the book and presents it as an intervention into the theater of the social, what Cicero coins as the acting of the real. From this beginning the subsequent tradition of emblem books becomes much more obviously a popularizing theater of norm and law illustrated and disseminated for learned and unlearned alike to see. These are our illusions, and it is this form that is rapidly taken up in the reprinting and translations of Alciato's *Emblemata*. Take, for example, Bonhomme's 1551 edition of the book.[22] The title page shows Moses at the top, his image in the form of a highly embellished stage arch. Bowed figures of strong men are shown supporting the columned arch, and between the arches is hung a screen with title inscribed. Below, on the stage, the figure of a winged Mercury with a sword in one hand and the head of a slain wrongdoer, severed head held by the hair, in the other. While the content of the emblem may seem clear, the theatrical staging of each emblem is less obvious or commented and this despite several works of moral emblematizing that take "Theater" as their title.

The French scholar Perrière can serve as one example. His book, *Le Theatre des bons engins*, a work of moralizing emblems, has as its title page image an ornate stage with a small stage, replete with players and musical instrument.[23] Add to this the fact that his preface is itself prefaced by and concludes with images of blank tableaux, and the theatrical reference of the title and image becomes more apparent. If we move back to the lawyers, the critical example and illustration is that of the jurist Pierre Cousteau, whose *Pegma cum narrationibus philosophicis* has recently been reproduced in part and lengthily analyzed by Valérie Hayaert.[24] The *pegma* of the title, refers to the machinery for staging plays, as well as to the scaffold and other public sites of spectacle. Most anciently the *pegma* was the pedestal and casing for the images, the wax death masks of the ancestors that were kept in the atrium of Roman houses. It is again, however, the reference to staging and to the theater that should capture attention because it is neither accidental nor necessarily obvious to contemporary eyes. It is the legal staging of the real, of the play – the illusion – of the social that returns time and again.

One last example, the English barrister George Wither's book of emblems has a magnificent frontispiece in which society as concept and whole is pictured in the form of twin peaks.[25]

The image is the path and stages of human life: two mountains rise into the heavens while the natural stage of human life is placed between the skies and a dark and subterranean underworld. Again by chance or artifice it is the printer who invented this frontispiece and Wither disapproves it as revealing secrets that prudence suggests should remain covered. The theater of this emblem is for Wither too much. The emblem, the image, should remain an enigma: "And hee that can unriddle them, to us, / Shall stiled be, the second Oedipus." Bad poetry aside, the emblem offers a conspectus of the social, of Church and state, good and evil, nature and culture, belief and law. These are matters contained in and carried by images that the learned will unpack but which the unlearned can also view, enjoy, recognize, copy, embody and learn from. This is the legal form, in its day, of an inscribed videosphere, a theater of legal images springing from the pages of books.

— Conclusions: stage to screen

Last stage in the argument, step two and a half, we must recognize that the social spectacle of law, lengthy though its image history may be, has moved from the stage, from *pegma* or theatrical device, from the theater of the legal text to the screen and monitor. It is well enough to argue that the graphosphere was in some considerable measure a nascent videosphere but this now surely changes with the new media and the chimerical and evanescent public spheres generated on television and the web. Law, as Alain Supiot has recently spelled out, now seems to disappear into an amorphous and indeterminate global realm of *html*, of universal text, and private computer portals.[26] Economics governs, law declines, the symbolic collapses.

No room then, and here I return to my opening remarks, for literature and law as an inter-sub-field or academic indiscipline. It is over, an illusion that has disappeared. And of course there are solid and sound grounds for believing that in some instances and circumstances this is true. There is a precious or simply miscellaneous use of literary texts as a diversion from law. There is a nostalgic and thoroughly retro interest in great books that extends in an apologetic fashion to the black letters of the law just as those letters vanish, turn red, flicker and shimmer before changing shape on screen. If literature has not disappeared, it is in the process of vanishing, shifting from page to liquid crystal display or high definition digital relay. Is this nemesis for law and literature, deluge for dogmatics as Supiot suspects, the end of a disciplinary mode of tourism? Here my answer is at least in part affirmative. It is time to move on.

It is time to track the literary in the legal at a different or more fundamental level. What should be in issue, and what I have traced throughout this discussion in terms of the image in and of the text, is the literary drive, the libidinal forces and erotic effects that join subject to law, affect to norm, the real and the illusion. That is the substrate of legal doctrine, the political protocol or diplomatic rhetoric of law and it is this deep hermeneutics, this affect inside legality that now becomes visible and cognizable by virtue of the videosphere, by dint of the becoming image of law. Here I want briefly to track that shift and to suggest that it is best understood as an internal division within law.

The theater of justice and truth, as I discussed it earlier, was concerned with legal doctrine in the dual sense of spiritual law and governance of the soul, which modern lawyers address in terms of justice, equity and the forum of conscience. Here and obviously enough, affect and mercy, the sense of justice and injustice, the visible sensibilities and legal emotions are put into play. This jurisdiction of justice is not identical with that of law but rather has its roots in the *lex amatoria* or laws of love that grow out of the Christian tradition in which, as St Paul coined it, *plenis legis est delictio* – love is the fulfillment of law.[27] Consider then and proleptically, as the visible representation of Pauline principle, the emblematic representation of emblem books of moralized love. What could be more important or immediate?

My first example is from 1653, and is the title page of Albert Flamen's book of amorous emblems. It has a very simple image. A plain blank cloth or screen hangs across what appears to be a stage, with cherubs peeking out from behind the curtain. The title and other prolegomena or threshold items are printed on this screen. Note first that this is clearly a version of theatrical curtain, announcing a play or display, an excitement or entertainment of an erotic but morally modulated kind. Note second, that the sheet hangs in mid or thin air. There is no visible means of support beyond the folded top corners, which are suspended *ex nihilo* or by divine providence in open space. Granted that curtains don't fly, there is something more here than meets the eye.

Take another example. Philip Ayres book of amorous emblems from the 1680s.[28] Here the title page appears in the form of a sheet held in mid-air by a winged angel. The scene is one of bucolic pleasure. Cherubs dance around a tree, while others bathe naked in the ocean. Two more mature lovers converse under a tree. All of the tropes of love here act as a visual introduction to the emblems of the book. We are again in the realm of images, in the air with a title that is caught if you will on the natural screen that shields and then opens upon the theater of life and love. Again note two points to this screen of amatory law. The image is one of a transition from tellurian to spectral, from the mundane to the spiritual, and its emblematic sign is a floating tableau, an imageless sheet. Accompanying the image, a poem titled Cupid to Chloe weeping, which ends "Strange tears! Whose power can soften all, / But that dear Breast on which they fall."

Those tears, *lachrymae amoris*, can perhaps provide a clue as to the theoretical significance of the image. Tears are a corporeal expression, a visceral illocution, speech without words. There is considerable doctrine on tears but my concern here is rather with their visibility and their evanescence. Tears are visible and they vanish. Like blushes and trembling, they express on the outside what is active inside. They are as close as we can get to seeing the soul. This then is the clue to the title page image. The sheet that hangs in the air is an emblem of the soul, a representation of a blank and chimerical cloth that captures things unseen, things in the air, not just images but moods and states of the soul, including love and attachment to nature and law. Here is the amorous jurisdiction, the theater of justice and truth, represented as it must be shown, as being of the air, spectral, floating and shapeless save when momentarily caught upon a screen as an image of unseen things. The soul, in other words, or not in words, moves from the visible to the invisible, from vision to faith.

Such is the theory of the spectral as relayed in law and love.

The early modern theologians had a term for evanescent images. The cross made in water on the forehead, the sign of the cross made by the hand in the air, these were "aereall" or vanishing signs. They flickered briefly, one could say, upon the spectral screen and then were gone. These aereall signs, however, were theologically the most powerful, they were the closest to the absent thing being signified, the spirit or invisible cause. They led, to quote a primary source, more swiftly *ab imagine ad rem significatem*, from the image to the thing, the hidden reality, signified.[29] Our author is clear that the image is always "a vanishing aereall shadow, like the ghost or shade of one dead" and it is in the likeness to the dead that the viewer sees and crosses over into the realm of shades and shadows. Strip Parker of his virulent theology and the point is that images transport, invoke the imagination and so play their pivotal role in the imaginary constitution of society. Their effect is their affect and this is as true for the libidinal economy of juridical images as it is of the sensual apprehension of literary texts.

Parker invokes the dead. Peters disquisits on the death of law and literature and specifically on the vanishing real. Carnage all around. I will end in my turn with a death. This time, however, it is not law and literature that is the object of disappearance but rather the death of a filmmaker that I want to invoke. It is my way of moving on. Theo Van Gogh was a Dutch artist and filmmaker who made a short movie titled *Submission* with a Somalian born activist Ayaan Hirsi Ali.[30]

The movie is ostensibly a critique of Muslim treatment of women. The monologue voice-over, in English, tells the story of a young woman who falls in love with an attractive but unsuitable partner. She is forced by her parents to marry an older man. She finds him repellent. He forces himself on her. The monologue is interesting mainly for being chanted, lyrical in sound, with Middle Eastern music in the back-ground. The power of the film, however, lies not in its rather unexceptional story but in its selection and use of images. The woman narrator is veiled in traditional Muslim manner. Here face is covered except for her eyes but her naked body is clearly visible through the thinnest of veils. More than that, in some scenes she is prostrate, splayed naked on the floor, a sheet over her middle with text from the Koran painted in black letters on the skin of her back. Blood, the welts from beatings, mingle with ink and show vividly the ultimate textual substrate of both interdiction and law.

Leave aside the death of the director at the hands of a Muslim militant. Others have dealt with this tragedy in their own terms.[31] I will focus on the image. The illusion. The image of the naked body seen through a veil is in theological terms both an illicit spectacle and equally a representation of the image as such. What is an image? It is variously, in our legal authors, a false truth, a woman, a strumpet, pollution, seduction, enigma, likeness or dissemblance, fraud or veil.[32] Here the religious costume tricks the viewer by displaying the body that the veil, the truth, is supposed to conceal and protect. Moving, however, to the bare skin with the text inscribed on it, what is evident is that the veil simply uncovers a further screen, another sign of things corporeal and in the end invisible.

The truth is a series of veils, in Nietzsche's depiction, and the body in this instance, serving as text is also and necessarily a screening of a law that will never be visible except obscurely, through further signs, through welts, blood, paint, letters, even skin. This, in other words, is theater playing and displaying the law, blood and paint, scars and letters. Here is the point. Where law and theater explicitly meet, there is always a dramatic negotiation, *otium* and *negotium* in the Latin, a confrontation between image and writing, imaginary and real. What is unbearable for some, moving for others, in the image of a holy text inscribed upon feminine flesh is precisely the raising of veils, the uncovering of the truth, the mixing of media and genre without the solemnized rituals of religious ceremony or legal form. The illusion lies in the element of play, the explicit pain and covered eroticism of the image, the juxtaposition of genres, pornography and politics, and not in the content of the letter or the fact of its being written.

Finally, return to the vanishing real. No question here. The real is, of course, vanishing. It is in the nature of the real to vanish, indeed its presence is always already shadowy, both aereall and spectral, mediated by the calculus and other signs through which we know it. What disciplines can aid in the legal study of such vanishing truths, such real but absconded things? To study the vanishing real or for that matter the collapse of the symbolic requires, indeed necessitates the illusion of interdisciplinary scholarship, the indiscipline of the study of law's use of figurative and visual media. Lawyers are not good with things that vanish, the juridical preference being for perpetuities, entailments, covenants and of course precedents whose essence is longevity and whose claim to reality is precisely their prior existence, their corporeality as part of the system or body of law. It is also true that jurists are less than comfortable with images, uneasy in the face of film or other spectral modes and media. They don't like illusions and hence the need for the assistance of philology, literary scholarship, and now media studies, cinematic acumen and psychoanalysis to help understand the drive behind the images, the affects and the effects of the theater of law.

1 Respectively, Richard Posner, *Law and Literature: A Misunderstood Relation* (Cambridge Mass.: Harvard University Press, 1988); Julie Stone Peters, "Law, Literature, and the Vanishing Real: On the Future of an Interdisciplinary Illusion" 120 PMLA 441 (2005); Stanley Fish, *Save the World on your own Time* (New York: Oxford University Press, 2007); Guyora Binder & Robert Weisberg, *Literary Criticisms of Law* (Princeton: Princeton University Press, 2006) suggest that cultural rather than literary criticism should take the stage.

2 Julie Stone Peters, *Theatre of the Book 1480–1880: Print, Text, and Performance in Europe* (New York: Oxford University Press, 2000).

3 Notably, if severally, James Bond White, *Justice in Translation: A Essay in Cultural and Legal Criticism* (Chicago: Chicago University Press, 1990); Richard Weisberg, *Poethics and Other Strategies in Law and Literature* (New York: Columbia University Press, 1990); Maria Anstodemou, *Law and Literature: Journeys from Her to Eternity* (Oxford: Oxford University Press, 2000); Francois Ost, *Raconter la loi. Aux sources de l'imaginaire juridique* (Paris: Albin, 2004), Peter Goodrich, *The Laws of Love: A Brief Historical and Practical Manual* (London: Palgrave, 2007); Antoine Garapon & Denis Salas, introduction to *Imaginaire la loi: Le droit dans la literature* (Paris: Michalon, 2008).

4 David Evans, "The Inns of Court: Speculations on the Body of Law," *Arch–Text* 1 (1993); and most recently Subha Mukerhji, *Law and Representation in Early Modern Drama* (Cambrigde: University of Cambrigde 2006). For an important study of French contexts of this relation, see Christian Biet, *Droit et literature sous l'ancien régime. Le jeu de la valeur et de la loi* (Paris: Champion 2002).

5 Sir John Davies, *Elegies and Epigrams*, cited in Mukherji, *Law and Representation*, 175.

6 Paul Raffield, *Images and Cultures of Law in Early Modern England: Justice and Political Power*, 1558–1660 (Cambridge: Cambridge University Press: 2004).

7 Florence Dupont, *L'orateur sans visage. Essai sur l'acteur romain et son masque* (Paris: P.U.F., 2000) 51–85. Specifically on the legal ban, see Dupont, "La scène juridique," 16 *Communications* 62 (1977); and Peter Goodrich, "Law" in *Encyclopedia of Rhetoric*, ed. Tom Sloane (New York: Oxford University Press, 2004).

8 Bradin Cormack, *A Power to do Justice: Jurisdiction, English Literature, and the Rise of Common Law 1509–1625* (Chicago: Chicago University Press, 2007); Shaun McVeigh, ed., *The Jurisprudence of Jurisdiction* (London: Routlegde, 2007).

9 Joannis Baptistae, *Cardinalis de Luca, Theatrum veritatis et iustitiae* (Cologne: publisher, 1689).

10 Sir Edward Coke, *The Second Part of the Institutes of the Lowes of England: Containing the Expositionof Many Ancient, and Other Statutes,-Whereof You May See Particulares in a Table Following* (1631), 380 and 537 respectively.

11 Bradin Cormack, *Power*, supra note 8, at 22–31 in particular, on epiphanies and bodies in law, see Anne Bottomley, "Theory is a Process and not an End" in *Feminist Perspectives in Law and Theory*, eds. Janice Richardson & Ralph Sandland (London: Cavendish Publishing, 2000).

12 Sir Edward Coke, preface to *The First Part of the Institutes of the Lawes of England. Or, A Commentarie upon Littleton,* (London, 1628).

13 Régis Debray, *Vie et mort de l'image. Une histoire du regard en Occident* (Paris: Gallimard, 1992), 221–254.

14 Erasmus, *The Adages of Erasmus*, ed. Dominic Baker-Smith (Toronto and Buffalo: University of Toronto Press, 2001); William Fulbeck, *Preparative to the Study of Law* (London, 1599).

15 On the theater of the chancelleries, see Cornelia Vismann, *Files: Law and Media Technology* (Palo Alto: Stanford University Press, 2008), 102.

16 Jacques Derrida's *Of Grammatology* remains one of the best discussions specifically on the metaphor of book and writing. So too his essay "Scribble: Writing-Power": 58 in *Yale French Studies* 1, 16 (1979), provides key insights into the politics of texts. Also worthy of mention, and equally extreme, is Pierre Legendre, *Les Enfants du texte* (Paris: Fayard, 1996), and *De la Société comme texte* (Paris: Fayard, 2001) amongst other works.

17 Peter Goodrich, "The Visial Line: On the Prehistory of Law and Film," 14 *Parallax* 55 (2008); see also Goodrich, "Visive Powers: Colours, Trees and Genres of Jurisdiction" 2 *Law and Humanities* 213 (2008).

18 The letter is reproduced in part and discussed in John Manning, *The Emblem* (2002), 38.

19 The definition is from Joannes Comenius, *Orbis sensualium pictus* (Cologne, 1672) sig. A33b.

20 Claude François Menestrier "Plan for Study of the Philosophy of the Image," repr. as an appendix in *L'Art des Emblèmes,* by Claude-Francois Menestrier (1684; facsimile repr., ed. Karl von Mòseneder, Mäander: Mittenwald, 1984).

21 Cicero, *De oratore* (Cambrigde, Mass.: Harvard University Press, 1942), voi Illi, lvi., 214–215.

22 Andrea Alciato, title page, *Emblemata* (Lyons, 1551). In many editions each emblem is itself reproduced as if on a stage, with columns to the side, above and below as frame or stage.

23 Guillaume de Perrière, *Le Théâtre de bons engins* (Toulouse, 1544); Also a theatrical reference: Pierre Coustau, *Pegma* (Toulouse, 1555).

24 Valérie Hayaert, *Mens Emblematica et Humanisme Juridique. Le cas du Pegma cum narrationibus philosophicis de Pierre Coustau* (Geneva: Droz, 1555) (2008).

25 George Wither, *A Collection of Emblèmes* (London, 1635).

26 Alain Supiot, *Homo Juridicus: On the Anthropological Function of Law* (London: Verso, 2007), 119–131. A similar argument can be culled from W. T. Murphy, *The Oldest Social Science: Configurations of Law and Modernity* (Oxford: Oxford University Press, 1992).

27 *The Tretyse of Love* (1494; repr. London: Oxford University Press, 1951), lines 19–20.

28 Philip Ayres, *Emblemata amatoria* (London, 1686).

29 Robert Parker, *A Scholasticall Discourse against Symbolizing with Antichrist in Ceremonies: Especially in the Sign of the Cross* (London: 1607), 47–48.

30 *Submission* (Dir. Theo van Gogh, 2004).

31 See particularly Ian Buruma, *Murder in Amsterdam. The Death of Theo van Gogh and the Limits of Tolerance* (New York: Basic Books, 2006).

32 My preferred source here is the Toulousian lawyer Jean Coras, *altercación, en forme de dialogue* (Toulouse, 1558), 23–27.

Must Justice Be Blind? The Challenge of Images to the Law

— Martin Jay

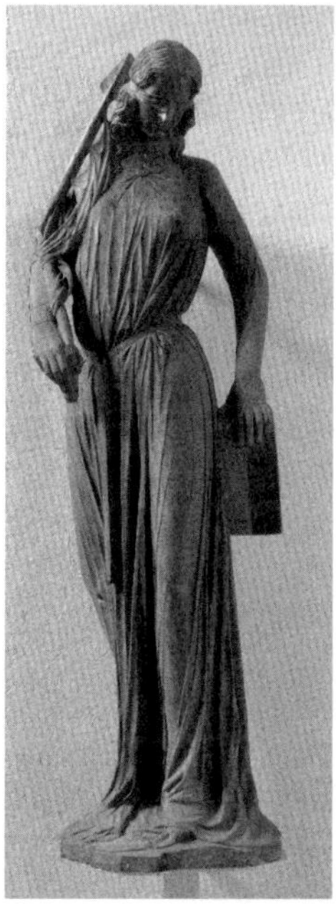

La Synagogue
Musée de l'Oeuvre Notre Dame de Strasbourg.
Photo M. Bertola

Allegorical images of Justice, historians of iconography tell us,[1] did not always cover the eyes of the goddess, Justitia. In its earliest Roman incarnations, preserved on the coins of Tiberius' reign, the woman with the sword in one hand, representing the power of the state, and the scales in the other, derived from the weighing of souls in the Egyptian Book of the Dead,[2] was depicted as clear-sightedly considering the merits of the cases before her. Medieval images of justice based on figures of Christ, St. Michael, or secular rulers likewise provided them with the ability to make their judgments on the basis of visual evidence.

But suddenly at the end of the 15th century, a blindfold began to be placed over the goddess' eyes, producing what has rightly been called "the most enigmatic of the attributes of Justice."[3]

Perhaps the earliest image showing the change is a 1494 wood engraving of a Fool covering the eyes of Justice, illustrating Sebastian Brant's *Narrenschiff* (*Ship of Fools*), which was rapidly reproduced in translations throughout Europe. Initially, as this engraving suggests, the blindfold implies that Justice has been robbed of her ability to get things straight, unable to wield her sword effectively or see what is balanced on her scales. Other medieval and Renaissance allegories of occluded vision, such as those of Death, Ambition, Cupidity, Ignorance or Anger, were, in fact, uniformly negative. The figure of the nude child Cupid, as Erwin Panofsky pointed out many years ago, was depicted blindfolded not merely because love clouds judgment, but also because "he was on the wrong side of the moral world."[4]

By 1530, however, this satirical implication seems to have lost its power and the blindfold was transformed instead into a positive emblem of impartiality and equality before the law. Perhaps because of traditions transmitted by Plutarch and Diodore of Sicily from ancient Egypt that had depicted judges as blind or handless, the blindfold, like the scales, came to imply neutrality rather than helplessness. According to the French scholar Robert Jacob,[5] the explanation may also have something to do with the reversal of fortunes experienced by the symbol of the Synagogue in medieval Christian iconography. Traditionally shown a blindfolded – as well as with a broken lance – to symbolize her resistance to the illumination of divine light, the Synagogue was negatively contrasted with the open-eyed Church, as in the famous early fourteenthcentury statue on the south gate of Strasbourg Cathedral.

What had been a sign of inferiority was, however, dramatically reversed when the iconophobic Reformation took seriously the Hebrew interdiction of images, the second of the Commandments Moses brought down from Mount Sinai. Now it was once again a virtue to resist what Augustine had famously called the "lust of the eyes." A blindfolded justice could thus avoid the seductions of images and achieve the necessary dispassionate distance to render verdicts impartially, an argument advanced as early as the jurist Andrea Alciati's influential compendium of emblems, the *Emblemata* of 1531.[6] According to Christian-Nils Robert, this impartiality was required by the new urban, secular, bourgeois culture of the early modern period, which left behind the personalism of private, feudal justice. It was not by chance that many statues or fountains of blindfolded Justitia were placed in town squares in Northern Europe next to newly erected civic buildings, in which a nascent public sphere was in the process of emerging.[7] Even in Catholic countries like France, where churches remained flooded with images, secular edifices began to grow more austere.

The law was now to be presented entirely in language and justice dispensed only through language, necessitating discussion and persuasion, rather than appearing in images, which might overwhelm through dazzlement. Along with the iconoclastic purification of courtrooms of their artworks and lawbooks of their illustrations, at least in countries influenced by Reformations iconophobia, went the frequent robing of judges in sober black and white and the replacement of colorful seals by simple signatures on legal documents.[8] No longer would signs from heaven, like those informing medieval ordeals, be sufficient; now the words of men giving testimony about what they knew or had witnessed and then arguing about what rule might be violated would in most instances suffice. Although it is true that law was to be increasingly codified and preserved in written form, which has been interpreted by some as reflecting the modern privileging of sight because of its frequent use of visual metaphors,[9] the nonhieroglyphic script of Western languages meant that visual revelations of the truth, illuminations of divine will, were no longer relevant to the decision-making process. Along with the invisible "hidden God" of the Jansenists, who increasingly left the world to its own devices, went a justice that applied general rules and norms rather than looked for indications of divine dispensation. As with the later prohibition of laws referring to specific people with proper names, famously banned in the American Constitution as "bills of attainder," so too the interdiction on images was designed to thwart favoritism or personal vengeance. With the blindfolding of Justitia, we are well along the road to the modern cult of the abstract norm in juridical positivism.

If that road is paved with the prohibition of concrete images, we have to ask, however, whether or not building it had hidden costs, which we may still be paying today. In what follows, it is precisely this question that will occupy us. One place to begin an answer would be Max Horkheimer and Theodor Adorno's celebrated accusation in the *Dialectic of Enlightenment* that the modern notion of justice was still beholden to a mythic assumption: the fetish of equivalence, the desire for perfect commensurability, the domination of the exchange principle:

> For mythic and enlightened justice, quilt and atonement, happiness and unhappiness were sides of an equation. Justice is subsume in law... The blindfold over Justitia's eyes does not only mean there should be assault on justice, but that justice does not originate in freedom.[10]

Unexpectedly, in the light of the Frankfurt School's often-remarked embrace of the Jewish taboo on idolatrous images as a mark of resistance to a prematurely positive utopian thought, Horkheimer and Adorno here register a protest against the complete banishment of images. The preservation of the ability to see they cryptically associate with freedom, a freedom that is threatened when justice is reduced to law. What, it has to be asked, is this freedom which the blindfolding of Justitia denies? How does the reduction of justice to law threaten its very existence?

One explanations is suggested by the famous argument developed by Lessing in his classical treaty on aesthetics, *Laocoon*, in favor of the Greek regulation of images, an argument drawing the critical attention of W. J. T. Mitchell in his influential study of images, texts and ideologies, *Iconology*.[11] According to Lessing, images should be kept under legal control because of their capacity to depict monsters, those indecorous amalgams of the human and divine or the human and the bestial that are a scandal to the alleged order of nature. Mitchell interprets Lessing's iconophobia as symptomatic of an anxiety over proper sex roles and adulterous fantasies, but it might be just as plausible to see it as a fear of boundary transgression in general, especially the boundaries that define and circumscribe our bodies. Lessing's visual monsters are an affront to the law because they depart from the assumption that the boundaried categories we use to order the world are ones under which all its particulars can be subsumed. The image of a hybridized creature, at once man and beast, divine and human, male and female, confounds our reliance on conceptual subsumption by refusing to be an exemplar of a general rule.

The freedom of which Horkheimer and Adorno speak is thus the ability of the particular, the unique, the incommensurable, the improper to escape from the dominating power of the exchange principle that is manifested in universalizing concepts and in the reduction of justice to the law of equivalents. The eye, by far the most discriminating of the senses in its ability to register minute differences, must therefore be closed to produce this reduction. Justitia's vision is veiled so that she is able to maintain the fiction that each judgment before her can be understood as nothing more than a "case" of something more general, equivalent to other like cases, and subsumable under a general principle that need only be applied without regard for individual uniqueness. That general principle is understood to hover somewhere above specific cases, recalling the origin of the word justice in the Latin *iubeo* (to command). This is a version of justice, as Vassilis Lambropoulos has recently pointed out, that can be understood as "the right command, the command that rightfully deserves obedience. What is right is what is decreed as straight, the line of the ruler and the regime directing from above, the regal control, the reign of the supreme direction.... 'Justice' comes from above, form the realm of certainty."[12] It is thus unlike the Greek notion of *Dike*, which in certain of its acceptations involved a dynamic, polemical balance between contraries, an agonistic ethos based on proportion and analogy that could not be subsumed under a single *nomos* or law.[13]

It will doubtless have occurred to many of you that achieving this effect of regal control required not merely a blindfold, but also one placed over the eyes of a specifically female deity. Granted, as Christian-Nils Robert has argued,[14] Justitia may be a somewhat androgynous figure, at least to the extent that she wields a powerful symbol of coercive authority, a sword fit for swift decapitations. Traditional religious iconography had, in fact, permitted its use only infrequently to women, the most notable instance being Judith, the slayer of Holofernes, in the Old Testament. The stern and vaguely menacing statues of Justitia in front of the Palaces of Justice in early modern Europe were certainly a far cry from the maternal images of the forgiving, mediating Madonna that populated so many medieval churches. Nor were they reminiscent of so many sainted, suffering female martyrs, whose assigned role was that of passive victim bearing witness to their faith, even if one might detect a certain symmetry between the blindfolded criminal condemned to die and the image of blindfolded executioner.[15] As a result, Justitia may plausibly be interpreted as a symbol of the very temporal power, firmly in male hands, that sought to displace the spiritual power that had accrued to the cult of Mary in the late Middle Ages. Neoclassical images with martial overtones were, after all, the source of this allegory, not religious ones.

And yet, it must be acknowledged that blindfolded Justitia, with all of her warlike attributes, was still primarily a female figure, as had been the Egyptian Maat (not only the Goddess of justice, but also of truth and order) and the Greek Dike, who was the daughter of Zeus. Male images of divine justice, such as that of God at the Last Judgment or St. Michael, had not been prevented from exercising the power of vision. Solomon famously could see how the two contesting mothers felt about the dividing of the child they both claimed as their own. What was the implication of preventing a female judge from seeing? What power might still be lurking beneath her blindfold, which, after all, does not permanently rob the Goddess of her sight?

What that power may be is suggested by the traditional reading of another image from a slightly later era, Jan Vermeer's *Woman Weighing Pearls* of 1662–1663. Depicted in front of a picture of the Last Judgment, thought to be by Cornelisz Enhelbreecht, the woman with the delicate scales in her hands appears to be looking soberly and carefully at the individual pearls in each tray, as if she were contemplatively pondering their particular value. Or at least so the traditional interpretation of the canvas has assumed. Whether or not she is actually doing so is a question to which I will return shortly. But whatever the target of her gaze, there is no trace of judgemental harshness or vindictiveness in her visage; indeed these seem to be traits that the blissfully serene Vermeer was simply incapable of depicting. As with the souls whose salvation is judged in the scene behind her, each pearl, that precious object mirroring the world around it so often at the symbolic center of Vermeer's paintings, seems worth careful, deliberate scrutiny. The setting, moreover, is a typical Vermeer interior, a private, intimate, humble realm, far from the public space of the early modern statues of Justitia.

The goddess' gender as mediated by this comparison with Vermeer's painting is relevant here if we recall the contrast between male and female variants of moral reasoning posited by feminists like Carol Gilligan and Seyla Benhabib against moral theorists like Lawrence Kohlberg and John Rawls.[16] Whereas male judgment often tends to be abstractly universalist, decontextualized, and formalistic, its female counterpart, they tell us, is more frequently sensitive to individual detail, narrative uniqueness, and specific contexts. Instead of acknowledging only an imagined "generalized other," it focuses instead on the actual "concrete other" before it. The blindfolding of Justitia is thus not a thwarting of the gaze per se, but of the specifically female gaze, or at least of those qualities that have been associated with it in our culture.[17] It is thus ultimately in the service of the disembodiment, disembeddedness, and decontextualization that a legalistic justice based on the reductive equivalence of the exchange principle requires.

The complete victory of what has recently been dubbed "algorithmic justice"[18] because it involves following binding rules decreed from above is, to be sure, substantially modified in a legal system such as the Anglo-American, in which concrete precedent is often as important as statute as the basis for judgment. Here Kant's well-known contrast between reflective and determinant judgments, the former applied to aesthetic issues, the latter to cognitive and moral ones, might be invoked to justify the paradigmatic value of prior specific examples over abstract rules that are universally binding. But there is still in the law of precedent the presupposition of at least analogical commensurability from case to case. Even reflective judgments, after all, draw on the presumption of a *sensus communis*, a shared sentiment that goes beyond the arbitrary whim of idiosyncratic taste. If not by subsumption, then by analogy, what is different is somehow compelled to become similar through resemblance. In addition, the common law of precedent can be said to collapse the temporal difference past and present in its search for a replicable standard of measurement.

Although images can, of course, themselves be the object of such judgments, their initial, brute impact on the beholder's sense of sight may well be prior to any evaluation, reflective or determinant, of their meaning. Even Kant's a priori categories do not, after all, include a necessary mechanism of cultural, symbolic commensuration. If Horkheimer and Adorno are right, mute visuality retains traces of a mode of interaction between humans and the world, which is prior to conceptual subsumption or the rule of common sense, a mode they call mimetic. This is not the place to launch a full-fledged analysis of the vexed concept of mimesis in their work, an analysis I have tentatively attempted to make elsewhere.[19] Suffice it to say that they understood mimesis to involve a non-dominating relationship between subjects and objects in which the world was not "subjected" to categorical determination or even intersubjective consensus. Mimesis meant a more passive affinity between perceiver and perceived rather than a hierarchical control by one over the other. Affinity, it should immediately be noted, does not mean identity or equivalence, as the mimesis between subject and object maintains a certain, irreducible difference between them. Insofar as images and their referents, representations and originals, perceptions and objects, may be similar, but not ontologically identical, they resist the full power of the exchange principle. Thus the image need not be of an imaginary monster, transgressing natural boundaries, to do its work of resistance; it need merely evoke the primal power of mimetic affinity, which acknowledges differences even as it seeks similarities, against the counter-power of conceptual subsumption, which seeks to suppress the remainder left behind in the act of subsuming.

What ultimately distinguishes mimetic from conceptual behavior, according to this argument, is the absence of violence in the former, the symbolic violence, that is, of categorical subsumption, which finds an echo in the potential for literal force heard in the phrase to "enforce the law." Justitia, it should be remembered, is never depicted without her unsheathed sword.[20] As Jacques Derrida has recently pointed out in his meditation on Walter Benjamin's famous essay "Critique of Violence," there may well be a moment of originary violence or brute force in the foundation of even the most legitimate of laws: "Applicability, 'enforceability,' is not an exterior or secondary possibility that may or may not be added as a supplement to law," he writes. "It is the force essentially implied in the very concept of *justice as law*."[21] Here we can detect an echo of the argument from Horkheimer and Adorno's *Dialectic of Enlightenment*: that a justice reduced to a law of equivalence based on the subsumption of individual cases under a general rule, the "algorithmic justice" produced by commands from above, involves violence and restricts freedom. A different justice that would evade the binding force of the algorithm would follow instead the logic of the gratuitous gift, bestowed without an expectation of reciprocity, rather than that of the debt paid to even out a score, the primitive act of vengeance that Nietzsche famously saw at the root of modern notions of exchange.[22] It would be incalculable, impossible to capture in definitions, irreducibly aporetic, perhaps even dangerously mad. Always either a memory of what may have been or a hope for a future that can perhaps be, but never actually is, it haunts the project of fully realized justice in the present, a justice based on blinding one's eyes to the absolute alterity of each of its alleged cases, a justice reduced to nothing but the positive, formal, abstract law. As such, it is the basis not only of religious notions of divine justice, but also of every defense of a revolutionary "political justice" that can claim the right to suspend the laws prevailing in a system that can itself be deemed unjust.[23]

But both dialectical and deconstructionist modes of thinking, as we know, resist simply binary oppositions, and so too this overly abstract dichotomy must itself be shaken. Allegedly non-violent, gratuitous justice based on respect for absolute particularity and the benign mimesis of nature cannot be placed entirely on the other side of a divide from the putatively sinister, coercive force of law as command from above. In "Critique of Violence," Benjamin had in fact juxtaposed a divine violence, which destroys laws and transgresses boundaries, to a mythical one that makes and conserves them.[24] Although he cryptically described the former as "lethal without spilling blood,"[25] the troubling implication was that a justice beyond the law of formal equivalence, the life-affirming justice of absolute qualitative singularity based on the logic of the gift, was not itself somehow beyond coercion. For without any rules or criteria at all, what was to prevent a *soi-disant* divine justice from descending into nothing more than the principle "might makes right." As Derrida himself uneasily concludes, "in one form or another, the undecidable is on each side, and is the violent condition of knowledge or action."[26]

Similarly, Horkheimer and Adorno were never willing to pit mimetic affinity against conceptual reflection as if they were simple opposites, one inherently superior to the other, one the singular locus of freedom, the other of mere repression. Discussing the residue of mimetic behavior that can be found in the work of art in his *Aesthetic Theory*, Adorno wrote,

> The desideratum of visuality seeks to preserve the mimetic moment of art. What this view does not realize is that mimesis only goes on living through its antithesis, which is rational control by art works over all that is heterogeneous to them. If this is ignored, visuality becomes a fetish.[27]

In art, he argued, it was important to avoid the either/or of sensuality vs. spirituality, which simply repeats the alienation characteristic of modern life. Instead, the paradoxical mixture of the two must be preserved, for what lurks behind the false synthesis called aesthetic vision is a rigid polarity between spirit and sensuality, which is inadequate. At the center of the aesthetic of vision is the false, thing-like notion that in the aesthetic artifact tensions have been synthesized into a state of rest, whereas in fact those tensions are essential to the work.[28]

If we return to our point of departure, the blindfolding of Justitia, we can now understand that it was perhaps not entirely without some reason that vision was denied even to a female gaze in the name of impartiality and the banishment of monsters. Like the other "fools" in medieval tales, who often speak a higher truth, the fool who blindfolds goddess on Sebastian Brant's ship may have known what he was doing after all. For like the false synthesis of the aesthetic artifact, a practice of judgment based solely on the power of an immediate visual apprehension of irreducible singularity risks succumbing to the illusory potential that always accompanies sensual perception, however acute.

There is also another powerful justification for the allegorical images of the blindfold. Because her eyes are covered, Justitia must walk cautiously into the future, not rushing headlong to judgment.[29] Vermeer's open-eyed, female weigher of pearls can be shown without a blindfold because her judgment is allegorically linked to that of the Last Judgment in the canvas depicted behind her. But a secular judgment that is anything but the last, a justice of mere mortals, cannot pretend to possess so clear-sighted a sense of whose soul merits salvation and whose does not. It must acknowledge that imperfect general laws and the concrete judgments of those who apply them somehow always fall short of an absolute and final justice, and yet that both are necessary means in the endless struggle to realize that unrealizable goal.

It must furthermore accept the fact that even the most comprehensive notion of justice contains within it a pluralism of distinct logics that may sometimes be in conflict.[30] Procedural notions of justice within an established order, those that subordinate it to positive law, are likely to be in tension with compensatory, distributive, restitutive and retributive alternatives that may well point beyond that order. A justice that remembers and tries to redress the wrongs of the past and one that hopes to create a truly just society in the future can easily be at odds with formal procedures in the present, as any observer of the heated debate over affirmative action in the United States can well attest. Rather than a single over-arching criterion, there may be several that cannot be perfectly reconciled, but this does not mean that it is better to throw out general considerations altogether and judge decisionistically.

Unexpectedly, this point is suggested in visual terms by the same Vermeer painting discussed earlier as an example of a benign woman's gaze at concrete particulars. For recent scientific analysis of the pigments on the canvas has revealed that the scales do not, in fact, contain pearls, as has traditionally been thought, but are empty instead.[31] What shines is apparently only the light reflecting off the trays. Rather than directed at individual cases, the woman's contemplative gaze, we now can appreciate, falls on the apparatus itself, as if she were weighing its merits as an impartial mechanism of fairness, albeit one then used to judge the worth of each pearl.

A justice, in other words, that tries to see only concrete, contingent, incommensurable particularity and judge without *any* abstract prescriptive criteria whatsoever – such as that recently defended, for example, by Jean-Francois Lyotard in *Just Gaming*[32] – may – paradoxically be as blind as one that pretends to be entirely algorithmic. What is needed, as Adorno points out in the case of aesthetic judgment, is a creative tension between the two, a justice that can temper the rigor of conceptual subsumption, or more precisely, several such subsumptions, with a sensitivity to individual particularity. The unresolvable paradox of the relationship between law and justice, as the Slovenian philosopher Jelica Šumič Riha has recently argued, may, in fact, require a certain measure of blindness. "We know," she writes,

> that law as such is not and cannot be just. However, if we accept that and behave according to this knowledge, we will have lost not only justice, but also law. Law is namely conceived as an instance that appeals to justice which means that a law that does not refer to justice is simply not a law. It is therefore in some way necessary to blind ourselves to this knowledge. In Derrida's terms: even if justice cannot be reduced to rule-governed activity we must respect rules. We must respect them because in the very undecidability of justice on the one hand and the groundlessness of law on the other lies the danger that the right to do justice can be usurped by bad legislators.[33]

Perhaps it is best, therefore, to imagine the Goddess Justitia neither as fully sighted nor as blindfolded, but rather as she was once visually depicted at the threshold of the modern world, in a mid-sixteenth century frontispiece to J. De Damhoudere's *Praxis rerum civilium*: Justitia, that is, as a goddess with not one face, but two. The first has eyes that are wide open, able to discern difference, alterity, and non-identity, looking in the direction of the hand that wields her sword, while her second, facing the other hand with the calculating scales of rule-governed impartiality, has eyes that are veiled. For only the image of a two-faced deity, a hybrid, monstrous creature which we can in fact see, an allegory that resists subsumption under a general concept, only such an image can do, as it were, justice to the negative, even perhaps aporetic, dialectic that entangles law and justice itself.

Martin Jay "Must Justice Be Blind. The Challenges of Images to Law" in *Law and the Image. The Authorithy of Art and the Aesthetics of Law*, eds, Costas Douzinas and Lynda Nead (London: The University of Chicago Press, 1999), 19–35. Republished with the permission of The University of Chicago Press and the author.

1 O. E. von Möller, "Die Augenbinde der Justitia," *Zeitschrift für christliche Kunst*, 18 (1905): 107–122, 141–152; Otto R. Kissel, *Die Justitia: Reflexionen über ein Symbol und seine Darstellung in der bildenden Kunst* (Munich: Beck, 1984); Dennis E. Curtis and Judith Resnik, "Images of Justice," *Yale Law Journal*, 1727 (1987); Christian-Nils Robert, *La justice, vertu, courtisane et bourreau* (Geneva: Georg, 1993); Robert Jacob, *Images de la justice: Essai sur l'iconographie judiciaire du Moyen Age àl'âge classique* (Paris: Leopard d'or, 1994).

2 Herman Bianchi, "The Scales of Justice as Represented in Engravings, Emblems, Reliefs and Sculptures in Early Modern Europe," in *Images et representation de la justice du XVie au XIXe siècle*, ed. G. Lamoine(Toulouse, U. of Toulouse-Le Mirail, 1983), 8.

3 Christin-Nils Robert, *La Justice*, 13.

4 Erwin Panofsky, *Studies in Iconology: Humanist Themes in the Art of the Renaissance* (New York: Harper and Row, 1967), 109.

5 Robert Jacob, *Images de la Justice*, 234f.

6 Andrea Alciati, *Emblemata cum Commentariis* (New York: Garland, 1976).

7 Christin-Nils Robert, *La Justice*, 37f.

8 Bernard J. Hibbitts, "Making Sense of Metaphors: Visuality, Aurality, and the Reconfiguration of American Legal Discourse," *Cardozo Law Review*, 16, 2 (December 1994): 255–56. He interprets these changes in terms of the growing ascendancy of an abstract, Cartesian visuality over the more concrete variant that reigned in the Middle Ages.

9 Ibid. 241. Hibbitts, however, acknowledges that in the early modern period, when most people were still illiterate, texts were meant mainly to be read aloud rather than silently (256).

10 Max Horkheimer and Theodor W. Adorno, *Dialectic of Enlightenment*, trans. John Chumming (New York: Continuum, 1972), 16–17.

11 W.J.T. Mitchell, *Iconology: Image, Text, Ideology* (Chicago: University of Chicago, 1986), 108f.

12 Vassilis Lambropoulos, "The Rule of Justice," *Thesis Eleven*, 40 (1995): 18.

13 See the entry on Dike in F.E. Peters, *Greek Philosophical Terms: A Historical Lexicon* (New York: New York University Press, 1967). For more sustained discussions, see Eric Havelock, *The Greek Concept of Justice: From Its Shadow in Homer to its Substance in Plato* (Cambridge, Mass., Harvard University Press, 1978); Michael Gagarin, *Early Greek Law* (Berkeley: University of California, 1986).

14 Christin-Nils Robert, *La Justice*, 65 f.

15 For a comparison, see Christin-Nils Robert, *La Justice*, 92.

16 Carol Gilligan, *In a Different Voice: Psychological Theory and Women's Development* (Cambridge, Mass.: Harvard University Press, 1982); Seyla Benhabib, *Situating the Self: Gender, Community and Postmodernism in Contemporary Theory* (New York: Routledge, 1992).

17 Hibbitts cites certain feminists scholars, who claim that the power of the gaze is inherently male, whereas women's culture is more aural, and uses their arguments to buttress his claim that at least the American legal order until only recently was both ocularcentric and phallocentric. (267). I would qualify this generalization to the extent that a female gaze is not a contradiction in terms and it is precisely its occlusion that may be complicitous with the type of visual regime that he shows dominated American legal theory. That is, without essentializing the gender differences, there may be a link between realizing the abstracting potential in vision and patriarchal domination, which functions by repressing the more concretizing alternative latent in the "female gaze" denied Justitia.

18 Alan Wolfe, "Algorithmic Justice," in *Deconstruction and the Possibility of Justice, eds.* Drucilla Cornell, Michel Rosenfeld and David Gray Carlson (New York: Routledge, 1992). He criticizes it for lacking an appreciation for "the rule-making, rule-applying, rule-interpreting capacities of human beings and an emphasis instead on the rule-following character" (366).

19 Martin Jay, "Mimesis und Mimetologie: Adorno und Lacoue-Labarthe," in *Auge und Affekt: Warhnehmung und Interaktion,* ed., Gertrud Koch (Frankfurt: Fischer, 1995).

20 This raises the question of the status of images or representations of violence (or threatened violence, as in the case of the brandished sword). If they are understood as more mimetic than conceptual, does this mean that the violence in them is modified or even cancelled? Or can images participate in another kind of violence beyond that of subsumption? For a consideration of this theme, see Paul Crowther, "Violence in Painting," in *Critical Aesthetics and Postmodernism* (Oxford: Oxford University, 1993).

21 Jacques Derrida, "Force of Law: The 'Mystical Foundation of Authority,'" in *Deconstruction and the Possibility of Justice*, eds. Cornell et al., (New York: Routlegde, 1992), 5.

22 Friedrich Nietzsche, *The Birth of Tragedy and The Genealogy of Morals*, trans. Francis Golfing (Garden City, N.Y.: Double Day, 1956).

23 For a classic account of the dilemmas of political justice, see Otto Kirchheimer, *Political Justice: The Use of Legal Procedures for Political Ends* (Princeton: Princeton U., 1961). For a more recent discussion, which considers Kirchheimer's position with relation to Carl Schmitt, see William E. Scheuerman, *Between the Norm and the Exception: The Frankfurt School and the Rule of the Law* (Cambridge, Mass.: MIT, 1994).

24 Walter Benjamin, "Critique of Violence," in *Reflections: Essays, Aphorisms, Autobiographical Writings*, ed. Peter Demetz (New York: Harcourt, Brace, Jovanovich, 1978), 297.

25 Ibid.

26 Jaques Derrida, "Force of Law," 56. At the end of his piece Derrida acknowledges the frightening potential in Benjamin's attraction to divine violence, an annihilating, expiatory violence, to become a perverted justification for the Holocaust. For differing opinions of how successful Derrida himself has been in thwarting this potential, see Dominick LaCapra, "Violence, Justice, and the Force of Law," *Cardozo Law Review*: 11, 6–6 (1990); Drucilla Cornell, *The Philosophy of the Limit* (New York: Routledge, 1992), chapter 6; and Gillian Rose, *Judaism and Modernity: Philosophical Essays* (Oxford: Blackwell, 1993), chapter 7.

27 Theodor Adorno, *Aesthetic Theory*, trans. C. Lenhardt, eds. Gretel Adorno and Rolf Tiedemann (London: RKP, 1984), 141.

28 Ibid. 143.

29 This metaphor of blindfolded Justice walking cautiously is taken from M. Petitjean, "Un homme de loi semurois: l'avocat P. Lemulier," *Annales de Bourgogne*, LXII, 245, quoted in Christin-Nils Robert, *la Justice*, 130.

30 On this issue, see Michel Rosenfeld, "Restitution, Retribution, Political Justice and the Rule of the Law," *Constellations*, II, 3 (January, 1996): 309–332.

31 Arthur J. Wheelock, Jr., and Ben Broos, *Johannes Vermeer* (New Haven: Yale University Press,1996), 141–142.

32 Jean-Francois Lyotard and Jean-Loup Thébaud, *Just Gaming*, trans. Wlad Godzich (Minneapolis: University of Minnesota, 1985).

33 Jelica Šumič Riha, "Fictions of Justice," *Filozofski* Vestnik, 2 (1994): 80.

Sublime Law: On Legal and Aesthetic Judgments

— Costas Douzinas

Religion, ethics and law have a long history of policing of images. This normative control of the visual takes the form of an economy of permitted images and a criminology of graven, dangerous, threatening and fallen images or idols. It was argued in an earlier essay which started the clearing of the ground towards the developments of a "legal iconology" that each epoch develops its own peculiar and historically changing "regime of visuality."[1] Such regimes form a combination of iconoclasm and iconophilia and amount to a complex administration of an era's available ways of seeing.[2] These epochal regimes received an early formulation in the Byzantine iconoclastic controversies and later in the Reformation; they still occupy a central part of legal operations. The strategic intervention in the field of vision has been organized primarily around the regulation of the relationship between beings, images and language. While this relationship has been examined in relation to art, its central contribution to the constitution of the subject has been neglected.

The claim of legal iconology is that the stakes behind the close link between law and vision are high.[3] Subjectivity is created in the field of vision, to be a self is to be seen. I look from one position, but I am looked at from everywhere. The "social gaze" looks back at me from the place of the others and inscribes otherness in the midst of self. It is not the look of any particular other, but the visual, photographic action of otherness which places me within a field of vision as I turn towards others and look at them. The operation of normative systems (religion, morality, increasingly law) interposes a "legal screen" between the subject and the social gaze, filtering the objects of vision and determining the way in which we see and are given to the world to be seen.

The screen is a collection of authoritative images and material practices which offer a repertory of approved representations through which social identity is inscribed. It determines how each of us is given to the world to be seen, as handsome or ugly, pleasant or nasty, polite or boorish. The pre-modern religious "chain of icons" was such an institutional arrangement; our own cultural wars over obscenity, blasphemy, (im) proper and (im)moral images and the society of the spectacle are others. These historically changing imagistic regimes bring together the fleshy body and approved imagery and create what can be called the "normative" body of the individual.

These "regimes of visibility" involve three vital anthropological tasks. The first is about the internalization of absolute otherness and the domestication of death. The second organizes the field of representation, defines what passes as true or false, natural and authentic or artificial and false. The last is more detailed, flexible and historically changing. It is about positive evaluations of certain images which are ascribed a culturally specific normative superiority against others. The first establishes the human subject; the second influences what passes as true and false in a society; the third determines what is accepted as good or beautiful. The law contributes to all three despite the aesthetic abstinence alleged by orthodox jurisprudence and the courts of law which have dealt with art and images.

This essay continues the development of legal iconology. Its central argument is that aesthetic question of representation or mimesis is influenced by normative considerations. The theory and practice of representation involves ontological assumptions and is closely associated with questions of form and judgment. Despite surface differences and conventional thinking, legal and aesthetic judgments are close to each other. They both derive from a common source, the *sensus communis*, and they mirror each other in form and substance. We will illustrate these points through the discussion of a court case involving the relationship between an architectural "landmark" and an artistic "masterpiece."

— I.
The idol of the altar with an excursus on a phenomenology of the image

The church of St Stephen Walbrook was built in the City of London by Sir Christopher Wren on classical lines, after the Great Fire. St Stephen is the first domed church in England and is considered as Wren's masterpiece. In the late 1960s, Peter Palumbo, a churchwarden and patron of the arts, commissioned Henry Moore to design a circular, central altar, similar to the dome. Moore sculpted a massive 10-ton marble piece. Objections were raised against its installation, and as a result, a "faculty," or permission, had to be obtained from the London Consistory Court. The Court refused the faculty on both doctrinal and aesthetic grounds but was reversed by the Court of Appeal.[4] The most amazing feature of both judgments, handed down in 1987, is that they faithfully reproduce the arguments of the iconoclastic controversies, with a late twentieth-century gloss.

The law was asked in this case to judge both the ecclesiastical propriety and the aesthetic value of the artwork. All the main arguments about images which dominated the iconoclastic controversies during the Reformation were rehearsed in that case and offer a perfect example of law's *iconomachia*. In the iconoclastic idiom, only full correspondence between image and prototype "validates an image as 'true'."[5] Insofar as an image resembles the original, it partakes of its nature. But this train of thought is madness, concluded the image breakers, and the iconophiles are as deluded as the birds who flew down, according to legend, to eat the grapes realistically portrayed by the classical painter Zeuxis. Icons and other plastic forms are material objects and by definition different from the spiritual nature of divinity. The belief that icons resemble or represent divinity was twisted into the claim that they share the divine substance, and was condemned as blasphemy. Similar arguments were used in relation to the sacraments, which were closely associated with icons as two forms of representation of the spiritual world. The Eucharist of the unreformed church was the highest representation of divinity; the host resembled the body of Christ and symbolized his sacrifice. "Sacraments should have likeness to the things for which they are sacraments," wrote a ninth-century bishop.[6] For the iconoclasts, the claim that the host is like Christ is the worst idolatry. "The idol of the altar, the papist 'god of bread' was the most pagan perversion of the Christian faith."[7] The art, *peinture* and statuary of the Eucharist was seen as idolatrous because the iconoclasts portrayed the unreformed church as claiming that images, forms and the host are the complete and accurate representation of the original, the material expressions of the soul.

The first instance court adopted fully the iconoclastic position and condemned the artwork following canon law and doctrine. The Court declined the faculty because the sculpture looks like an altar and therefore cannot be a table. But an altar "signifies a place where a sacrifice is to be made, a repetition at every Mass of the sacrifice of our Lord at Calvary."[8] Accepting this close connection between prototype and copy, original and image, the court argued that the Moore sculpture is heretical because for the reformers the "holy communion was not a renewed sacrifice of our Lord, but a feast to be celebrated at the Lord's table and as the latter view prevailed the result was that altars were removed from churches and tables substituted."[9] The huge, marble sculpture cannot be seen as a table for eating meals. While the table of the reformed liturgy dissimulates the sacrifice, the Moore altar simulates it and must therefore go. The appeal court reversed. The relationship between prototype and copy, the court argued, is much more complex. "I do not think myself that even at the most superstitious time before the reformation any Christian, except a madman, could have conceived of the altar as a place of real immolation."[10] The judge echoes Thomas More:

> There is no dog as mad but he knoweth a very coney from a coney painted and carved. [The simplest fool] will call an image an image, and she will tell you the difference between the image of an horse and an horse indeed.[11]

The image does not share the substance of the original. The Eucharist "signifies" and "represents," it does not re-enact the sacrifice.[12] The altar, through its likeness, reminds us of the sacrifice of the Lord, but at the same time, in being used as a table, it dissimulates the sacred ground.

The most striking aspect of the disagreement is that both courts interpret the dogma of the Eucharist in similar terms, as one should expect even from the Church of England. Yet, they reach opposed conclusions through their conflicting approaches to the metaphysics of representation, both of which derive from the iconomachic controversies. For the Consistory Court, the representative presents its *representatum*, it brings it into presence. The sculpture as altar calls for sacrifice and must therefore be sacrificed. For the Court of Appeal, it resembles the primordial altar but it is also totally removed from the place of sacrifice. The representative does no longer make the original present, but it signifies an absent original, it does not represent but misrepresents.

In these clumsy judicial musings, we can detect an implicit understanding of the peculiar qualities of the image which can help us move towards a phenomenology of the image. I use the term image here in its essential meaning: the image is the perceptual support and helps organize language.[13] We see through the windows opened by the imagistic perception of the external world; according to structural linguistics the signified in its arbitrary link with the signifier forms images through which we understand the sign/concept. In this sense the image is the foundation and essence of all other types of images such as icons, pictures, photographs, artworks etc. Images give visual form to the invisible and make present what is absent. But the image does not represent the absent, it presents it. The image is distinct, distanced from the thing, it must be detached from the thing and placed in front of the eyes in order to work as an image. The image is different from the thing, it is a thing, which is not the thing, it distinguishes itself from it. A phenomenology of the image would analyze therefore how the image discloses things, brings them into presence. The primary meaning of the expression "this is the image of something" is not that the image comes after the thing, in a sequence where the thing leads to the image. The image unveils the thing for us, assembles it for our eyes and thus brings it into being. The image poses the thing for a subject. In this "presencing," the thing is assembled into being. To resemble a thing, the image must first assemble it for a subject and in so doing, both the thing and the subject are called into life.

Without the image there would be no thing, no presence and no subject. In this ability of disclosing things, the image is a prodigious and forceful entity. It confers unity and identity to the thing, by arranging it for us and reducing its multiplicity. I am "Costas" because another sees my image/visage. This image announces to the other a unity and therefore an identity, by forcing the chaotic disorder of existence and consciousness into a singularity. I come to existence and subjectivity through the image you now have of me and the gaze, this photographic and ubiquitous look that targets me from everywhere and nowhere.

But what the image discloses is not things with ontological solidity. The image brings to presence and withholds Being at the same time. I am my image for the other but this image is not who I am. The image stays distant both from the world of beings it brings forth and from the possibilities of availability and utilization it opens. The image presents the absent but also the absence in the thing, the fact that the thing cannot exist without the action of the other through its image. This double absence reminds us that the birth of what we can call the artistic image must be associated with the experience of death. Archaic images adorn graves and *mausolea*, they are an attempt to defy the trauma of loss and soothe the sadness of mourning. By painting the image of the departed, in death masks, on mummies, in funereal sites or the Roman *imagoes*, a double or replica is created and death is defied. The first ritual images of the Greeks were called *eidola*. These archaic idols, which have no negative connotations, included dream images, apparitions and visitations and the phantoms of the dead. The ghost who visits the living is called the *psyche* (the psyche of Patroclos visits Achilles in the first Act of the *Iliad*). In the economy of the eidolon, the image is a double. It does not share only the shape, color and form of its model but its voice, life and soul, its ontological qualities except for its material existence. It can be seen but cannot be touched.

The image therefore inhabits the gap between the thing and the subject it brings into being. This gap, the image as gap between Being and beings, what opens beings out of Being is always captured by power and influenced by normative rules and regulations. The history of this gap is the history of our world. Our case indicates that the two major strategies of representation as presencing (co-substantiation) or as simulation (semiotic circulation) are deeply involved with the legal doctrine on icons. Not only is the question of representation and mimesis normative; its main answers have been sketched in the religious-legal tradition.

— II. Sublime Law

Yet behind the triumph for modern art, in the Appeal Court, stands law's fear of the image. When Peter Palumbo offered Moore the commission, he asked him to

> forget any altars he had ever seen ... and to think of something going back to the dawn of history, something primitive and inseparable from man's search for a meeting place with God. I implored him to think of the stone altar on which Abraham was prepared to sacrifice Isaak.[14]

Moore's inspiration responded in kind. According to the court, the likeness of the altar to the primordial place can lead to revelatory experiences. The altar "says things not expressible in words, but to limit the understanding to the easily expressible is to limit understanding indeed."[15]

This is the language of the sublime, the modernist idiom *par excellence*. "The sublime is not strictly speaking something which is proven or demonstrated, writes Boileau, but a marvel."[16] The sublime artist, the genius, is possessed by the memory of something he never experienced, and in his quest for the meeting place with God, the altar strikes him in the same way that Abraham is ready to strike Isaak at the behest of the invisible God. The viewer of sublime art does not feel a simple aesthetic pleasure, but an intensification of emotion and concept, an ambivalent delight "associated with an ontological dislocation."[17] According to the court, the altar can become "the germ of what religious writers call a conversion."[18] But the altar is not just sublime; it stands for sublimity.

Kant was fascinated with the sublime nature of the biblical prohibition on images. The Kantian sublime is closely associated with an absence of images and the inability to see, with a special type of blindness. In his discussion of the genius, Kant gives another example of the sublime that is similar to the Second Commandment.

> Perhaps nothing more sublime was ever said and no sublimer thought was ever expressed than the famous inscription on the temple of Isis (mother Nature): 'I am all that is, and that was, and that shall be, and no mortal hath raised the veil from before my face.'[19]

This latter example occurs in the course of Kant's discussion of the key category of "aesthetic ideas" in the *Analytic of the Sublime*. These ideas are representations of the imagination which "strain out beyond the confines of experience ... and no concept can be wholly adequate to them." They are "sensible forms," the "*attributes of* an object, the concept of which, as an idea of reason, cannot be adequately presented." The examples given are poetic attempts to present "invisible beings, the kingdom of the blessed, hell, eternity, creation" or the way in which "Jupiter's eagle, with the lightning in its claws, is an attribute of the mighty king in heaven, and the peacock of its stately queen."[20] In this line of argument, we can understand the importance of Jehovah's command and of Isis' statement that no one can see her face. The classical tradition associates sublimity with the presentation of God and more generally with metaphysical concepts. The two examples are divine laws about the presentation of divinity. They are the most sublime utterance because God cannot be represented. He is non-representable and the proscription recognizes this non-representability.

Kant uses the proscription on images and the associated blindness to answer the objection that if his idea of the law and of moral freedom were deprived of sensual representations, they would lose their "force or emotion," would be "attended by lifeless and cold approbation" and would be unable to move people.[21] But not so. For Kant, the sublime feeling is created as a reaction to the presentation of the non-representable. The imagination casts aside the barriers of the sensible world and, in this presentation of the non-iconic, of the infinite, it ascends to a feeling of being unbounded by the senses. In the same way the sublime Jewish prohibition leads to the pleasure and terror of an imagination unrestricted by the senses, so too does the law without the need of idols.

> For where nothing any longer meets the eye of sense, and the unmistakable and ineffaceable idea of morality is left in possession of the field, there would be need rather of tempering the ardor of unbounded imagination to prevent it rising to enthusiasm, than of seeking to lend these ideas the aid of images and childish devices for fear of their being wanting in potency.[22]

The sublime presentation is therefore abstract and negative; its proper form is that of law and its proper content the proscription on representation. And not only is the form assumed by God's dislike of images legal, the law itself cannot be properly represented through "images and childish devices."

We find similar ideas in the writings of Edmund Burke, whose empiricist theory of the sublime and the beautiful stands at the opposite side of Kant's metaphysics. Both in his early essay "On the Sublime and the Beautiful" and in his later "Reflections on the Revolution in France,"[23] Burke develops a political and aesthetic theory which associates the sublime with language and verbal expression, while the beautiful with vision and imagery. The sublime is the feeling generated before ineffable, distant, terrifying power. People submit to the figure of God, King or Father because they generate terror and pain. These male figures of power are awesome. They make us submit through an overwhelming force which cannot be fully comprehended. But this political aesthetic of sublimity must be protected from visualization. An image or a painting gives a clear idea of its object, leaves nothing to imagination and doubt and can be judged according to conventional criteria of aesthetic beauty. The sublime is obscure, it overawes but also creates intense pleasure in the attempt to comprehend what overwhelms the mind and defies reason.

Burke uses his analysis of the sublime to reinterpret the symbols and emblems of the aniconic tradition. Invisibility, darkness and visual deprivation are the political signs of sublimity: "Despotic governments keep their chief from the public eye, heathen temples are dark and barbarous temples keep their idols in a dark place."[24] In Burke's hierarchy of the sublime, language comes before imagery and unwritten law, convention and custom before written positive law. Saxon customs operated better than laws and provided the basis for later laws and the Constitution. Written laws only fashion or finish what had been created by the oral tradition. Indeed, Burke argues that the Constitution should not exist in visible form; a visible, written Constitution is "criminal."[25] The real constitution is an organism, a living body, a community of sense with powers and privileges, a mixture of natural and conventional behavior preserved by immemorial custom.

Kant and Burke agree that both transcendent power and absolute secular sovereignty are non-representable and that the proscription on representability is the most sublime of all laws. The modern sublime is abstract and negative, its proper form is that of law and its proper content the proscription on representation. And not only is the form assumed by God's dislike of images legal, the law itself cannot be properly represented through "images and childish devices." The absence of icons of the God and of law leads to the creation of the images of eagles, peacocks and serpents. In a paradoxical fashion, the prohibition on images becomes the transcendental condition of representation, of imagery and of the law. This is the crucial moment at which the idea of invisibility passes from the divine to law and from theology to jurisprudence. The law becomes the absolute or transcendent force of modernity, expressed in the theory of the sublime. The immanence of the divine in history, exemplified by the economy of the holy icon, becomes the immanence of law. We are surrounded by laws, codes and regulations, but like Kafka's man from the country "Before the Law," we do not know where or what the law is. As God withdraws from history, the law succeeds in the key function of bringing the modern subject into existence and the law becomes sublime itself.

In philosophical terms therefore, Moore's altar is the presentation of the non-representable. The law, as much as the sublime, demands blindness in order to turn from image to text, from the light of vision to the darkness of hearing. The eyes are sacrificed to the inner eye and to the ear. The altar celebrates the triumph of law over the image and becomes as sublime as the commandment of Moses or Michelangelo's Moses in Freud's reading. Before the law one is blind; the law is given and obeyed before we know its commands. The law is heard and can only be seen in its inadequate representations and in the pathetic garments of its servants and doorkeepers. The inadequacy of divine images frees religious imagination in the same way that the inadequacy of legal imagery frees the love of the text.

— III. Legal and aesthetic judgments

The intellectuals and learned men of the late Middle Ages were either jurists or cognizant of the law. As a result, medieval theories of art were influenced by political and legal theology. The artist, a key Renaissance notion, is seen as both creator and imitator of nature, he is modeled on the metaphysics of *ingenium* and the genius. The prototype artist, the original creator, is the Pope. The first reference to the Pope as "someone who makes something out of nothing" is found in a papal decretal of 1220. This papal power to create *ex nihilo* referred almost exclusively to legal matters: he could make new law except that it could not be contrary to faith or natural law. Furthermore, the Pope could waive the strict application of the law, reversing the relationship between justice and injustice: "[The Pope] can make an illegitimate legitimate, and can make a monk a canon" states a typical gloss.[26]

These creative powers and prerogatives were eventually claimed by and transferred first to the Emperor and then to Princes. The divine inspiration of the Pope was arrogated to the secular lawmaking and law dispensing power. The King, like the Pope, imitated nature by applying its laws but he was also the only person who could make new laws according to the changing circumstances and therefore create *ex nihilo*. A parallel development in juristic writings extolled the way in which the law could create world-making fictions. One such legal fiction was the institution of adoption, in which strangers could imitate the natural function of the family. Legal fictions imitate nature and create important effects. It was through a legal fiction, for example, that the law could create *ex nihilo* a *persona ficta*, a corporation or the *corpus mysticum* of the Church and breathe into them a life of their own. These important fictions were invented by the jurist and jurisprudence was seen as an art which both imitates and creates nature.

This idea became generalized in the sixteenth century. The legislator invents the particular way in which general natural law is to be applied, recreates nature in a limited way and thus, he partially resembles God. He is therefore an artist who both creates and imitates nature by following the universally valid Natural Law. "As the jurists and political theoreticians asserted time and again [the legislator was] the *sicus deus in terries.*"[27]

Dante was the first to compare the poet with the Emperor. The analogous nature of their powers was emphasized during Petrarch's coronation in 1341. The poet was called the *officium poetae* and was compared to an *ex officio* Emperor. Horace's *Ars Poetica* further extended the creative power of the poet to painters and sculptors all divinely inspired. Through a series of equivalences the power to create *ex nihilo* was passed from God to Pope, to the secular powers of the legislator and the jurist and eventually to the "individual and purely human abilities and prerogatives which the poet, and eventually the artist at large, enjoyed *ex ingenio.*"[28] The artist's creativity was presented on the analogy of the legislator and the jurist.

The similarity between law and art was still apparent in Renaissance humanism and was still evident in the fifteenth century. But the progressive professionalization and positivization of law gradually removed its study and scholarship from the humanities. Positivist jurisprudence started presenting law as the preserve of a specialist science-like expertise, without spiritual claims or emotional investment and set into motion the inexorable process of separation between art and law. In a process encapsulated by the trope of chiasmus, the artist moved from the position of a simple craftsman to that of a genius on the analogy of the legislator; art progressed from skilful *techne* to being the main depository of creation and imagination. Law, on the other hand, concerned now with regulation and application regressed from the god-like position of world-making to that of craft and technique. In a curious reversal, the law mimics art in an attempt to claim creativity while the judge tries to mirror the artist or the art *connoisseur*.

Let us return to *St Stephen Walbrook* to examine how these attitudes to representation, aesthetics and judgment are played out in contemporary law. Art criticism and history, aesthetics more generally, have acquired sufficient importance since the Reformation. The court was asked to judge the aesthetic merits of the sculpture in the context of the masterpiece of Wren. But legal attitudes to aesthetics share law's ambiguity towards the image. On the one hand, the courts claim that they do not deal with aesthetics and that judgments of taste are not their proper domain. The courts place a clear line of separation between law and art and insist that they did not decide the dispute on the basis of "aesthetic considerations"[29] nor did they examine the "matters of taste" and the aesthetic conflicts between the two sides "on the basis that either was or could be shown to be right or wrong."[30] "There are hardly ever any rights or wrongs in matters of aesthetics. There are differences of opinion."[31] Art and the subjective responses it evokes are diametrically opposed to the reasoned and objective resolution to questions of doctrine and law.

But while the law explicitly sets itself apart from aesthetics and judgments of taste, the process of legal judgment introduces back again into the domain of law those elements law needs to keep away. For the Consistory Court, the architectural genius of Wren created a work of great geometrical precision based on the tension between the circular dome and the square space beneath, in which the Moore altar would be placed. Beauty is natural, a result of "numerical geometry," the juxtaposition and congruence of pure forms. But if beauty has its own eternal criteria which determine questions of style, in the same way that unalterable principles of doctrine decide matters of law, the opinions of the judges of taste are as authoritative as those of the judges of law. These judges are the aesthetes and the connoisseurs, who cannot be wrong if the dispute is seen as strictly technical. The objectivist aesthetic of form allows the expert to distinguish amongst the various opinions those that "may be attributable to fashion or personal preference rather than to the application of more enduring criteria of judgment."[32] The law turns this judgment of taste into its own, because both aesthetics and aesthetes mimic the operation of law. Aesthetic and legal judgments are formally homologous and their subjects, the judge and aesthete, are involved in the same process of applying universal principles. Art criticism simulates the self-identification of law and thus gets its legal recognition.

But there is another way of bringing together legal and aesthetic judgments by making the legal emulate the aesthetic. According to the modernist aesthetic, beauty in art is created not through formal congruence and harmony, but through the complex intertwining of many formal elements. Its appreciation is the result of the energy created and the interpretative acumen necessitated by the ambiguity and polyvalence of the many possible readings. The interpretation of a work changes according to historical period and understanding and depends crucially on changing social needs and expectations. Art history is a progressive evolution towards modernism and modern experts and aesthetes are the best judges of the nuances and excellencies of art throughout the centuries. As Clement Greenberg, the greatest modernist critic, put it "modernist art continues the past without gap or break.... What modernism has shown is that though the past did appreciate the [great] masters justly, it often gave wrong or irrelevant reasons for doing so."[33] The modernist sculpture therefore, rather than being incongruent with the classical Wren design, "gives the church what it has always needed, a central altar, something out of the question when it was built, but fully consonant with modern liturgical developments."[34] In more formal terms the church had always had the need for "a 'sense of the centre' which did not require nevertheless the centre to be empty."[35] But how can the law decide amongst the conflicting opinions of the experts who represent the openness of interpretation and the difference in aesthetic appreciation?

We associate aesthetics with form and the beautiful and we distinguish between the determinant judgment of law and the subjective responses to art. But both aesthetics and judgment have a common source in the Aristotelian aesthesis, the senses and sense perception. Until early modernity, philosophy and theology believe that judgment is a matter for the senses. The senses distinguish light from dark and pain from pleasure. This first external judgment is then organized by the internal faculties of the soul, such as fantasy, memory and recollection, which deal with mental images. These are lower types of reason which bring the senses together and compare individual forms. Behind the senses, as Chapman argues in 1595, lies a *sensus communis*, a sense, common to all of them and which judges. Higher or right reason organizes those judgments of sense and compares universal forms. But this particular judgment of sense is very close to practical reason. The pre-modern domain of law is that of the particular, the individual situation and the unique litigant, the response of conscience to mental images and past narratives. Practical judgment is the discourse of the particular, in the various versions of *phronesis*, in the casuistry of the Church and of course in the casuistry of the common law. Before the academization of aesthetics, art too was judged as right or good in a way similar to the judgment of law.

Early modern aesthetics was conceived as the science of these lower faculties of the soul, the *sensus communis*, and its task was to discover the rules of its constituents, intuition, imagination and memory. It was the impossible science of sensate life, of affects, emotions and phantasms, an attempt to understand and control the way through which the body is inserted into and reacts to the world. The partial abandonment of this grandiose project is symbolized in Kant's redefinition of the *sensus communis* from a faculty of the soul into the transcendental horizon for the operations of reason. The judgment of sense or taste withdraws to the subjective sensibilities of the aesthete. But her twin sister, the judgment of law, continues the same project, of administering images and disciplining the senses. The Consistory Court recites an answer well-known to aesthetics but now abandoned: "Voltaire once wrote: 'On dit que Dieu est toujours pour les gros bataillons.' Possibly this is true on some battlefields, but it is not necessarily true in a court of law." The Court does not follow the "gros bataillons" of the experts, heavily in favour of Moore's sculpture, but its contradictory explanation has already opened the way for the overturning of its decision. "In a court of law ... it is weight and cogency that tell."[36] The court must put the weight and importance of the expert witnesses on the two sides of the scales and give victory to the heavier of the two. A greater number of art critics, of the great and the good presented to the court are on the side of the altar. The altar is legal because a majority of experts and judges finds it "beautiful."

In discussing aesthetics, we have moved from matters of doctrine and exegesis to the question of judgment. The legal and the aesthetic appear to mirror each other. The question of judgment is either about the application of enduring criteria of principle (legal) or about the affect of the object or case on the judge (aesthetic). In the first case, judgment is immanent in the object and the judge acts as the mirror, the reflection of the harmony of nature, doctrine or art. In the second, judgment is the subjective disposition of the judge, either the judgment of the senses of the critic or the judgment of sense of the jurist. The law acknowledges the characteristics of mastery or expertise of artist or critic, and at the same time performs them by assigning to them their special juridical status. Yet, this acknowledgement of art as law's other is circular or fraudulent. What is at stake in this legal recognition and performance of originality is the mirroring process through which the law in regulating art claims for itself the insignia of authenticity and subjectivity. In mirroring the artist or the critic, the judge presents law's desire. When the judgment mirrors the genius of Wren or the mastery of Moore, the judge imitates the status and natural excellence of the master.

> The genius imitates nothing, it identifies itself with the productive freedom of God.... There is an analogy therefore between genius which creates a second nature ... and God who creates the first nature and produces the archetype which will serve as example and rule.[37]

When again the judgment reflects the technical expertise of the aesthete, the judge imitates the urbane style and sensibility of the sensus communis. In both instances, in the naturalism of doctrine and the casuistry of the senses, judicial authenticity or authority, is celebrated and concealed. The judge's subjection to the law is counterbalanced and redeemed by the presumed subjectivity and originality of his counterpart and companion, the artist or critic. But at the same time, in turning our gaze from judge to artist, the judgment presents the judge as an executive organ or copy of the immemorial power of the law and makes us forget its own materiality. The stake behind this contemporary war of the image is the assertion about "the genius of our law," law's image as transcendent and original and of the judge as subjected and subjective.

St Stephen Walbrook represents the legal ontology of modernity. While legal regulation proliferates and penetrates every aspect of social and private life, "the law," unknown and unknowable, attempts to mimic lost sublimity and appropriate its affective power. While jurisprudence maintains a strict distinction between legal argumentation and judgment and judgments of taste, St Stephen Walbrook indicates that these two forms of predication and decision are intimately related. By deciding which images are legitimate (true, right, beautiful) and which not, the law is intimately involved in constituting subjectivity. The task of legal iconology is to explain how power and normative systems frame what and how we see, to develop a critique of regimes of visuality that will complement the critique of ideology.

Costas Douzinas "Sublime Law: On Legal and Aesthetic Jugdements," *Parallax*, Taylor & Francis, (January 11, 2008).

1 Jacques Rancière has developed the concept of "artistic regimes." This is also an epochal concept but its application is limited to art and aesthetic considerations unlike my "regimes of visuality," which covers all aspects of imagery and vision. See Jacques Rancière, *The Politics of Aesthetics*, trans. Gabriel Rockhill (London: Continuum, 2004), 7–46.

2 Costas Douzinas, "Prosopon and Antiprosopon: Prolegomena for a Legal Iconology," in *Law and the Image*, ed. Costas Douzinas and Lynda Nead (Chicago: Chicago University Press, 1999), 36 –70.

3 Ibid. 61–67. See also Costas Douzinas, *Nomos kai Aesthetike* (Athens: Papazissis Press, 2006), chap. 2, 3 and 4.

4 *Re St Stephen Walbrook* [1986] 2 All ER 705 (London Consistory Court) and [1987] 2 All ER 578 (Court of Ecclesiastical Causes Reserved).

5 Moshe Barasch, *Icon: Studies in the History of an Idea* (New York: New York University Press, 1992), 271.

6 Margaret Aston, *England's Iconoclasts* (Oxford: Clarendon, 1988), 6.

7 Ibid. 8.

8 *Re St Stephen Walbrook* [1986] 2 All ER 705 (London Consistory Court), 709.

9 *Re St Stephen Walbrook* [1986] 2 All ER 705 (London Consistory Court), 709.

10 *Re St Stephen Walbrook* [1987] 2 All ER 578 (Court of Ecclesiastical Causes Reserved), 582.

11 Thomas More, *The Complete Works of Sir Thomas More* (New Haven: Yale University Press, 1963–1989), vol. 6, i. 56, 231–32.

12 *Re St Stephen Walbrook* [1987] 2 All ER 578 (Court of Ecclesiastical Causes Reserved), 582.

13 I was influenced in the development of this phenomenology of the image by Jean-Luc Nancy, *The Ground of the Image*, trans. Jeff Fort (New York: Fordham University Press, 2005), chapters 1, 2 and 3.

14 *Re St Stephen Walbrook* [1986] 2 All ER 705 (London Consistory Court), 709.

15 *Re St Stephen Walbrook* [1987] 2 All ER 578 (Court of Ecclesiastical Causes Reserved), 588.

16 Jean-François Lyotard, "The Sublime and the Avant-Garde," in *The Lyotard Reader*, ed. Andrew Benjamin (Oxford: Blackwell, 1989), 196–211 (and 202).

17 Ibid. 206.

18 *Re St Stephen Walbrook* [1987] 2 All ER 578 (Court of Ecclesiastical Causes Reserved), 589.

19 Immanuel Kant, *Critique of Judgement*, trans. J.C. Meredith (Oxford: Clarendon, 1988), 179.

20 Ibid. 176 –177.

21 Ibid. 127.

22 Ibid. 127–28.

23 Edmund Burke, *Reflections on the Revolution in France*, ed. J.G. Pocock (London: Hackett, 1987).

24 Edmund Burke, *A Philosophical Enquiry into the Origins of the Sublime and the Beautiful*, ed. James T. Boulton (Notre Dame: University of Notre Dame Press, 1958), 59.

25 Edmund Burke, *Appeal from the New to the Old Whigs*, quoted in W.J.T. Mitchell, *Iconology* (Chicago: University of Chicago Press, 1986), 141.

26 Ernst Kantorowicz, "The Sovereignty of the Artist," in *Selected Studies* (New York: J. J. Augustin, 1980), 352–65 (and 360).

27 Ibid. 356.

28 Ibid. 363.

29 *Re St Stephen Walbrook* [1986] 2 All ER 705 (London Consistory Court), 711.

30 *Re St Stephen Walbrook* [1987] 2 All ER 578 (Court Ecclesiastical Causes Reserved), 594

31 *Re St Stephen Walbrook* [1987] 2 All ER 578 (Court Ecclesiastical Causes Reserved), 603.

32 *Re St Stephen Walbrook* [1987] 2 All ER 578 (Court Ecclesiastical Causes Reserved), 595.

33 Clement Greenberg, "Modernist Painting," *Arts Year Book*, 4 (1961), 101–08 (and 103).

34 *Re St Stephen Walbrook* [1987] 2 All ER 578 (Court Ecclesiastical Causes Reserved), 602.

35 *Re St Stephen Walbrook* [1987] 2 All ER 578 (Court Ecclesiastical Causes Reserved), 593

36 *Re St Stephen Walbrook* [1986] 2 All ER 705 (London Consistory Court), 712.

37 Jacques Derrida, "Economimesis, *Diacritics*, XIX (1981): 325 (and 13).

Law and the Evidential Image

— Piyel Haldar

Courts make use of a range of images as proof objects. This paper highlights the doctrinal assumptions that the image is a clear and perspicacious representation of a (probable) truth and that the ideal image would be the result of an acheiropoietic process. In contrast to judicially defined doctrine, evidential practices of looking at images tend to surrender to a clutter of detail and impurities. Images are rather examined and scrutinized with meticulous precision. The works of Ravit Reichman, Carlo Ginzburg, and Jacques Derrida have already done much to radicalize and re-house the concept of the detail. The argument here will be that an understanding of "detailism" as it reveals itself in the evidential practice of looking at images might help provide an alternative understanding of how the trial operates.

> Ah, by the way, how should Moses have written the second commandment had he not misinterpreted it? ... my bet is that a safer reading would be 'Thou shall not freeze-frame any graven image!'
>
> Bruno Latour[1]

— I

How do lawyers treat or confront the image? Certainly, consideration of such matters as ownership, privacy, and obscenity are relevant juridical areas of inquiring into aspects of the relationship between the law and the image.[2] But such areas of inquiry do not offer us any indication as to the manner in which lawyers are able to view, read and scrutinize the image *qua* image. Such considerations rather, and most obviously, fall within the province of evidential concerns. Given the myriad, sometimes byzantine, possibilities that have been opened up by recent studies into "law and the image" the image as evidence might seem a colder, more narrow aspect of theoretical focus.

Nevertheless, the professionalized legal reception of images alerts us to an interesting tension within the law that might indeed reflect the more quarrelsome aspects of Byzantine culture. On the one hand, as shall be shown in more detail, appeal judgments assume that the veracity of images is based on technological and scientific values. The image represents an event, or an identity, as if it were a stable descriptive medium. Even if, as these judgments are bound to concede, images are mediated by adversarial techniques of cross-examination it is only because the image holds within itself the potential to tell an objective truth. On the other hand, judges (and evidence scholars) misconstrue and underrate the empirical encounter with the image as proof-object that takes place in the trial courts themselves. Evidential practice necessarily proceeds by focusing on the image as a collection of details. In this sense, images are rather anatomized into constituent parts. What matters are the tiniest of details otherwise overlooked by those too keen to see the whole picture. In order to acquire meaning, it shall be argued, images have to be torn apart and rendered unstable. Or, put differently, a form of iconoclasm is enacted under evidential examination according to which images are defaced and destroyed in a manner that seems to contradict the judicial faith in images.

Concentrating on evidential images (photographs, photofit and video images etc) this paper will explore such tension. In what follows, these two methods of approaching an image will be contrasted as belonging to two radically incompatible traditions of inquiry. The argument begins by examining the doctrinal evaluation of the use of evidential images. It then proceeds to focus attention on the adversarial and forensic scrutiny of the image. Examples are provided of the manner in which evidential images are inevitably assessed in terms of their details from which a more nuanced theory of "legal epistemology" emerges. That the evidential image is one which is ruptured in order for meaning to emerge as proven posits the detail as an alternative paradigm to legal objectivity. So that, finally, this article will attempt to contextualize evidential practice within an underground, or fallen, tradition that guides law's relationship to images and the world of events. What emerges from this analysis, in other words, is a need to reassess the epistemic methods of the trial.

— II

Legal questions regarding the admissibility and use of images in the trial raise few difficulties. The primary concern for the courts is to establish the image – typically a photograph, video or a photofit (sometimes referred to as a composigraph) – as "real" evidence thereby distinguishing it from hearsay documents.[3] The status of "real" evidence attaches to objects that the law defines simply in terms of their tangibility. Physical materials implicated in a case might be examined during trial as mere objects that directly testify to some fact in issue. The possibility that an item of real evidence might be fabricated, by one or other of the parties, is one that might be eradicated or confirmed during the trial itself. Where its provenance is questionable, an evidential image will be tendered for inspection, examination and cross-examination with supplementary proof of authenticity. Take, by way of illustration, the appeal judgment in *R.v. Cook* that centers around the admissibility of a photofit image.[4]

The photofit in question had been pieced together by a police artist based on statements made by a witness about the physical characteristics of the defendant. At first glance, all the requirements seem to indicate the hearsay nature of the composite image. The original statements regarding identity were made out of court, processed by the police into the form of the photofit, and tendered as truth of the defendant's identity.[5] The old common law rules against the admissibility of hearsay stressed the dangers that such material might be unreliable or even manufactured; such flaws might well apply to composed images.[6] It was held by the appeal judges, however, that along with other images (photographs, video, close circuit television, artist impressions etc.) photofits must be regarded as falling outside the scope of hearsay. All such evidence overcomes the usual suspicions leveled against hearsay statements since they are the result of mechanical or technological reproduction. Technology guarantees the reliability of photo-evidence to the extent that they might be regarded as direct and real media. To borrow a term from

Patristic theology, the ideal image would be acheiropoietic. That is, it would be free of any mortal intervention, the product of pure scientific provenance.

In the case of photographs, television or video images, such reliability derives from the idea that the resulting image was achieved in contemporaneity with the event itself. Hearsay is based upon the repetition of an original statement and the process of repetition opens up uncertainty as to its accuracy. The photograph, on the other hand, repeats without any loss of memory or veracity. Technology might even help bring out aspects of that event that might otherwise be hidden from ordinary human view. Thus the judgment in *R v Maqsud Ali*:

> For many years now photographs have been admissible in evidence.... The prints as seen represent situations that have been reproduced by means of mechanical and chemical devices. Evidence of things seen through telescopes or binoculars which otherwise could not have been picked up by the naked eye have been admitted.[7]

Given that computer images are more easily manipulated, it might be supposed that the digital revolution ushers in stronger doubts about the reliability and manufacture of the image. The evidential problems posed by digital formatting have been the subject of the House of Lords Select Committee on Science and Technology.[8] While recognizing the ease with which digital images might be copied and modified, the committee concluded that the evidential benefits conferred by them far outweigh any concerns over authenticity. Compliance with relevant standards for image storage, system logs, the use of digital watermarks and digital signatures ensure that a modified image is easily detected. Computer technology thus provides even further guarantees of accuracy.

The benefits enumerated by the select committee confirm judicial opinion and trial practice over the evidential value of images. Digital images provided by such devices as traffic enforcement cameras offer a much more efficient way of taking, processing and storing images than analogue film. In addition to their use as evidence in court, these digital images can be loaded straight to an image databank, stored on computers, and used to aid immediate detection and expedite processes of identification. Moreover, since digital cameras do not store film, they are easier to use in covert surveillance. Hardware is smaller and "can be disguised in anything from mirrors and pictures to smoke detectors and clocks." Finally, reflecting the judgment in *R v Maqsud Ali*, the select committee report stresses that the images themselves may be enhanced to become clearer.

— III

There are obvious practical benefits to the use of photographs and photofit images in the trial, but the theoretical assumptions made about these benefits upon which judicial evaluation rest seem to underestimate the actual evidential and adversarial practice of reading the image. We shall deal with the practice of reading, analyzing and dissecting the image in the following section. First, it is necessary, for the purposes of this argument, to summarize the above justifications according to these broader theoretical and philosophical assumptions. Such a summary, at the very least, provides an explanation as to how or why judges might misconstrue the manner in which images are received as proof-objects. What seems to emerge, perhaps surprisingly for an empirically minded institution such as the common law, is a model of imagistic and visual representation that is based on certain key traits of Cartesian modernity.

These traits (the centrality of a particular model of representation, the technologically mediated method of doubt, and the sovereignty of visual sense perception) can be analyzed in turn as follows. First, alongside oral testimony and written depositions, the image takes its place within a culture of representation and representative forms. As the arguments surrounding the suspicion of hearsay suggest, the photograph is to be distinguished from the phenomenon of orality. Indeed, contrary to Sir Matthew Hale's assertion that common law adversarialism is to be celebrated for its tradition of orality, the photo-image might be considered more reliable than oral testimony.[9] While the justifications for orality privilege the living voice over the dead life of letters,[10] cross-examination of witnesses cannot eradicate the vagaries of poor memory or the potential for undetected perjury. And, the risk of raising further collateral issues that might prolong the duration of the trial is far greater when dealing with speaking subjects. Furthermore, orality relies upon the ephemerality of sound. A tribunal of fact has to rely upon its memory of a particular witness or upon further (and potentially unreliable) mnemonic devices before reaching a verdict. At this level of analysis, the image shares with the printed document an ability to be archived, indexed, retrieved, examined and cross-examined. Copies can be handed out and subject to ongoing analysis either in the court or in the jury room.

However, in being placed alongside other forms of representation, what is at stake is not so much the efficacy of the image over that of orality or documentary forms. Rather, the comparisons are based on the supposition that the function of representation is descriptive. The image is consequently endowed with a rational capacity to describe the world; it is taken to be a medium of direct transparency to the object of its description. It does not reveal so much as demonstrate to the court the constitution and properties of its referent. It describes and designates that which is, in grand Benthamite tradition, assumed to have an objective life independent of the court.

This representative model of the perceptible world is resolutely Cartesian. It is a model according to which the image provides the Cartesian ideal of a systematic and mechanical representation of the world and according to which the particular and preferred mode of representation is deemed to be description. The image is simply no more than the world of events as it is described on its surface. It is no more than a document, a record, a measurement of the perceptible world. Rational discourse or legal judgment about the world can emerge only once that world has been described through the image. The second point is that the descriptive function of imagistic representations (in particular, photographs and video images) is guaranteed by virtue of a technological process. Photographs at least allow for the contemporaneous fixing and recording of moment. The image conserves a faithful memory by establishing itself with immediacy through a chemical or digital process. That is to say that such processes are ideally mint and free of human contact and intervention. Such images, according to Patristic formulation, might properly be categorized as *acheiropoietic*; borne of non-human process, they become the nearest thing to the event itself, or, the closest thing to an identity. At this level of analysis, it is assumed that technology guarantees a causal link between (or even an immanent fixing of) the presence of an event as it is experienced outside the court and its subsequent representation.

Indeed, digital processes attempt to further minimize the distinction between the event, or the object, and image. This fidelity to an event or to a person's likeness is assumed to establish a direct copy of the world and attempts, in its most ideal formulation, to leave little room for doubt. It is through technology that evidence attempts to bridge the gap between high probability and absolute certainty that characterizes modern epistemology. Again, a certain Cartesianism is inherent in this reliance upon the mimetic processes attributed to image technology. The Cartesian method of proof, of course, begins with the process of eradicating doubt. The "truth" of a matter arises once we are left with clear and distinct ideas.[11]

Technology transforms an object of knowledge that is otherwise prone to the defects of probable knowledge into a clearer and more distinct representation as free from doubt as one can achieve in the limited sphere of moral certainty. In attaining what is considered to be a high degree of probative force, the image as proof-object achieves a paradigmatic and privileged status among all other forms of testimony. Finally, the doctrinal assumptions regarding the evidential use and value of images obey a certain consistency with modern philosophical principles (again inaugurated by Descartes) that privileges ocular sensation. Crucial is also the question of the *visibility* of the image. The photograph is an object, an item, and, like any item, a residue of light that has to be seen. It may well be, as Charles Goodwin has argued, that the standard of visible perception is professional, selective and perspectival (and therefore far from being value free or neutral).[12] It may well be that the image can only be apprehended having been first mediated by adversarial techniques. Nevertheless, by whatever means it is transformed into an object of legal knowledge, the image enters the trial arena as an object to be looked at and scrutinized.

As a paradigm of visible object, the image exemplifies what is at stake across the whole of evidential practice. The court is raised to the level of a Cartesian *ego affirmo* whereby distance is placed between perceiving subject and the referent; it distinguishes between subject and material object. It renders the first active and transcendental, the second inert. It privileges the subject over any referent/object as a disinterested, disengaged viewing machine living entirely outside the world it feels able to objectify. Seen in this light, common law judgments regarding the admissibility of the image ought not to be so surprising. For, what the image does is to establish a position for the subject, the court, the judge, the jury within a symbolic and ordered register. That is to say, that even as a medium of description the image retains a specular function according to which subjectivity is positioned and affirmed.

— IV

What the above justifications of admissibility fail to address is the manner in which the evidential image necessarily entails a particular mode of reception and reading based upon its atomic detail. This failure is surprising since, as shall be argued in more theoretical terms later, the scrutiny of details within an image might even contradict the Cartesian and scientific pursuit of objective representation. It also subverts the Cartesian position of the active subject who super*vises* over a world of objects. If the image is assumed to be a clear and stable representation, if it minimizes doubt, one might argue that the admissibility of the photo image rests on the presupposition that it be clear of obfuscatory detail; "only the things I conceive clearly and distinctly have the power to convince me completely."[13] Yet, any photograph, even a photofit image, contains within its frame a clutter of trivialities, details and sub-images. Evidential technique rests on the close scrutiny of the image in which the image is divided and its elements isolated. It requires the image to be full of clutter. Elements are divided and divorced from each other. In a recent article, Ravit Reichman highlights the manner in which the more general aims of judicial methodology attempt to sacrifice trifles, small irrelevant details, and superfluous elements in favor of clearer scientific methods based on clarity and prediction.[14]

Details, argues Reichman, have little to do with the administration of justice and clear-headed decisionism. We might note that Reichman's focus on the inter-relationship between law and culture (specifically the detective story as a cultural mediation of law) allows an alternative analysis of legal knowledge to emerge. Here, she argues that the cultural and literary analysis of law that develops outside the courtroom by way of detective and mystery novels allow for smaller details to rise to the surface. Broader cultural affection for the details that beset the investigative process is one that explains and allows for a "cultural pleasure" in law as an antidote to dry legalism. It is in fine detail rather than fine print that the reader of detective fiction achieves textual delights.

The same argument regarding the sacrifice of detail *might* be made of the judicial evaluation of the evidential image. In attempting to minimize the measure of doubt inherent in all probabilistic reasoning, evidence, after all, depends upon perspicuity and clarity. What renders the evidential image such a stable and technologically reliable medium is its supposed or relative freedom from obfuscation and undecidability. It eradicates the very thing that might form the referent of the photograph; chaos, chance, happenings.[15] But are such "smaller details overlooked (or explicitly cast off) by legal discourse." The etymological roots of that betray the ocular, visual register of evidence (*evidere*) simultaneously alerts us to another pattern of enquiry that cannot easily be reconciled to the Cartesian epistemology that requires the sacrifice of detail in order to achieve clarity in order to judge. *Videre/visio* also lends its meaning to another mode of evidential inquiry based on division (*dividere/divisio*).[16] To divide and individuate is to distinguish, to see things in detail, to forget the whole picture or object and to concentrate on the part. Is such a process of particularization not already prevalent within trial methodology? Independent of judicial pronouncements regarding the quality of the image as a form, is the court itself not already an anti-Cartesian forum? Does it not already participate in a long tradition that recognizes the epistemological effects of chance encounters with details?

— V

Let us return to the evidential use of images such as photographs or photofits. Trial issues surrounding images as proof-objects center not upon the authenticity of the image but rather upon the manner in which these images are endowed with meaning. As stated, the image is already a clutter of detail. A photograph taken of a car crash might be scrutinized not for its overall depiction of the crash but for the manner in which the metal has twisted thereby providing a clue as to the causes of the crash, the speed with which the car was traveling (perhaps as it enters a tunnel) or the force of its impact. A photograph of an assassinated president might be examined in microscopic detail in order to assess the ballistic path of the fatal bullet. To provide a further example, consider the manner in which the video footage was used in the first trial of the police officers accused of using excessive force in the beating up of Rodney King.

Instead of playing the video in actual time, defense lawyers were able to dissect its representative qualities with the most detailed precision. Images were frozen, aspects of a frozen image were encircled and isolated and through such techniques it became possible to conclude that Rodney King's body was a threatening one. Rather than viewed as one whole event unfolding in time, the video image was atomized into infinitesimal movements of a leg muscle, a rising buttock, an angle of a foot. As one commentator puts it: "In actual time, King's movement from the ground was closely linked to the blows of the batons and the jolts of the taser, but slow motion and a frozen video produced a different reality."[17] Consider again the judgment of *R v Maqsud Ali*; reproduction might even bring out aspects of the original which are invisible to the naked eye. The image, in this sense, is considered more real than the intelligible world it purports to describe as a faithful copy. Such an observation about the image is already recognition that the image contains within it atomic details, particles, that might otherwise be overlooked. The court is asked to hone in on one specific element that might make sense of the whole. The value of the image rests upon suspending normal everyday vision in order to give attention to certain elements. Cartesian methodology assumes the viewer of the image to be in control. The effect of the dictum in *R v*

Maqsud Ali suggests otherwise that it is rather the image itself that renders details visible; details that would otherwise have been ignored jump out, catch our attention, arrest us.

Take the case of photofit images as a further example of what Reichman usefully terms "detailism." New computer-based wizardry has now established systems in which an image can be "evolved" on screen following statements made by witnesses. Using genetic algorithms, the computer begins with a database of thousands of variations of facial features; eyes, noses, chins, hair types and styles etc. In addition to these principal components, software is able to add skin tone, wrinkles, blemishes and so on. Once a possible solution is provided, the computer then repeatedly evolves the image until it best satisfies the witnesses' recollection. The final face can then be dismantled into its constituent parts so that a new nose, or new chin can be added to the database in order to be used in the future.[18] Both the systematic compilation of the photofit and the process of identification rely not on an overall interpretation of identity, but rather on subordinate, even pedestrian, features. Far from sublimating the centrality of details, the photofit demands an appreciation of a seemingly endless proliferation of constituent parts that make up a face. The overall coherence of identity rests upon recalcitrant details that can never be exhaustively or totally archived.

Such a practice of detailism is one that already has a long history in evidential practice of the courts. It focuses upon the minimal signatures, the minutiae and seemingly insignificant detail. In attending to the visual nature of micro details that informs evidence, it could be argued that all evidence is imagistic in nature.[19] Historically, what saves a document from the status of hearsay are excessive visual minutiae that adhere to the surface of a document. They are what convert an otherwise anonymous letter into anonymous text. Such details – notarial signs, flourished pen work, initials, obligatory Latin mottos, wafer seals – are not essential to the document; they do not spell out any meaning.[20] They are, however, the condition of its reception. Seals, for instance, (which may contain the impression of a fingernail, a garment, or a heraldic insignia) are both safeguards against interference and the very token by which an agreement or instruction can be said to have taken place. They both close and complete a document and grant it a meaning by placing it within a recognizable symbolic register.

The place of "detailism" can be expanded further in order to state that the oral witness himself can be understood in more imagistic terms. In his defense of the oral tradition of the common law, Matthew Hale turns the witness into an imagistic being composed of visual indicia; indeed it is the unconscious mannerisms of a witness that supports his argument: "Many times the very manner of a witness delivering testimony will give an indication whether he speaks truly or falsely."[21] What matters in the ascertainment of the truth value of a witness statement rests upon those visual indicia that leak out of the bodies of even the most schooled of witnesses. Indeed, rather than focus on the idea of the living pneumatic voice, it is precisely these visual details that form the *consilia* on oral testimony by the fourteenth-century jurist Baldus, "we blush to say many things which we do not blush to write ... One must see in a witness with what trembling he speaks, what there is in the visage, if he hesitates ... there is a popular adage which says, speak and I will recognize you."[22] Or, as in the context of the modern doctrine of "real" evidence: "The blush of nervousness or occasionally shame, the gape of stupidity, the gesture of annoyance, all have evidentiary value."[23]

In short, what applies to a reading of images extends to an analysis of all proof objects. Evidence rests on such detailed visual indicia. Returning to the specific context of images as real evidence, a question arises concerning the extent to which the forensic activity of the courtroom can be reconciled with doctrinal justifications for the admissibility of images. Does the practice of teasing apart images, isolating particularities, proliferating worlds within worlds contradict the assumption that the image is as near as possible an exact representation of its referent? What might be proposed is that instead of providing a *description* of the world, the image in its detail rather *explains* that world to us. Thus, the suggestion that an image in its detail might bring about aspects of an event that would otherwise be imperceptible to unmediated vision, rests upon the idea that the image is able to reveal to us, and explain, the true cause of an event. Such an idea, that the image helps to reveal hidden causes, resists the characterization of mere similitude that might form the doctrinal grounds of admissibility.

— VI

In what sense might this practice of detailism be considered to provide a radical alternative system of methodology to the one assumed by common law judges? One of the charges that might be leveled against detailism is that it does not necessarily subvert the Cartesian distinction between subject and object. Details require that a subject confronts them in an act of supervision. The Aristotelian process of reasoning, after all, rests on the fundamental proposition that details and particularities are inherent entities to an object. The imagistic detail is simply one further, albeit smaller object contained within a larger object (a photograph or video). A portion of an object remains an object to be viewed; the frozen and highlighted image of Rodney King's foot is still a foot and might be treated as an objective fact in its own isolated terms. The point is made by the art historian, Georges Didi-Huberman.[24] For him, the detail is a nameable element of a painting. They are the all too visible; threads, needles, pins etc (in Vermeer's *The Lacemaker*). However miniscule, such details are merely hidden among other details waiting to be discovered by the "skilled art theorist who wishes to behave like a fetishist."[25]

Nevertheless, an important albeit unintended point seems to arise from Didi-Huberman's observation. For, what a skilled art theorist who behaves like a fetishist (Didi-Huberman's terms) actually does is to apply a fine scalpel to a philosophical tradition that seeks to repress the radicality of details by denying a distinction between substance and detail, or between the whole and the part. Indeed to render the detail an objectifiable element of a whole surrenders to a Cartesian fusion between substance and detail (or accident).[26] Nothing about the evidential practice of honing in on details allows for such a collapsing of a distinction between the whole and its part.

These two features (the skilled art theorist who behaves like a fetishist, and the relationship between detail and substance) can be looked at in more depth in order to allow the radicality of image detailism. In fact another tract of inquiry opens up if we were to ask more profoundly what the skilled artist who behaves like a fetishist does. Put differently, what might be proposed is that the forensic examination of the image requires that members of a court or jury confront the image (or is confronted by the image) rather in the manner of a fetishist or a connoisseur. The term "connoisseur," as the art historian Edgar Wind reminds us, should not be used simply to name a character of refined taste.[27] Such a designation was an eighteenth-century import into the English language. Rather, the term is to be understood as an alternative *cognoscitorem* to describe one who is skilled in the evidential practice of attribution. Connoisseurship designates the practice by which the correct painter's name can be attached to an otherwise anonymous (or falsely anonymous) picture with precision; "as a skilled technician, the modern connoisseur knows by what signs to distinguish the genuine from the counterfeit; he can demonstrate authenticity."[28] Such skills, according to Wind, are based upon a rationalized set of techniques and methods defined initially by Giovanni Morelli.

This Morellian procedure, as it has become known, rests on "a meticulous technique of visual dissociation."[29] This technique avoids the mistake-ridden business of inspecting an overall picture for its themes and subjects of depiction. Poussin might favor certain biblical themes, but so do countless others whose paintings might look as if they were painted by Poussin. Similarly, and more obviously, Rembrandt shares motifs with other painters from the "school of Rembrandt." What then allows for a distinction to be drawn between a real and pretend Poussin, or Rembrandt. For Morelli, this "normal" aesthetic reaction rather has to be suspended. The connoisseur has to step back from the painting's overall depiction in order to hone in on the most telling of details. What might be considered insignificant or inessential thus becomes a loaded index of assigning meaning. As Wind asserts; "to identify the hand of the master, and distinguish it from the hand of a copyist, we must rely on small idiosyncrasies which seem inessential, subordinate features...: the shape of a finger nail or the lobe of an ear."[30] A century after, it feels like small wonder, as Carlo Ginzburg notes, that Morelli's techniques influenced the technique of Freudian psychoanalysis. In his essay

"The Moses of Michelangelo" Freud explicitly acknowledges his debt to Morelli:

> It seems to me that his [Morelli's] method of inquiry is closely related to the technique of psychoanalysis. It, too, is accustomed to divine secret and concealed things from unconsidered or unnoticed details, from the rubbish heap, as it were, of our observations.[31]

Uncovering the specific skills of the analyst, or the connoisseur, who proceeds by analyzing the symptom or detail, allows us to be a little more specific about the nature of those details that inhere in the image. What the connoisseur does in fetishing the detail is to recognize that the detail bears characteristics radically distinct from those that philosophers, or indeed lawyers attribute to substance.

In an essay that expands on the theme of random atomism inherent in language, Derrida muses on the character of the detective Dupin specifically as he is portrayed in "The Murders in the Rue Morgue."[32] Dupin, so Derrida stresses, is precisely the type of analyst for whom "all is symptom and diagnostics."[33] He "examines the countenance of his partner ... [h]e notes every variation of face ... gathering a fund of thought from the differences in expression."[34] For Derrida, such details, such clues, are more closely linked to a family of similar particles consisting of symptoms, clinamen and atoms. What links the detail to symptoms or atoms, or what establishes this family of particles is that they are both incidental and accidental. Put in more straightforward philosophical terms, Derrida returns the detail to a position in which it has to be divorced from substance. That is to say that the accident has to be understood in a broader sense as that which may be deemed extraneous to the purported essence or meaning of an image or a statement. The color, taste, smell and texture of an object are merely incidental. While they might "cleave" to a substance or a subject, they are simply "casual" effects and could be detached from an analysis of the essence of such things.[35]

Such incidentals may well attach to a substance, to a document, or to the oral performance of a witness, but they are in themselves non-essential qualities. They are separable and supplementary. A true analysis of an object, as judges would have it, would require details and accidents to *fall away* from the gaze of inquiry. Indeed, the accident, Derrida reminds us, is what *falls* from the order of the world. Again, etymology refers us to a series of connections (or what Derrida claims to be fortuitous chances) relating to the fall. The words "case," "casual," "occasion," "occident," "deciduous," "cadaver" are all related to "accident" through *cadere*, or *kad* (in centum languages). They all refer to a fall, or a lapse away from a system, a form, an order, the sky, a tree or life itself; they are all *casualties* of a post-lapsarian system of thought that celebrates verticality and hierarchy (or a system of thought that attempts to repair man's fallen status). As Derrida puts it, the accident "affects the upward stance and vertical position by engraving in [the subject] the detour of a clinamen" (the clinamen refers to the Lucretian theory describing the swerving of atoms as they fall).[36] Similarly, the detail also shares the sense of fall with the word "symptom," "a word meaning a sinking in or depression, a collapse but also a coincidence, a fortuitous even..."[37]

Derrida's analysis of chance ought to read as part of his broader concern with the relationship between aleatorics and representation, or rather with the aleatoric rupture of representation.[38] Such concern receives its most poetic and famous elaboration in *The Post-Card*[39] according to which representation is structured like a postal network; that is, the relationship between signifier and signified is structured according to channels that might link transmission to reception. And like postal systems, like any transmission from sender to receiver, the destination (or, in metaphysical terms, "destiny") of meaning is prone to ambush, delays and chance occurrences. Letters go astray. Failure is always possible. Chance intercepts and introduces a rupture in the relationship between signifier and signified, between image and referent. Representation is a decidedly dicey enterprise always open to the possibility that the relationship between signifier and signified comes away detached. There is always the possibility that the message does not arrive.

It must be stressed here that Derrida is not concerned with the disorder of representation but rather with those hidden chance features that prevent closure of meaning from the outset. Where appellate decisions regarding the admissibility of images might be regarded as an attempt to control meaning, and to close meaning within coded convention, the clinamen introduces the fatal possibility of erring. The detail always opens up the potential of swerving away from the proper juridically perceived destination of images. Details that inhere in images thus belong to those other spatiotemporal figures unearthed by Derrida as constituting the radical grammar of texts (traces, supplements, interruptions, blankspaces, cinders); endless profusions that defeat any attempt to fix meaning or to control the future of the image.[40] It might also be noted, and indeed as Derrida himself points out, that the theme of arbitrary detail is one that belongs to a repressed (or fallen/lapsarian) tradition that could be said to harbor this fallen collection of particles; "never forget that through-out the history of Occidental culture the Democritian tradition, in which the names of Epicurus and his disciples are recorded, has been submitted since its origin (and initially under the violent authority of Plato) to a powerful repression."[41]

What is important to bear in mind is that this Democritian tradition that Derrida wishes to highlight theorises the miniscule detail, the symptom, the atom, or the clinamen as those elements which escape intentionality and destiny, and which fall away from systems and code. In other words, what renders the image's detail so radical to methods of inquiry that stress objectivity and calculative rationality is precisely that they inhabit a register of what is potentially oblivious to consciousness. As Bachelard puts it:

> On the level of the detail, Thought and Reality seem to come undone, and we might say that by distancing itself from the order of magnitude in which we think, Reality somehow loses its solidity, its constancy, its substance. To sum up, Reality and Thought founder together in the same nothingness, in the same metaphysical Erebus, sons of chaos and night.[42]

Returning to the evidential confrontation, it is clear that in its detail the image as proof object is not an object of representation and that it resists the mimetic basis upon which testimony and proof rest. Even in attempting to be precise, the viewer of a detail only condemns himself to the tyranny of a non-exhaustive list of interferences and conjectural questions. (Which details are important? What exactly are we looking for, or at? What is the starting point of our examination?). Rather, the image transforms itself from a descriptive representation into a medium through which explanations about the world might be reached.

— VIII

An examination into the legal use of images uncovers two antithetical approaches. Where doctrine stresses the acheiropoietic purity of images, empirical practice offers no such respect. Images are pulled apart and their details proliferate. Two broad points might be made by way of a conclusion. First, what has been stressed throughout this article is that evidential approaches to the image cannot easily be reconciled with the Cartesian suppositions on which judicial pronouncements about admissibility rest. Rather, they seem to propose another paradigm for discovery based upon the sovereignty of details. Against the massive determinacy that is superimposed upon the descriptive surface of an image is a practice that proceeds from the fallen or underside of the photographic image, from its chances and accidents. Following Ginzburg's essay on connoisseurship, which suggests that connoisseurship shares its epistemological practice with a constellation of similar disciplines, the use of the evidential image attests to the survival of conjectural or divinatory paradigms.[43]

To stress the conjectural domain that arises in the encounter with the image is to suggest that the court is placed not so much in a position of a Cartesian viewing subject. Rather, all activity proceeds from the detail. It is the detail that arrests and forces us into a suspension of the normal critical or perceptual faculties that might otherwise allow us to impose meaning upon an object of inquiry. The second point that might be made is that, by virtue of its distinction from the whole, as well as by virtue of its distance from transparent meaning, the detail is always in danger of letting the image collapse into non-meaning. Here it is not simply the case that the detail arrests and suspends judgment. Accidents and chance happenings that fall within a frame do not elicit an infinite number of possible interpretations, nor do they render the image an anarchic medium.

Detailism should not be rendered a species of Quinian anti-essentialism which assumes that objects have no properties and only accidents. While, accidents are opposed to facts, and, viceversa, interpretation opposes chance, a structural relationship between the detail and the image has to be maintained. As Georges Didi-Huberman reminds us, images have a structure. But this structure, he states, is open. "The 'world' of images does not reject the world of logic, quite the contrary. But it plays with it ... it creates spaces there."[44] What the detailed reading of images alerts us to is the potential that beyond all questions of authenticity, the image may be more profoundly unreliable than mere hearsay.

Acknowledgements:

Although they may not recognize them I have to acknowledge with gratitude that many of the ideas contained in this paper were developed during and after conversations with both Marty Slaughter and Anton Schutz. Further, thanks to the comments provided by the anonymous referee. Also, for encouragement when it was much needed, thanks to Peter Fitzpatrick, Patrick Hanafin, Elena Loizidou, Les Moran and Helen Reece.

"Law and the Evidental Image" was first published in *Law, Culture and Humanities*, vol. 4, no 2 (June 2008), 139–155 Copyright 2008 by *Law, Culture and Humanities.*

Reprinted by the permission of SAGE.

1 Bruno Latour, "What is Iconoclash? Or is there a World Beyond the Image Wars?" at www.bruno-latour.fr/livres/cat_icono_chap.html. Last accessed August 7, 2011.

2 This paper is more concerned with the status of the image as an object (or proof-object). An alternative formulation of the relationship between law and the image focuses on the idea that the law itself requires itself to be received in terms of its own image. Thus Peter Goodrich states: "The law is a system of images." In this sense, the image of law is more than the surface indices that constitute the type of images analyzed in this paper. The sinister Victoriana of court rooms, the somber wigs and gowns that clothe the pinky flesh of self-indulgent judges, the light–starved atmosphere are all details subject to change and modernization; court rooms are being updated, there is a broader ethnic range of judges who are able to do away with the robes, strip-lighting has replaced the old gas lamps etc. The strength of Goodrich's argument lies in the stressing that the image of law is in fact the very idea of law itself. The image of law refers more to its national geography, to its language, to its visible presence, to its structure, than to the empirical particularities of its texture. Such arguments are crucial to the study of institutional life, and to any critical engagement between the study of law and images and the study of subjectivity. See Peter Goodrich, *Languages of Law, From Logics of Memory to Nomadic Masks* (London: Weidenfeld and Nicolson, 1990), 210.

3 As Joel Snyder has recently uncovered, early nineteenth-century American cases had to deal with arguments raised against the admissibility of photographs that they were nothing more than "hearsay of the sun." This astonishing argument rests on the complaint that the ultimate author of a photograph is none other than the sun. Given the necessary exclusion of the sun (and, indeed, sunlight) from the trial, the photograph rests on an out of court assertion. It is according to Snyder's analysis secondhand testimony. Joel Snyder, "Res Ipsa Loquitor" in Lorraine Daston, *Things that Talk* (New York: Zone, 2004), 195, 221. The phrase "hearsay of the sun" is a statement used by counsel for the plaintiff in *Howland Will Case* [1870] 4 *American Legal Review* n 625, 644–53 discussed in Snyder, 214 et seq.

4 *R v Cook* [1987] 1 Q.B. 417. For similar judgments see *R v Dwyer* [1925] 2 K.B. 799; *R v Goss* [1923] 17 Cr. App. R.; *R v Melaney* [1924] 18 Cr. App. R.; *R v Halsham* [1925] 19 Cr. App. R.; *R v Hinds* [1932] 2 K.B.; *R v Seiga* [1961] 45 Cr. App. R.; *R v Constantinou* [1989] Crim. L. R.; *Jones v Wright* [1991] 1 All E.R.; *The Statue of Liberty* [1968] 1 W.L.R. 739.

5 The definition of hearsay is usually given as "an out of court statement (oral or otherwise) made by a person and tendered to prove the truth of its contents." See *Wright v Tatham* 7 Ad. & E.L. 313.

6 The old common law rules have now been superseded by the Criminal Justice Act 2003, which attempts both to liberalize and codify rules regarding the admissibility of hearsay evidence in criminal trials.

7 *R v Maqsud Ali* 1966 1 Q.B. 688 at 701.

8 House of Lords Select Committee on Science and Technology: *Fifth Report (Digital Images as Evidence)* 1998, available at www.parliament.the-stationery–office.co.uk/pa/ld199798/ldsctech/064v/st0501.htm. On the benefits of digital imagery for broader schemes such as the National Identity Register see *the House of Lords Select Committee on Science and Technology* (Project Iris Review), 2005: www.parliament.uk/parliamentary_committees/science_and_technology_committee/scietecfuidcard.cfm

9 The often-cited doctrine of *Ore Tenus* is to be found in Sir Matthew Hale, *A History of the Common Law of England* (Chicago University Press: Chicago, 1971), 163.

10 See, for example, John Wigmore, "A Brief History of the Parole Evidence Rule, "*Columbia Law Review*, vol. 4, no. 5 (1904): 338–355.

11 The relevance to evidential reasoning of the Cartesian method of doubt is expressed by Lord Brandon in *Rhesa Shipping S.A. v Edmunds* 1985 1 W.L.R. For a fuller account of the influence of Cartesian methods of doubt on the common law evidence, see John D. Jackson "Theories of Truth Finding in Criminal Procedure: An Evolutionary Approach, "*Cardozo*

Law Review vol. 10, n. 3 (1988): 514–29. There is clearly a contradiction between doubt as the first principle of this methodology and the doctrinal presumption of innocence. However, the limits of the present paper are such as to prevent further analysis of this point.

12 Charles Goodwin, "Professional Vision," *American Anthropologist*, vol. 96, no. 3 (1994): 606–33.

13 Rene Descartes, "Fifth Meditation" in *Discourse on Method and Meditations* (Harmondsworth: Penguin, 1985), 147.

14 Ravit Reichman, "Making a Mess of Things: The Trifles of Legal Pleasure," *Law, Culture and the Humanities* 1 (2005): 14–34.

15 Thomas Thomas, *Dictionarium Linguae Latinae et Anglicane* (Cantebridgiae: T.Thomasii), 1587.

16 Reichman, 16.

17 John Fiske, "Admissible Postmodernity: Some Remarks on Rodney King, O. J. Simpson, and Contemporary Culture," *University of San Francisco Law Review*, vol. 30, no. 4 (1996): 917–31, 918.

18 *New Scientist* March 19, 2005. Available at www.newscientist.com/article.ns?id_dn7143.

19 Or, as one judge puts it "Every object seen with the natural eye is only seen because photographed on the retina ... What we call sight is but the impression made on the mind through the retina of the eye, which is nature's camera." *William Eborn v George B. Zimpleman, Adm'r & c.*, 47 Texas 503 (1877), quoted in Joel Snyder, "Res Ipsa Loquitor," 219.

20 That signatures, wax seals, stamped leather fixes the identity of the witness is treated in more historical fashion by Jean-Phillipe Levy, *La Hierarchie des Preuves dans le Droit Savant du Moyen Ages* (Paris: Annales de L'universite de Lyon, 1939). A more philosophical treatment of the status of the signature as a mark of transcendental presence (or nowness) is of course famously provided by Jacques Derrida, "Signature, Event, Context," in *Margins of Philosophy*, trans. Alan Bass (London: Harvester Wheatsheaf, 1982), 328.

21 Sir Matthew Hale, *History of the Common Law of England* (Chicago: University of Chicago Press), 1975.

22 Baldus, cited in G.D. Nokes, "Real Evidence," 65 *Law Quarterly Review* (1949): 62.

23 Nokes, 67.

24 Georges Didi-Huberman, *Confronting Images; Questioning the Ends of a Certain History of Art* (Pennsylvania: Penn State University Press, 2005).

25 Ibid. 268

26 Treated generally in the sixth meditation.

27 Edgar Wind, *Art and Anarchy* (Chicago: Northwestern University Press, 1985).

28 Ibid. 31–32.

29 Ibid. 32.

30 Ibid. 36.

31 Sigmund Freud, "The Moses of Michelangelo" in *Collected Papers* (New York: Harper Collins, 1959), 4:270–71, cited in Carlo Ginzburg, "Clues: Roots of an Evidential Paradigm" in *Myths, Emblems, Clues* (London; Hutchinson Radius, 1986), 99.

32 Jacques Derrida, "My Chances/*Mes Chances*: A Rendevous with some Epicurean Stereophonies" in Joseph H. Smith and William Kerrigan, *Taking Chances: Derrida, Psychoanalysis and Literature* (Baltimore: Johns Hopkins University Press, 1984), 1–32.

33 Ibid. 12.

34 Poe, cited in Jacques Derrida, op. cit.,13.

35 The terms "casual" and "cleave" are often used by sixteenth and seventeenth century books of logic to describe the relationship between accident and substance. Thus "[An accident] is a voice or worde signifying thinges casuall, cleaving to substance or subjects." Blundeville, *First Book of Logike* (1599), 9. Similarly; "An accident depends upon a substance for its existence. It is that which cleaveth to a substance." Zachary Coke, *The art of Logic* (1654), 27.

36 Derrida, "My Chances/*Mes Chances*: A Rendevous with some Epicurean Stereophonies," 5.

37 Ibid. 6–7.

38 See Jacques Derrida, "Telepathy," trans. Nicholas Royle, *Oxford Literary Review* 10 (1988): 3–41.

39 Jacques Derrida, *The Post Card; From Socrates to Freud and Beyond*, trans. Alan Bass (Chicago: University of Chicago Press, 1987).

40 On the spatio-temporal figurations in Derrida's work see J. Hillis-Miller, "Derrida's Destinerrance," 4. *MLN* 2006: 893–910.

41 Derrida, *The Post Card*, 18.

42 Gaston Bachelard, "Essai sur la connaissance approchee," 257, cited in Georges Didi-Huberman, *Confronting Images*, (Pennsylvania: Penn State University Press, 2005), 234.

43 Ginzburg, "Clues," 117.

44 Didi-Huberman, *Confronting Images*, 142.

The Testamentary Whimper

— Avital Ronell

Somewhere between the imperatives of reality testing and the interrogatory title "What Is Called Thinking?" Jean-François Lyotard institutes phrase regimens – events that surpass the holding capacity of a linguistic act.[1] Here, language and proof have met their reciprocal limits. Exploring the failure of speculative thought to supply relief to victims of colossal as well as minute, unclassified historical grief, phrase regimens go to the heart of injurious wrongdoing. They underscore the weakness of evidence and of probative restitutional acts. "A wrong," writes Lyotard, "is a damage accompanied by the loss of the means to prove the damage."[2] Prior to the confirmation that a right has been infringed upon, and earlier still than the recognition of the human, Lyotard inquires about the impossibility of human rights. Beyond hypothesis yet in some cases legally short of proof, the desolating ordeal to which Lyotard addresses this inquiry concerns evasive turns of law when called on to perform justice. On the one hand, Lyotard's work comes to the aid of those who, unable to manipulate the rules of cognitive discourse, are left stranded by speculative thinking; those who phrase according to the rules of other genres are stripped of the very power to speak. On the other hand, rescue and relief cannot be guaranteed, for every phrase in itself is capable of offending another phrase and thus runs an inevitable risk of wrongdoing. What happens to those among us who make existence claims that, according to the rules of cognitive discourse, cannot be validated? What about those whose distress has not been proven, whose rights have not been recognized, and whose pain has yet to be legally seared into our living memories?

In *The Differend* everything is staked on the plight of a phrase whose regimen excludes cognitive verification. Lyotard examines the nearly closed cases of those whose discursive fragility is legendary, and for whom no test of heterogeneous phrasal regimens has been devised. They include the perpetually contested, the historically harassed victims of rape, or those survivors whose claims concerning the existence of gas chambers has been rejected by an emissary or mask of a Faurisson – the revisionist historian whose demand for proofs opened a notorious "debate." (Can the existence of gas chambers be debated and, if not, why not? If so, in what terms? Does the resistance to debate already indicate a grave political problem, or is debate itself a subterfuge, a simulated solution – or worse, an offense, to the extent that it puts a historical occurrence up for discursive grabs?) Lyotard shows how the demand to establish the reality of a phrase according to normative procedures can wrong a witness, can produce unsolvable conflicts or radical differends. One problem is that the revisionist historian monopolizes and appropriates cognitive discourse, comfortably finding critical support in the workings of speculative thought. The victim asked to account for the reality to which she points, sometimes mutely, is under pressure to produce reference. She becomes witness but also structurally assumes the place of *plaintiff*. The circumstance of seeking what has since been californianized into "validation" puts the victim in the position of a plaintiff before a public court. The differend is "owed to the impossibility faced by the plaintiff of demonstrating the existence of what is in question. The kind of demands for verification that are made of him stifle the plaintiff 's ability to furnish proof."[3] Reality, writes Lyotard, "is always the plaintiff's responsibility."[4] What this means is that the plaintiff must shoulder the burden of establishing the existence of the referent. In the terms and logic that Lyotard confronts, it becomes even the burden of the victims of the Shoah to *prove* the extermination, to supply proof for the reality of gas chambers. Reality, whether of a historical or more personally cut nature, is not pregiven, and cannot by any means be taken for granted but recurrently foregrounds the contestability of the referent. Reality is "always potentially in suspense, or in dispute."[5] Sometimes the value of an asserted referent achieves consensus, legitimacy. But even a successful plea for the referent can only be temporary, "until further notice [that] it has not been falsified."[6] More people than one cares to count live in such worlds of unprovable distress. These worlds, each time singular, resist comparison, though somewhere they pile up like abandoned shoes.

As with all cognitive claims, it is expected that others will be able to verify or falsify the referential proposals put forward, at any time and any place. The expectation of the public nature of verification for the anchoring of a stated contention meets the traditional expectations of Western thinking. Ever since Socrates stopped passersby to make his philosophical points and to harass the truth into the open, truth claims have become a matter of public display, complying with a serious stage direction of street theater. The scenography of openness, the demand for intelligibility and consensual accord is what Plato called *logon didonai*.[7] The scene changed when dialectical disclosiveness abandoned the streets of early urban philosophy. Truth moved out of Socratic neighborhoods, clearing the way for turf wars requiring a new level of arbitration. With reality shaky and reference elusive, the question became one of assuring consensus; appeals were made to an implicit third party – a public forum, a tribunal or court. At the same time, the Platonic solution to "finding a consensus about the adducing of proofs concerning a referent [became] the living dialogue between two, the *dialegesthai*."[8] Lyotard asserts, "We believe in the decision of the third party in matters of reality."[9] This, for instance, is why human rights commissions are important, part of the package deal of a testamentary ethics. The status and stakes of reality are thus addressed to a third party: they become in sum and summation a matter of testimony and attestation. Testimony implies another degree or logic of reality testing, the requirements of which are often satisfied with the appearance of truthfulness or *veracity*. Irreducible to a strictly verifiable result, testimony embraces the instability of reference while seeking to establish the veracity of its claims. Still, witnessing, which necessarily bypasses cognitive checkpoints, poses a host of problems even as it swears itself in.

There must be a way to distinguish between the person whose testimony is about having been abducted by space aliens and the one or many whose narrative – whether shared or silently withheld – names extreme oppression or even the event of extermination. Between fiction (I think) and a traumatic event not available to the purposeful aims of the cognitive empire and its empirical satellites, something happens in the world of philosophy to the way stories get told and heard. The internal collapses in the discursive capacity to yield truth bear on legal considerations as well, particularly when evidence fails instantly to feed the referential scanner. Winning an argument depends on its own steam, attached to some fixable substance only by ever-vaporizing contingency. Given the "loss or decline of the referent's reality" – the threat that nothingness could be a real possibility – we have come to the point, since Gorgias's refutation of Being, where by dint of paralogical operations or dim-witted tenacity weaker arguments trump stronger ones: "We allow the lesser argument to prevail, under the right conditions."[10] Lyotard's work responds to this genuinely contemporary issue; it also takes on, as a measure of the difficulty of submitting a satisfying response to the gravity of the questions with which he struggles, the related problem of the sublime, which elicits only a stuporous witnessing of the unpresentable. How can one bear witness to the ontological sublime if it endlessly slips out of view? We'll get to Lyotard's redescription of the sublime momentarily.

Very often victims of torture, indignity, and pain are abandoned to phrases whose regimen excludes cognitive verification. Or, in the case of traumatized survivors, they are rooted to a phrase whose only recognizable quality is what we call silence. The silence of Holocaust survivors has been held against them by the revisionist historian. This is why Lyotard includes silence as the possibility of phrasing. Phrasing is expansive, generous, even as it gets drained by word privation. The phrase can consist in a fleeting blush, a flicker of anxiety, a tapping of the foot, a shrugging of the shoulder, a blink. A silence can also serve as a phrase.[11] Silence offers its own syntax of testimony. Yet it runs counter to the traditional adducement of proof – the constitutive demand of cognitive discourse, "the demand to prove the existence or reality of the claim one makes according to established rules, so that they can be verified by others."[12] The "others" upon whom the referent depends for some measure of solidity convokes a select crowd derived from the *dialegesthai*, essentially a dialogue among friends, for it is careful to exclude idiots, hostile interlopers, as well as infirm brutes and in fact "anyone who is in bad faith."[13] This means that, in the

Platonic partnering up of solutions, there remains an excluded negativity, a party who abstains from the obtained consensus, maybe capable in the end of sabotaging its premises by his mere existence. The so-called idiot can run with his own logic, jumping the boundary of the friendly Platonic dialogue into the future of aberrant assertion – with good and bad results, depending on who's breaking away from the dialogue of friends. The runaway idiot could be a Faurisson. Or a luminous singularity could break the consensus. In any case the status of friendship has been sufficiently complicated by Bataille, Blanchot, Derrida, and others as to give pause to the selective fraternal construction, the ancient boys' club, that determines the cases before them.

In Plato the consensus about adducing proofs or stabilizing reference depends on the fragile construction of amicable colloquy: the agreement has to be made prior to the accord, verification prior to proof. The buddy system has preapproved the reality checks to be issued, in effect offering a group discount on veracity claims. All this would be inoffensive if it were not for the fact that scientific discourse is based on these premises, which is to say, the genre of discourse that "seeks to institute the rules for what we call scientific discourse – that is, the rules for our prevailing mode of thinking in the West" depends on the values of clarity and public openness from which our procedural sense of propriety, linked to and based on scientific method, issues.[14] Yet the expectation and indeed requirement that the reality of a phrase's referent be established according to unanimously agreed upon procedures can in themselves wrong a witness or plaintiff, resulting in recalcitrant conflicts or extreme differends. These results come in even though, as Gasché argues, the "demand in itself is rational, [one] without which thinking (in its cognitive mode, at least) is not possible."[15] The demand that testimony be bolstered by material evidence, that phrases bulk up on tried and proven evidentiary supplements, encounters a snag. One is wronged, Lyotard reminds us, when a damage is "accompanied by the loss of the means to prove the damage." Stranded with an unprovable reality, one has lost all recourse or means of appeal, since to this privation "there is added the impossibility to bring it to the knowledge of others, and in particular to the knowledge of a tribunal."[16] In the famous words of Paul Celan, the witness needs a witness of which cognitive regimens, however, deprive him:

> Should the victim bypass this impossibility [of bringing the wrong it has incurred to the knowledge of a third party] and testify anyway to the wrong done to him or her, he or she comes up against the following argument: either the damages you complain about never took place, and your testimony is false; or else they took place, and since you are able to testify to them, it is not a wrong that has been done to you, but merely a damage, and your testimony is still false.[17]

There is, however, a further Kafkan twist to the strained requisite of stating one's case despite the referential odds. Testifying to the reality of the horror of injustice as if one were perpetually standing trial, one is structurally trapped. The victim's sense of being on trial with no testable ground, with phrases that collapse under the pressure of cognitive bullying, creates a situation where the test of obliterating contestation has been summoned to defeat the victim once again. This dilemma has been established with painful clarity by Lyotard.

—

You're making it up, you're faking it, you can't prove it!

As cruel and common as they are, these statements offend not only because they come from a hostile or institutionally appointed space of exteriority; they belong to another curl of conspiratorial anguish. The disbelieving persecutor is not the only one who tries to reduce an inassimilable reality to a matter of testability. You yourself, as lacerated victim, cannot believe this has happened, is still happening to you. To you. Language fails you. It is not as if one has mastered trauma so well that one can get out from under its flaying machine or see or speak or know or understand. That severe, ego-built part of you responsible for reality testing shudders to a halt. Remember, K. from *The Trial* could not tell what was happening to him; he tried to play by the rules of cognition, went to court, submitted to the test, if that's what it was, until he was a dead man walking metamorphosed into a piece of executed dog. What I am trying to say is that the victim is rolled into an ongoing surprise attack, shaken down by a sudden spread of anxiety that bears the caption, "Is it happening?" Can this be true? This "*Arrive-t-il?*" of which Lyotard writes hits you in and as the foreign language region of your being, even in its most homegrown aspect of terror. What I am trying to say is that the persecutory reality continues to slap the victim around and does not come with a "how to tell and get over it" kit. There is only something that Lyotard calls a *feeling* – a terrible, startling feeling for which philosophy needs to find a phrase, a link, a support. Philosophy has to stop testifying for the institutionally self-satisfied defense team, stop kissing up to state-sanctioned power plays, and instead get into the untested regions of new idioms, new addresses, new referents; it has to abandon its conciliatory habits. Rather than continue its traditional pursuit of conciliation, philosophy, more or less according to Lyotard, needs to be invaded by new inconsistencies and to saturate itself with the feeling of the damaged. The differend must be put into phrases with the understanding that such an act cannot yet be accomplished. In sum, philosophical thought must come up with a link to the feeling-tone of the unaccounted for, and offer privileged protection to the unaccountable refugees of cognitive regimens. The Platonic model, setting truth as an invariable – as that which remains detached from the plight of the addressers and addressees of phrases – serves no useful, pathbreaking purpose in light of the task that Lyotard sets for a philosophy of dignity and activist commitment. How can this new mutation in philosophical engagement stay intimate with those throttled by a dependency beyond dependency? If I am getting this right, Lyotard asks that contact be made with the real ravages of the impossible and that one move with the incessant punches of untamable horror. Even if the object seems elusive (especially when it eludes): one has to go there, be there, stand there.

Not always available to translation or in the least bit comprehensible, the "Is it happening?" tells you only that the impossible has become a real possibility. Adding shock to wonder, this dazed state of troubled residue that cannot be seized or comprehended reverts in Lyotard to a stuporous *Grundstimmung*, to a traumatic stupidity that resets the cognitive levers according to which we respond to catastrophic eclipses, inhibited by that which cannot as such be presented according to classical values of presentation. There is something senseless in the heart of things, provoking "a bewilderment, a stupid passion" that can no longer be resolved into tragic representation or protected by any recognizably edifying recuperation.[18] This is why, among other things, Lyotard is determined to offer a redefinition of the sublime as that which is no longer opposed to the beautiful. The task of philosophy no longer consists in neutralizing or domesticating the senseless, in rounding up the savagely unintelligible but in staying with the stupor of unaccountable excess and regressive brutality. Gasché comments,

> The task of thinking set by the stupor at the realization that non-being could prevail, cannot be fulfilled by schematizing the unpresentable into facile intelligibility. Thinking absolves its task of witnessing only if it encounters the unpresentable without resistance. The sublime feeling in which the impossible possible is acknowledged can therefore no longer be a sublime that plays by the rules of the beautiful.[19]

The evacuated site of non-Being, of the nothing, and the senseless "is only truly and properly acknowledged in a feeling of sublime stupor. In such stupor alone, philosophical thinking is true to its task."[20] It is not as though the "proper" of philosophy has now migrated to stupefying figures of the unpresentable. Lyotard does not originate a call for a new mystification, even in the form of some "truth of a task." Nor would he be likely to concur with his commentator that something like nonresistance is possible, given the irreversible vocabularies of psychoanalysis and rhetorical deconstruction. The sublime stupor is meant to stem the enticement of philosophical overreach, calling thought back to the sting of the unsayable: this is where phrasing, each time anew, stunned and dazed, begins to s-crawl.

—

Lyotard's work engages the quality of incommensurability that obtains between philosophical statement and what testimony can do. Bold and exemplary, his argument necessarily appears to leave some uncomfortable residue to the extent that the issues exceed the frame under which they are solicited: no matter how many precautions and subtleties are reflected in the effort to respond to his call – in the effort, precisely, to *enchaîner*, link on – one risks finding oneself inadvertently replicating the language of negationism, as if the Shoah were indeed unprovable, as if one had no choice but to parley noncognitive regimens in order to provide a semblance of credibility to corroborating claims. Meaning well and doing good, *The Differend* sets an unbypassable trap by which it has itself been quietly exploited. At least, the history of its reception has allowed for the trace of a trip-up, a confusion between what can be known and what can be proven. In another context, recognizing that in cases of extreme wrongdoing we come face to face with an event that annihilates its witnesses, Shoshana Felman has offered that not one direct witness can be summoned to claim the Shoah, which in the end cannot be understood as a single event in its totality.[21] For much of scientific thought the destruction of the witness would reveal the insufficiency of the case under consideration. However, this is not a matter of not knowing what we know or knowing what we don't know or rigorously lacking proof: there is knowledge here, material evidence has been established, and even Nazi testimony has confirmed time and again the existence of gas chambers. The death camp was an acknowledged fact since 1943. So the purported failure of material proof to manifest cannot in itself be the problem, philosophically speaking, nor is it what stirs us to return incessantly to a discursive crime scene.[22] No. What interests me is the way the damages tally up in the language of scientificity, something that Lyotard no doubt wants us to think about. The tenacity of revisionist prodding is due in large part to its ability to invoke the rhetoric of testing when it comes to the deconstitution of the Shoah as memory and knowledge. The discourse of Holocaust negationism is paradoxically coextensive with scientific discourse. In the case of Faurisson and others like him, the "question" of the existence of gas chambers – another crease in the perpetuating Jewish "question" – is raised in terms of hypothesis testing, as an assertion that cannot be proven wrong as long as it stays within the jurisdiction of the tenets of falsifiability. The recourse to hypothesis testing invites the inquiry into whether the extermination took place. The point I am making about the pervertability of testing and hypothetical positing raises only a hair of a differend with *The Differend*, yet it seems worth registering. Commentators whose intentions are not to be impugned readily fall in line with the phrase universe that scorns what is by all reasonable measure known, archivized, certified, agreed upon. If such slippage can happen, it is also because there is something irresistible at the core of the discourse of testing, which manages to seduce even the subtlest of philosophical sensors.

—

The counteroffer to this state of affairs, testimony, contains its own measure of destabilizers. In a work that leans heavily on the "test of testimony,"[23] Derrida indicates the degree to which testimony is structurally susceptible to falling under or into fiction. To the extent that testimonial language customarily engages the first-person narration, it takes up the old liabilities already schematized by Goethe in *Dichtung und Wahrheit* – testimony splits the honors between truth telling and its fictional support. A passion or experience without mastery, without active subjectivity, testimony, as passion, always renders itself vulnerable to doubt. It takes place as a "promise to make truth, according to Augustine's expression, where the witness must be irreplaceably alone ... testimony always goes hand in hand with at least the possibility of fiction, perjury and lie. Were this possibility to be eliminated, no testimony would be possible any longer; it could no longer have the meaning of testimony."[24] Given that Derrida links testimony to passion – even to the passion of a martyr who offers up her or his body in testifying – it always *suffers* its undecidable relation to fiction, perjury, lying while never "being able or obligated – without ceasing to testify – to become a proof."[25] The disturbing complicity between fiction and testimony cannot be erased or simply overcome. Thus, whereas the testimonial is by law irreducible to the fictional – this is what one swears to – there is still "no testimony that does not structurally imply in itself the possibility of fiction, simulacra, dissimulation, the lie, and perjury – that is to say the possibility of literature, of the innocent or perverse literature that innocently plays at perverting all of these distinctions."[26] Testimony does not need some outside perv to come in and bend its meaning, crush its horizon. The literary club ownership requires, when showing up to collect its dues, that the dissimulating propensities of the testifying act be honored and in some crucial way remembered. Testimony can never be expected to pass its own test if it suppresses the literary premises on which it stands. Unlike the discursive rallying that attempts to defeat it, testimony, while never abandoning the effort to scope veracity and say what it knows, remembers, sacrifices, and attests to, has no reliable test to back it up or make it back down, no accredited lie detector test tied to the stopwatch axioms of falsifiability. Testimony comes forward to pose a knowing without cognition, a memory without prosthetic or technical support, an irreplaceable exemplarity that must be repeated and replaced by more testimony without ever resolving itself into a proof. If testimony were to limit itself to establishing proof, information, certainty, or archive, "it would lose its function as testimony. In order to remain testimony, it must therefore allow itself to be haunted. It must allow itself to be parasitized by precisely what it excludes from its inner depths, the *possibility*, at least, of literature."[27] In the *Step Not Beyond*, Maurice Blanchot has written about this difficult border along which we would like to settle our thought, the border between testing and testimony, stalked by the living and the dead who carry each other as they burden and argue the language of our listening: "Silence carries us into the proximity of the distant. Word still to be spoken beyond the living and the dead, testifying for the absence of attestation."[28] It is as if the whole region were suffering from the default of test.

1 In significant articles devoted to Lyotard, Rodolphe Gasché defines the phrase event by distinguishing the phrase from a proposition: "Phrases, first and foremost, are occurrences. They are events before they are beholden to specific regimens, such as, for instance, the logical and cognitive regimen to which propositions belong." Rodolphe Gasché, "The Sublime, Ontologically Speaking," *Jean-François Lyotard: Time and Judgment*, a special issue of *Yale French Studies*, no. 99, (2001): 118.

2 Jean-François Lyotard, *The Differend: Phrases in Dispute*, trans. Georges Van Den Abbeele (Minneapolis: University of Minnesota Press, 1988), 72. See also Gasché's discussion of this statement, "The Sublime, Ontologically Speaking," 139.

3 Rodolphe Gasché, "Saving the Honor of Thinking: On Jean-François Lyotard," *Parallax* 6.4 (October 2000): 135.

4 Lyotard, *Differend*, 8.
5 Ibid. 8.
6 Ibid.

7 See Gasché's discussion of *logon didonai* in "Saving the Honor," 135.

8 Gasché, "Saving the Honor," 138.

9 Lyotard, *Differend*, 25–26.

10 Ibid. See also Gasché's discussion along these lines in "Saving the Honor." However, I must add a word of caution. If we allowed the weaker "argument" to prevail in the *stronger* sense, then testimonial arbitration would not pose such a consternating problem – the inability in some cases of the weak to produce argument or admissible language requires attentive analysis here.

11 See Lyotard, *Differend*, 70.

12 Gasché, "Saving the Honor," 134.
13 Ibid.
14 Ibid. 139.
15 Ibid.

16 Lyotard, *Differend*, 5.
17 Ibid.; see also Gasché, "Saving the Honor,"139–140.

18 Lyotard, *The Inhuman: Reflections on Time*, trans. Geoffrey Bennington and Rachel Bowlby (Stanford: Stanford University Press, 1991), 202.

19 Gasché, "Saving the Honor,"127.
20 Ibid.

21 Shoshana Felman and Dori Laub, M.D., *Testimony: Crises of Witnessing in Literature, Psychoanalysis, and History* (New York: Routledge, 1992). See also Ulrich Baer's haunting discussions of medial testimony in *Spectral Evidence: The Photography of Trauma* (Cambridge: The MIT Press, 2002).

22 The land of Descartes rather unavoidably has shown a receptivity to casting doubt on disaster-formation. Thus the bestselling *L'Effroyable mensonge*, ed. Guillaume Dasquié and Jean Guisnel (Paris: Découverte, 2002) put an undermining spin on the destruction of the World Trade Center. But dialectical turnovers being what they sometimes are, the so-called French have also put out the most compelling probes, setting up unavoidable question marks and in a certain unwearying way keeping the pain alive, on the agenda.

23 Jacques Derrida, *Demeure: Fiction and Testimony*, trans. Elizabeth Rottenberg (Stanford: Stanford University Press, 2000), 35. Compelled by a rhetoric of testing, Derrida also writes of the "test of the instant," "the linguistic test," and submits a number of hypotheses to the test in this work.
24 Ibid. 27.
25 Ibid. 27–28.
26 Ibid. 29.
27 Ibid. 30.

28 Maurice Blanchot, *The Step Not Beyond*, trans. Lycette Nelson (Albany: State University of New York Press, 1992), 76. See also Derrida's discussion of this passage in *Demeure*, 31.

CONTRIBUTORS

— Julie A. Cassiday, Ph.D., is a Professor of Russian at Williams College in Williamstown, Massachusetts. She is author of *The Enemy on Trial: Early Soviet Courts on Stage and Screen* (2000) and has published articles on theatre, theatricality, and cinema in Russian and Soviet culture. Her current projects include a monograph on gender and theatricality in early nineteenth-century Russia and research with Emily Johnson of the University of Oklahoma on the so-called cult of personality surrounding Vladimir Putin.

— Costas Douzinas is Professor of Law, Director of the Birkbeck Institute for the Humanities and Pro-Vice Chancellor at Birkbeck College, University of London. Educated in Athens, London and Strasbourg, Costas has taught at the Universities of Middlesex, Lancaster, Prague, Athens, Griffith and Nanjing. Costas is a founding member of the Critical Legal Conference; founding member of the Birkbeck Law School and the Birkbeck Institute for the Humanities; managing editor of *Law and Critique: The International Journal of Critical Legal Thought*; managing director of the publishing house *Birkbeck Law Press.*

— Peter Goodrich is Professor of Law and Director of the Program in Law and Humanities at Cardozo School of Law, New York. He teaches Law and Film, Visual Advocacy, and Forensic Rhetoric. He is currently working on a treatise on legal emblems and on a polemical account of the death of law in the videosphere. freregoodrich@gmail.com

— Piyel Haldar has been lecturing law since 1990. He was appointed lecturer in law at Birkbeck College, University of London in 1993. He received his doctorate in 1996. His research revolves around the historical evolution of legal institutions and legal subjectivity. These broad issues are given tighter focus with reference to a number of separate areas; namely, the historical studies of evidential practices, the establishment of common law jurisprudence in British India, and, more recently, the manner in which law distinguishes legal personality from animality. His work is informed by, and engages with, critical theory; aesthetics, cultural theory, post-structuralist philosophy.

— Martin Jay is Sidney Hellman Ehrman Professor of History at the University of California, Berkeley, where he teaches Modern European Intellectual History. Among his works are *The Dialectical Imagination* (1973 and 1996), *Marxism and Totality* (1984); *Adorno* (1984); *Permanent Exiles* (1985), *Fin-de-siècle Socialism* (1989); *Force Fields* (1993); *Downcast Eyes* (1993); *Cultural Semantics* (1998); *Refractions of Violence* (2004); *Songs of Experience* (2005); *The Virtues of Mendacity* (2010), and *Essays from the Edge* (2011).

— Richard Mohr has been Research Director of the Centre for Court Policy and Planning and Director of the Legal Intersections Research Centre at the University of Wollongong. Until 2011 he was managing editor of *Law Text Culture*. Dr Mohr maintains connections with the Law Faculty at Wollongong, the Institute for the Public Life of Arts and Ideas at McGill University and the Institute for Judicial Research in Bologna (IRSIG-CNR), where he publishes with Francesco Contini. He is principal of Social Research, Policy & Planning. rmohr@srpp.com.au

— Judy Radul's practice includes video installation, photography, sculpture, and performance. Her latest and most ambitious work is called *World Rehearsal Court*, a large-scale media installation. This work draws on Radul's research into the role of theatricality and new technologies in the court of law and questions the distinctions between experience, testimony, truth, and fiction that the law attempts to make distinct. Radul is currently Chair of the graduate program at the School for the Contemporary Arts, Simon Fraser University. She is represented by Catriona Jeffries Gallery Vancouver.

— Avital Ronell, Ph.D., University Professor and Co-Director for Trauma and Violence Transdisciplinary Studies at New York University. She is also Jacques Derrida Professor of Media and Philosophy, European Graduate School, Switzerland. Ronell is the author of several books, including *Fighting Theory* (2010), *The Test Drive* (2005) and the forthcoming *Loser Sons: Politics & Authority*. Her recent performances include nine lecture-installations at the Centre Pompidou in Paris, involving encounters with Werner Herzog, Judith Butler, Pierre Alferi, Laurence Rickels, and others. Ronell frequently teaches and provides media commentary in France and Germany.

— Eyal Sivan is a documentary filmmaker and Associate Professor in Media production and co-leads the MA program in Film Video and New Media at the School of Arts and Digital Industry at the University of East London. Known for his controversial films, Sivan directed more than ten feature length critically acclaimed and internationally awarded political documentaries. He also publishes and lectures on the Israeli-Palestinian conflict, documentary filmmaking and ethics, political crimes and representation, political use of memory, genocide and representation, etc. Sivan is the founder and chief editor of *South Cinema Notebooks.*

— Cornelia Vismann (1961–2010) is well known and deeply respected for her extraordinary work bridging constitutional law, philosophy and media. Cornelia Vismann was a Professor in Legal History, Public Law and Legal Theory at the Max-Planck-Institute for European Legal History in Frankfurt and then in 2007 became a Chair in Cultural Theory at the Bauhaus University in Weimar. Her last book was *Files: Law and Media Technology* (2008).

ARTWORKS

— René Magritte | p. 3

René Magritte
Not to Be Reproduced /
La Reproduction Interdit, (1937).

Magritte was a Belgian artist (1989–1967) affiliated with the Surrealists. This painting was commissioned by the patron of the Surrealists, poet Edward James and is considered to be a portrait of him. Throughout his oeuvre Magritte creates pictures that construct an expectation, which the image itself undermines or refutes. The veracity of the visual is thereby always in playful dispute in his work.

— Model Court | pp. 4/5 & 18/19

Model Court is as an ongoing body of work designed and produced by Sidsel Meineche Hansen, Lawrence Abu Hamdan, Oliver Rees and Lorenzo Pezzani. The project builds upon regular meetings with an international network of people (lawyers, judges, typists, courtroom artists) who inhabit the space of the courtroom as well as various filmmakers, architects and theorists whose work deals with the spatial, aesthetic and geopolitical aspects of legal protocols. The material produced by these meetings becomes exhibitions, lectures, performances and workshops. The first image included in this book is from an installation at the Center for Contemporary Art Glasgow (2009). It shows a to-scale sketch of the court, reminiscent of courtroom drawings. In many cases the drawing is the only public document available during the trial, before the verdict is published. In the U.K., cameras are not permitted in court while the jury is present, and the court artist is only permitted to take notes. As a technology, the drawing stands in contradistinction to the increasing resolution of digital representation devices.

The *Transcription and Subtitling* image is a document of a workshop (2010) in which Model Court screened Otto Preminger's *Anatomy of a Murder* (1959). Three different perspectives were suggested for the transcription of the film to the workshop participants: One transcription was to attend to the dialogue in the filmclip; another was to note the demeanor of the witness and the third was to describe the internal dialogues of both witness and prosecutor. Through these practical exercises and others, the group attends to the performative qualities of the trial and its relations to the cinematic.

— Les Levine | pp. 6–9

Much of Les Levine's prolific oeuvre concerns the effects and functions of media and information. As well as being an early practitioner of video art, Levine produced sculptures, performances and – as reproduced in this volume – photographs and billboards. The photo series *Using the Camera as a Club* (1979) includes image diptychs and series in which the accompanying text calls attention to specific aspects of the image, and thus alters the hierarchy of meaning in the picture. Since 1976, Levine has exhibited major media campaigns throughout North America, Europe and Australia. These often take the form of billboards, enlarged from his gouache paintings. The images have a hand drawn quality and the text is straightforward, yet open to multiple readings, and their acid humor and occasionally disarming humanism destabilize the language of mass advertising. Rather than to advertise a product, these billboards magnetize social and political anxieties. The *Law Order* billboard included here was one of 100 billboards in a 1992 media campaign in Cincinnati.

— Thomas Demand | pp. 10–13

On first view Thomas Demand's large photographs appear to be images of somewhat defeatured locations and scenes. On closer inspection they reveal themselves to be socially and historically relevant locations elaborately modeled in paper. The images reproduced here, *Embassy VI and Embassy VIIa* (2007), were shown under the exhibition title *Yellowcake.* Yellowcake denotes a form of uranium that may be enriched to make nuclear weapons. The allegation made by USA that proof existed of a contract for hundreds of tons of yellowcake to be sold by Niger to the Iraqi authorities helped validate the invasion of Iraq. However, as the story unraveled, it became clear that the evidence that had originated with the SISMI military intelligence agency of Italy was obvious a forgery. Thomas Demand accessed the apartment that serves as the Niger embassy in Rome, and through observation he reconstructed the site in his studio in order to create these images. This imagined epicenter of what became a deadly and politically fraught reality is depicted as a bland chaos of official papers. There is a notable absence of evidence of the cause of this upheaval; are we looking at everyday reality, the aftermath of a robbery, or a clean up operation?

— Rana Hamadeh | pp. 14–17

The artist Rana Hamadeh has an ongoing discursive research project that comprises a number of conversations, lecture-performances, installations, fictive narratives, and the like. The main focus of these associative forms is a damaged magazine. She writes:

> Among the objects I brought with me from Beirut when I first arrived in the Netherlands is an issue of an international magazine on graphic art called GRAPHIS (GRAPHIS 127, 1966, published in Zurich). The magazine, penetrated in its lower centre by a bullet during the Lebanese civil war, was for a long time part of my normal everyday possessions. (This is what my lectures begin with. A blown up, beamed image of a magazine with a hole in its lower centre projected on the wall. The actual object is never shown.) In its new European context, the magazine seems to have radically transformed from a "sheer" object into an explicit war document, something that can no longer escape or defy the historical event that marked it. The magazine with the bullet hole has since become an image determined by its loss.

This expansive work has included hundreds of handwritten reports, using various modes of assessment, such as damage to the text, damage to the paper and damage to the color. All of this to analyze this single object by which Hamadeh plays out a relentless scrutiny of the relation of object, evidence and narrative.

— The Atlas Group | pp. 20–23

The Atlas Group is a project of Walid Raad established in 1999 to research and document the contemporary history of Lebanon. As part of a suite of works the video *Hostage: The Bachar Tapes (#17 and 31),* from which the images here are captured, is catalogued in the Atlas Group Archive as "Files Type A" a category of files "that contain documents that we produced and that we attribute to named imaginary individuals or organizations." These files include videotapes attributed to Souheil Bachar "... a Lebanese national who was kidnapped in Beirut in 1983 and was held hostage for ten years. After his release, Bachar collaborated with The Atlas Group to produce fifty-three videotapes about his captivity. Souheil Bachar was the only Arab hostage to have been held captive with the American men who were kidnapped and detained in Lebanon in the 1980s."[1]

Many of the sequences we see in *Hostage* are first person testimonies given to the camera, in makeshift locations, by "Souheil Bachar." Here he describes his time in the same cell as Terry Anderson, Thomas Sutherland, Benjamin Weir, Martin Jenco and David Jacobsen – five Americans taken hostage in the 1980s in Lebanon. He reviews the push-pull of fear and desire and the racial projections that determined the relations between him and the other hostages. The plausibility of the document leaves viewers wondering why they had never heard of this sixth hostage – was it because he was just a low-level employee at the Kuwaiti Embassy in Beirut? While Bachar tells his story, a female voice offers an English translation. The effect of this voice speaking over his is the creation of another device of plausibility, which simultaneously acts as a form of erasure.

— Judy Radul | pp. 24–26 & 251

Judy Radul's multimedia installation *World Rehearsal Court* (2009), is a seven channel video installation, with a running time of four hours. The installation includes five servo-controlled cameras, a live camera position playback system, video monitors, dolly, track, plexiglass, together with various found and built objects. *World Rehearsal Court* is the result of research into new technological courts of law, such as the International Criminal Court in the Hague. In one gallery, the seven channel video presents courtroom scenes based on transcripts of International Criminal Tribunals. In the other galleries, through the use of computer choreographed live cameras, Radul stages an encounter between the real time perception of the viewer, and the machine vision of the cameras, which display their feed on several monitors and sometimes catch the viewer in their field of view. The space contains photographs and all sorts of objects, which may be taken as a kind of "evidence." *World Rehearsal Court* explores the tensions between experience, testimony, truth, and fiction – categories that the court attempts to make distinct.

— Ana Torfs | pp. 252–255

Ana Torfs' installation *Anatomy* (2006), originated with her research into a trial held in 1919, the "Case of the Murder of Dr. Karl Liebknecht and Rosa Luxemburg before the Military Field Tribunal of the Cavalry Guard Rifle Division in the Main Courtroom at the Berlin Criminal Court." The installation includes black and white slides projected in a thirty-four minute loop and color video on two monitors in a ninety minute loop. The text is spoken in German and an English interpretation is available via wireless headphones. Torfs selected statements from the trial to compose "A Tragedy in Two Acts" – the literary script for *Anatomy*.

The artist has cut up the case files into short scenes so that a "story" emerges, in which details from the same event are told from different angles, highlighting the relative nature of the narrative: the last hour of the lives of Liebknecht and Luxemburg, founders of the Communist Party of Germany. On video, twenty-five young actors act out these testimonies. Another group of seventeen actors are depicted in the black and white slide photographs. The scene is set in the demonstration room of the Anatomical Theatre in Berlin whose architecture evokes an atmosphere somewhere between a theatrical stage, a Greek amphitheatre and a court of law. In the installation, slide projections provide a more abstract visual counterpoint to the video images. Appropriately, Torfs process of dissection and analysis of text and image results in a complexity of perspectives rather than a singular verdict.

— Renzo Martens | pp. 256/257

Renzo Martens, *Episode III: 'Enjoy Poverty'*, (2009) is a ninety minute film shot by Martens as he travels from Kinshasa to the interior of DR Congo. Refusing to endorse the conventional humanitarian stance and commenting on current conditions such as the percentage of the Congolese economy accounted for by foreign aid, and the vested interests of journalists and aid workers, Martens exhorts the Congolese to accept the dialectics of their economy and understand their poverty as a kind of resource. Martens offers the harsh assessment that material conditions are unlikely to change anytime soon and films himself, journalists, aid workers, plantation owners, and Congolese people as they respond to his questions and provocations.

This provocative logic underpins his heroic yet self-disassembling enterprise to float a neon sign with the message "Enjoy Poverty (please)" down the Congo river. In the scene from which the images in this book were taken, Martens – in previous scenes having made the viewer aware of what foreign journalists are paid for local images – organizes local photographers. These photographers usually get a pittance for wedding photos and Marten's instructs them to take conventionally sensational photographs of the misery around them so they can have some possibility to profit from it. When they seek press passes and further accreditation for access to projects run by Doctors Without Borders and the like, they are dismissed using the circular logic, which insists that they aren't "real" photographers.

— Agency | pp. 258/259

Agency is the generic name of a Brussels-based agency established in 1992 by Kobe Matthys. Matthys describes his own project as follows:

> Agency constitutes a growing list of things that resist the split between culture and nature. These things are mostly derived from juridical processes, lawsuits, cases, controversies, affairs and so forth involving intellectual properties (copyrights, patents, trademarks, etc.). The concept of intellectual property relies upon the assumption of the division between culture and nature and consequently between expressions and ideas, creations and facts, subjects and objects, humans and non-humans, originality and tradition, individuals and collectives, mind and body, etc. Each thing on the list invokes the moment of hesitation in terms of those divisions. Agency calls things forth from its list via varying assemblies inside exhibitions, performances, publications, other forms. Each assembly speculates topologically on a different question of the performative consequences of the apparatus of intellectual property for the ecology of art practices, which pay attention to other types of agencies.[2]

For work included in this volume, the question concerns the legal status of a performance versus a recording. As the accompanying text documents, the court finds it impossible to consider Victor DeCosta's live performance durable or material enough to warrant copyright, but rather designates it a mere characterization, not protected by the legal frameworks granted a recording.

— Aernout Mik | pp. 260–263

Aernout Mik's three-screen video installation, *Shifting Sitting* (2011) creates a setting which is neither a portrait of the Italian Prime Minister, Silvio Berlusconi, nor a restaging of the accusations leveled against him by the Italian people. Mik's video installation does not refer to any specific trial. Rather, it renders visible the shifts that occur between political structures (as democratic formations and agents of power) and legal structures. It shows how these two levels are constantly intertwining; passing from spontaneous modes of popular organization to more fixed, ritualized forms.

Shifting Sitting also reflects on the various faces of democracy in Europe. It was filmed in Rome's EUR quarter (Esposizione Universale di Roma), which was built by order of Mussolini in the late 1930s. The installation shows five men being questioned in a court of law and the scenes depict different types of gatherings, contrasting rigid with more fluid structures of power.

— Stan Douglas | pp. 264/267

In Stan Douglas' recent body of work *Midcentury Studio* (2010), from which the images in this volume are selected, the artist has assumed the role of a fictional, anonymous photographer to create a series of images hypothetically produced between 1945–1951. For the project Douglas constructed a "midcentury studio" using authentic equipment and actors to produce carefully staged, black-and-white photographs that emulate the period's fascination with crime-scene reportage, exotic artifacts, magicians, fashion, dance, gambling, and technology. Douglas's writes, "*Midcentury Studio* chronicles the career of a photographer who was introduced to his craft during the war and tried to make it into a business in the postwar period. It is also a fragmentary portrait of a North American city being normalized after a war."[3] *Midcentury Studio* concocts images that in addition to their pictorial content depict a visual fascination in and of itself. The look, or style, of the image registers emotionally and reflects a way of seeing surprisingly conditioned by its era-specific "lens." Douglas' work also reminds us that this specificity can be painstakingly reconstituted and introduced into the present context.

— Harun Farocki | pp. 268–271

Harun Farocki's *I Thought I Was Seeing Convicts* (2000) is both a single channel projection and a two screen installation. The single channel version is twenty-three minutes long and consists of surveillance footage from the maximum-security prison in Corcoran, California, as well as computer-generated graphic tracking of the movements of shoppers in the aisles of a supermarket. The prison surveillance shows the prisoners in a concrete yard, the camera suddenly zooms in on a fight. Those not involved lay on the ground in anticipation of rubber bullets, followed by real bullets if the fight doesn't stop. The camera and the gun shoot side by side. The image is silent. It takes nine minutes for the convict, who has been shot and killed, to be taken away on a stretcher.

The confluence of visual technologies and their role in social control via shopping, sports, and the military have been material for several of Farocki's experimental documentaries and installations.

Additional credits:
Scriptwriter: Harun Farocki. Researcher, Cinematographer: Cathy Lee Crane. Editor: Max Reimann. Sound: Luis Van Rook. Production: Harun Farocki Filmproduktion, Berlin, Generali Foundation, Wien. With support from ZDF/3sat, Mainz – Inge Classen, Movimento, Paris – Christian Baute

— Dan Graham | pp. 272/273

Dan Graham's *Time Delay Room* (1974) is one of several installations using closed-circuit cameras and video monitors that the artist produced in the 1970s. In his characteristically denotative style, Graham describes the work and its effects this way:

> Two rooms of equal size, connected by an opening at one side, under surveillance by two video cameras positioned at the connecting point between the two rooms. The front inside wall of each room features two video screens – within the scope of the surveillance cameras. The monitor which the visitor coming out of the other room spies first shows the live behavior of the people in the respective other room. In both rooms the second screen shows an image of the behavior of the viewers in the respectively other room – but with an eight second delay. The time-lag of eight seconds is the outer limit of the neurophysiological short-term memory that forms an immediate part of our present perception and affects this "from within." If you see your behavior eight seconds ago presented on a video monitor "from outside" you will probably therefore not recognize the distance in time but tend to identify your current perception and current behavior with the state eight seconds earlier. Since this leads to inconsistent impressions which you then respond to, you get caught up in a feedback loop. You feel trapped in a state of observation, in which your self-observation is subject to some outside visible control. In this manner, you as the viewer experience yourself as part of a social group of observed observers (instead of, as in the traditional view of art, standing arrested in individual contemplation before an auratic object).[4]

— John Baldessari | p.274

John Baldessari is well known for his vast and diverse body of work. Many of his canvases and prints feature colored shapes, which negate an aspect of the image. Related image treatments isolating aspects of physiognomy such as noses and ears have long been of interest to the artist. The work reproduced in this volume, *Profile with Ear and Nose* (2006), finds a precursor in the 1965 painting *God Nose*, which shows a disembodied nose floating in a blue sky. The face is a constitutive focus for human perception, and the representation of the face and its features emphasizes the immediacy of the experience of physiology. One is reminded of the role of the face in constituting identity, and thereby guilt. The choice of ears and noses, over the more often reproduced eyes and lips, heightens awareness of the awkward aesthetic of the face, crowded as it is with sensory organs. The use of charged color, and negative space, introduces abstract generality – a puddle at the very point of individuation – yet the dissonance between the negated features and the present features may heighten rather than diminish our awareness of both.

---

1 Walid Raad, "About the Bachar File," *The Atlas Group Archive*. Last accessed August 23, 2011; http://www.theatlasgroup.org/data/TypeA.html

2 In correspondence with the artist, August 2011.

3 Stan Douglas, "Midcentury Studio," in *Stan Douglas Midcentury Studio*, ed. Tommy Simoens, (Antwerp: Ludion, 2011), 6.

4 Dan Graham quoted in Gregor Stemmrich "Dan Graham," in *CTRL[SPACE]. Rhetorics of Surveillance from Bentham to Big Brother*, eds. Thomas Y. Levin, Ursula Frohne, Peter Weibel (Cambridge, MA: The MIT Press, 2002), 68.

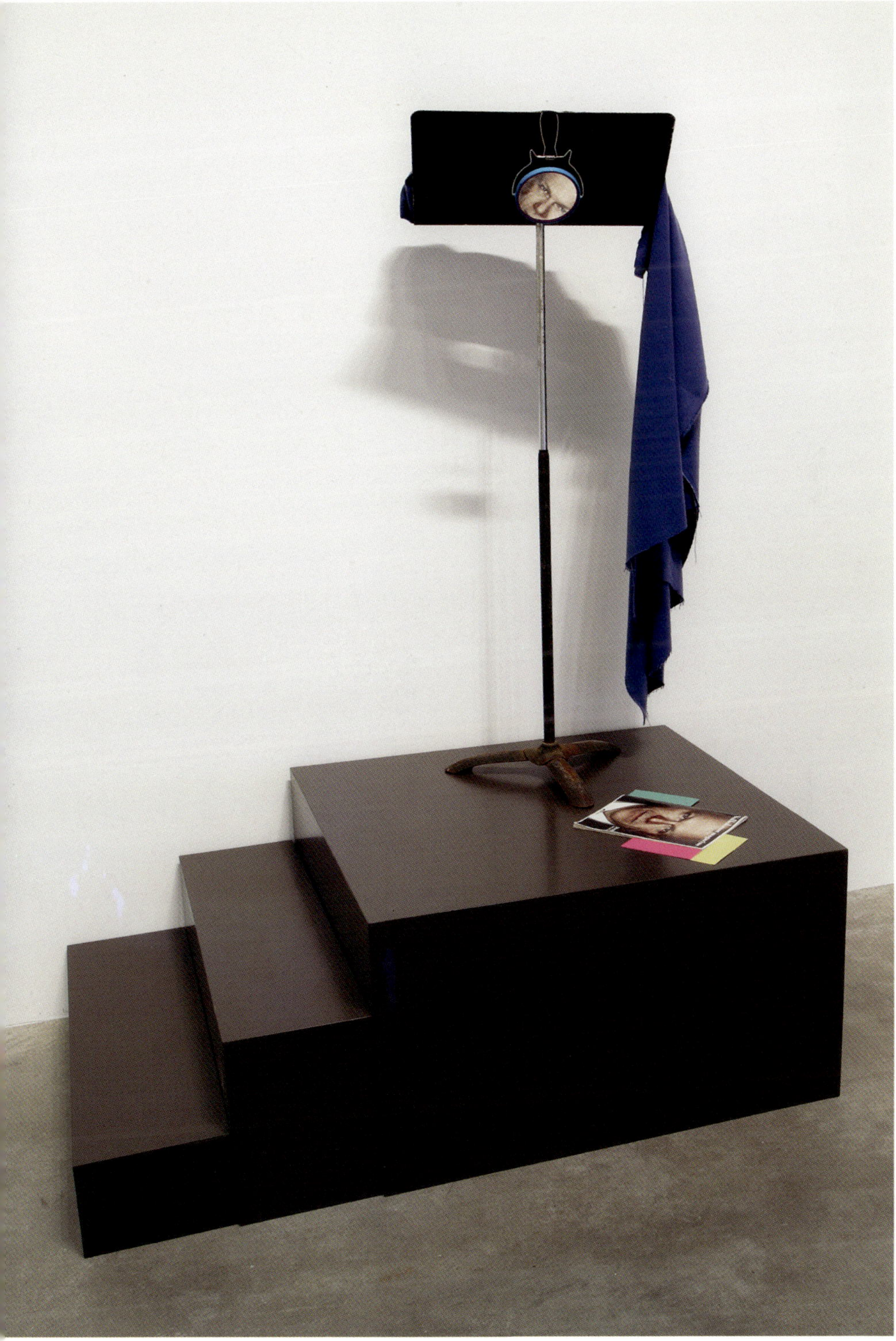

Judy Radul, *World Rehearsal Court* (2009). Multimedia installation, detail.
Courtesy the artist, Morris and Helen Belkin Art Gallery and Catriona Jeffries Gallery. [See p.247]

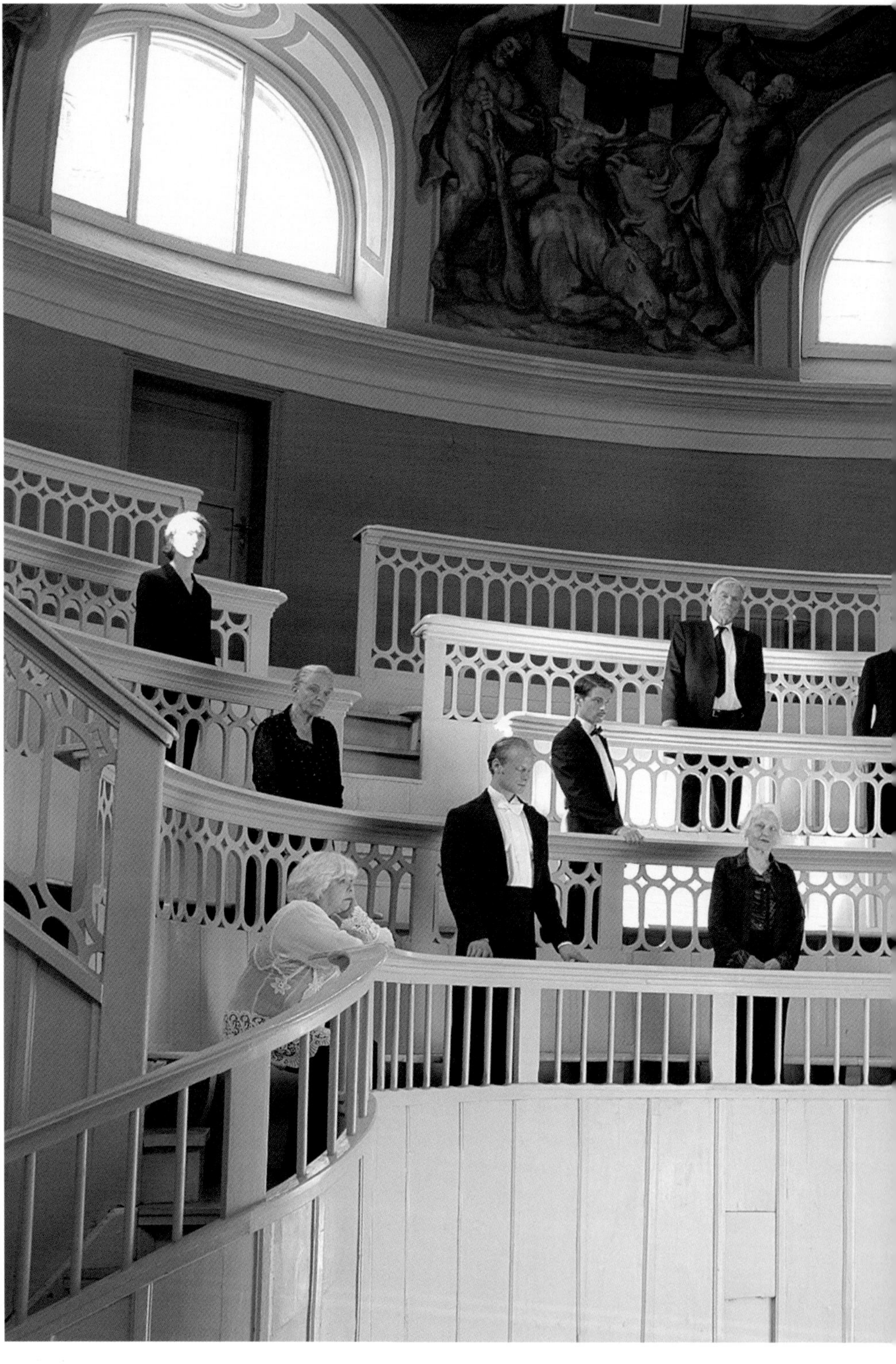

Ana Torfs, slide photograph, detail from *Anatomy* (2006). Installation.

[See p.247]

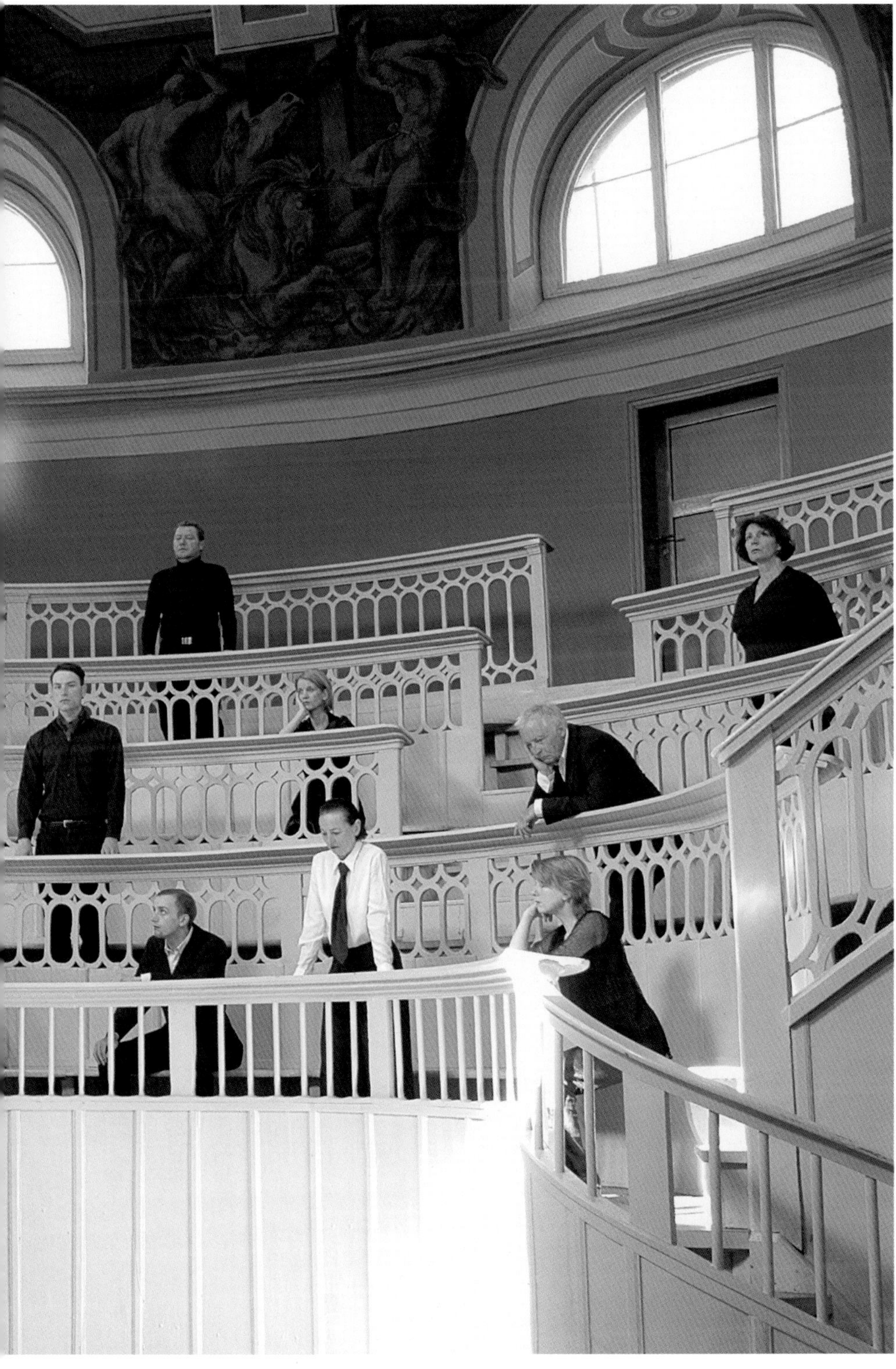

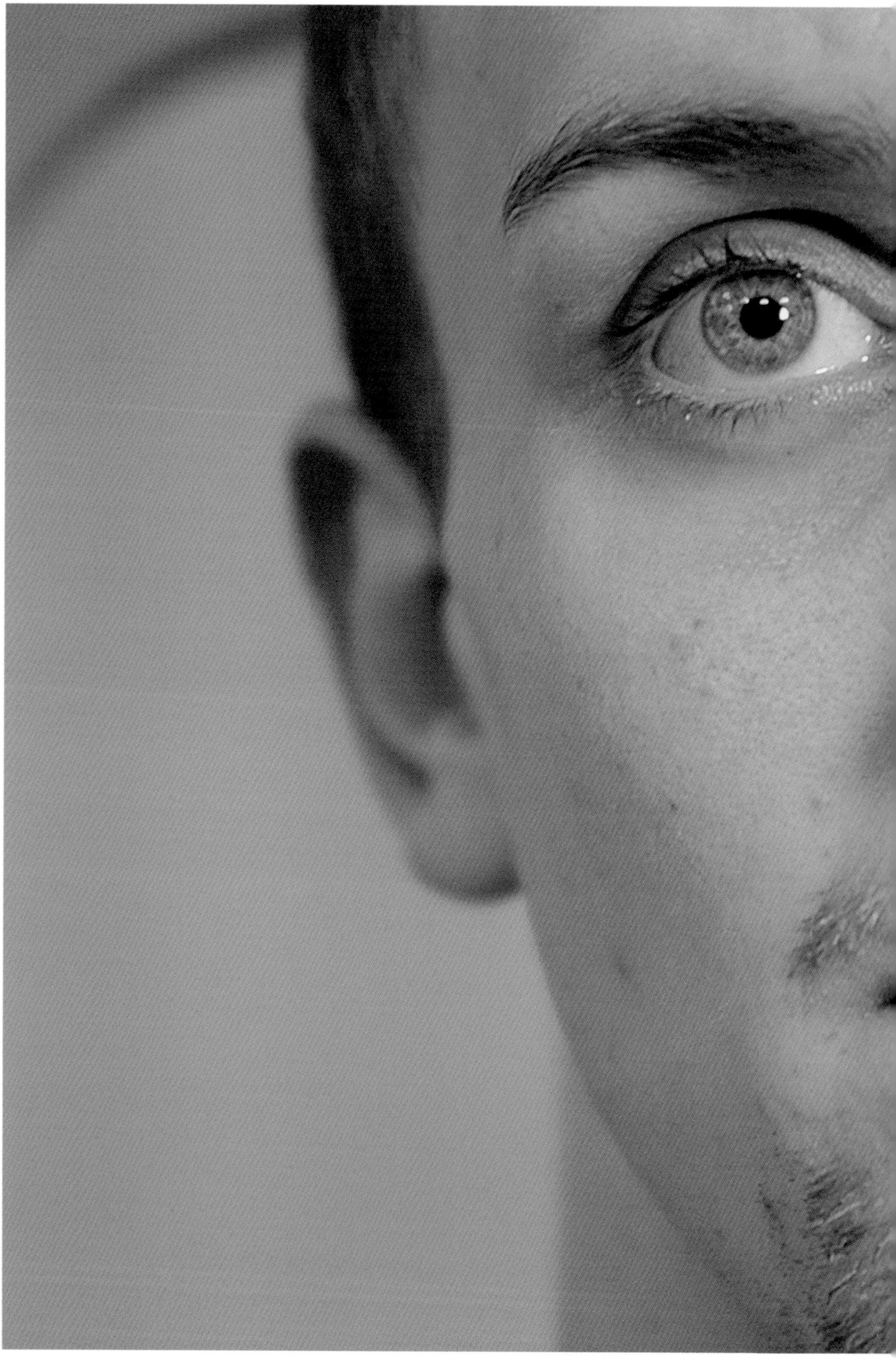

Ana Torfs, slide photograph, detail from *Anatomy* (2006). Installation.

[See p.247]

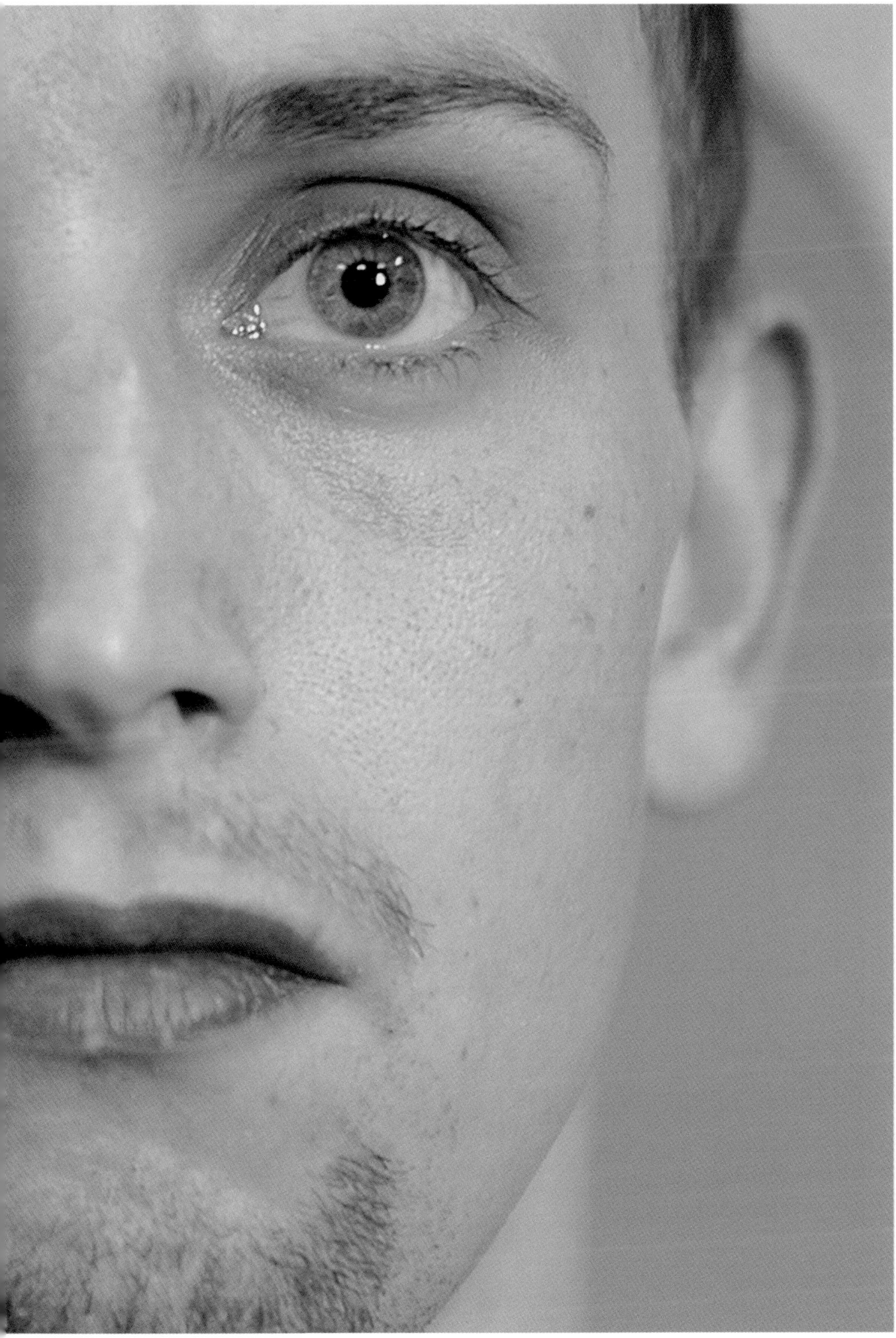

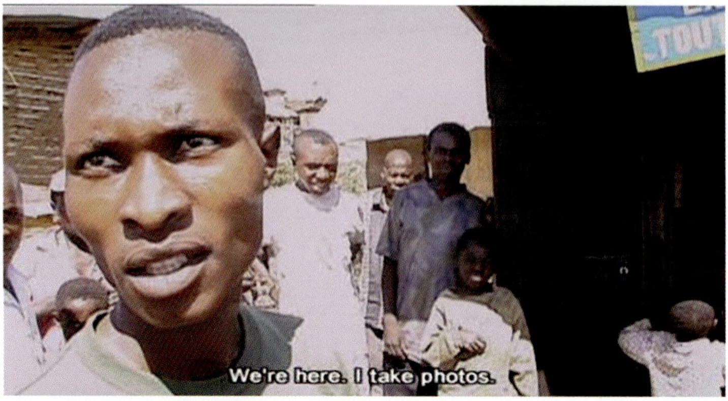
We're here. I take photos.

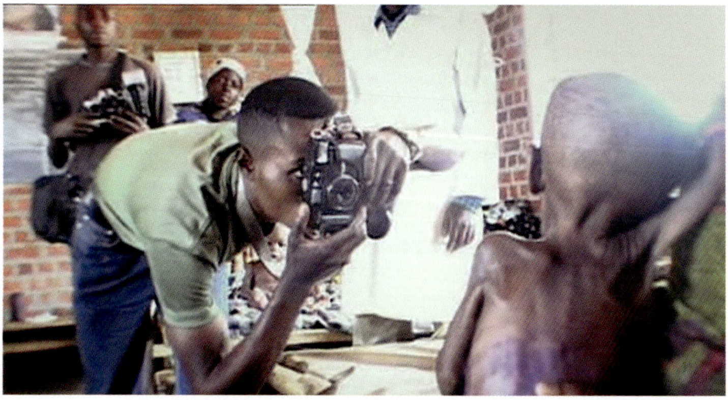

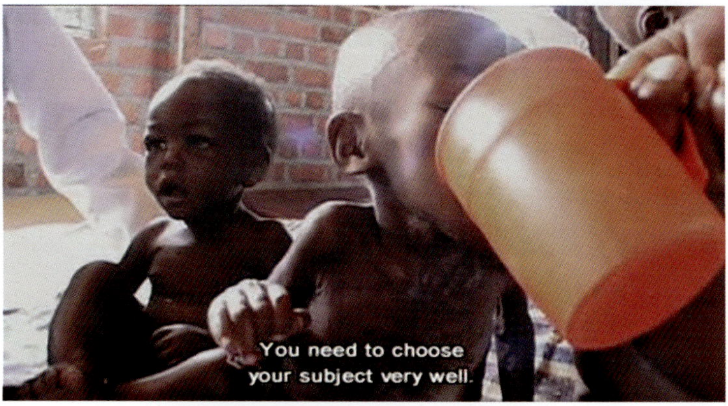
You need to choose
your subject very well.

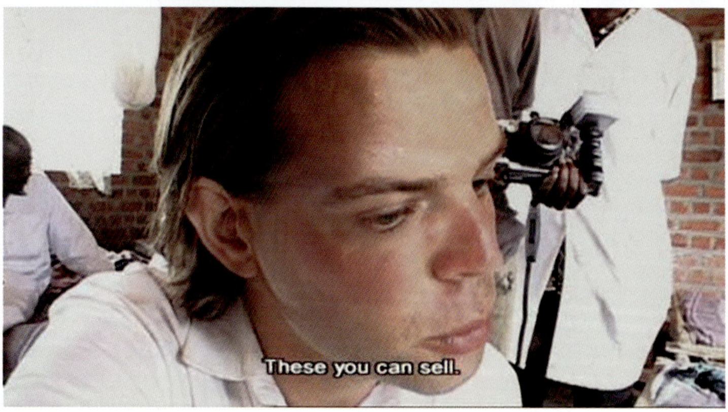
These you can sell.

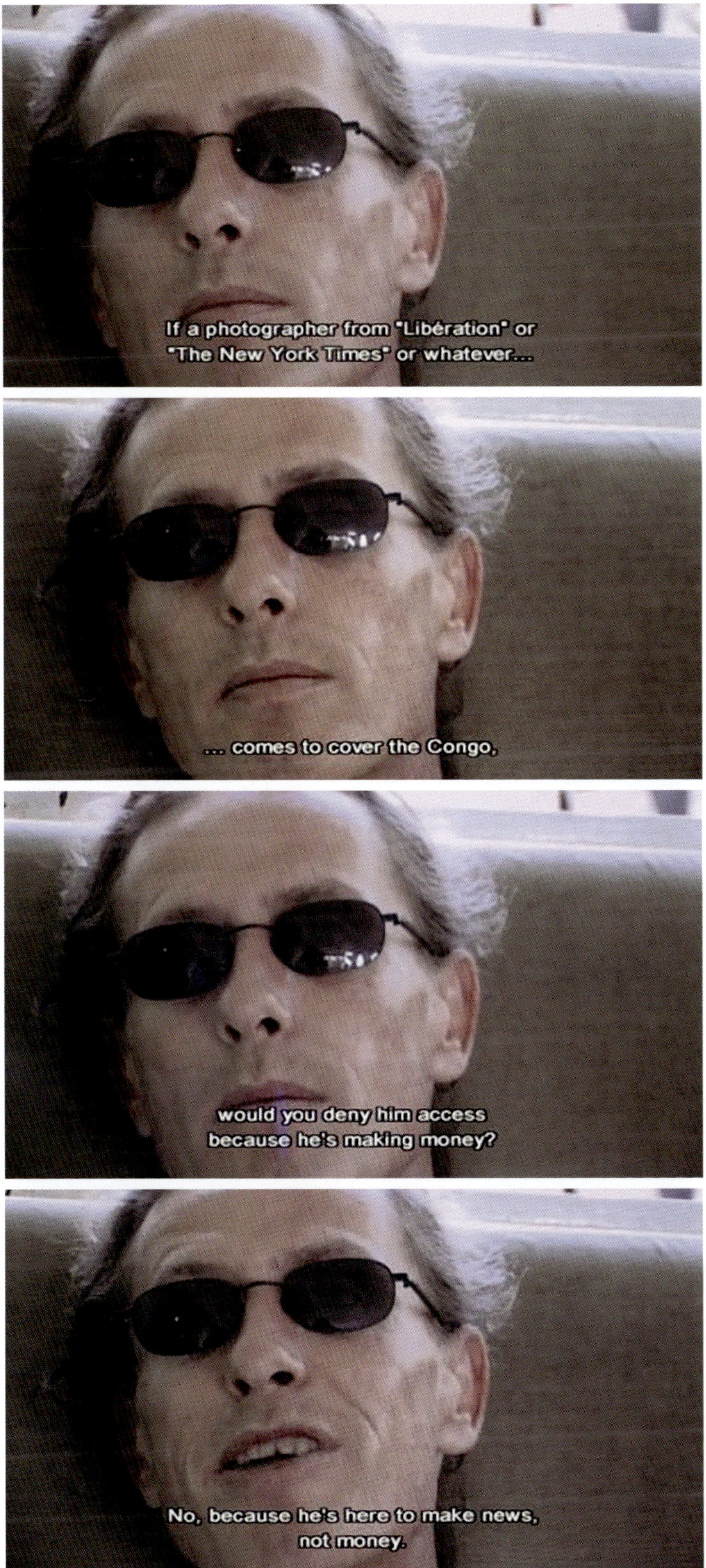

Renzo Martens, *Episode III: 'Enjoy Poverty'* (2009).
Video, 90 min, stills.
Courtesy the artist.

[See p.248]

Thing 000815 (*Have Gun - Will Travel*)

Since 1947 Victor DeCosta, a Rhode Island mechanic, participated in rodeos, horse shows, horse auctions, and parades. He had learned horse riding during the depression of the 1930s, when he worked as a range hand on a Texas ranch. For the shows, he dressed in a black shirt, pants, and a flat-crowned hat with a St. Mary's medal affixed to it. He named himself Paladin, after an onlooker of Italian descent had hurled "Paladino". One day when he had put on his costume in preparation for a horse show someone said "Have Gun Will Travel", a cry immediately picked up by the children present. DeCosta used a chess knight as his symbol, along with the words: "Have Gun, Will Travel, Wire Paladin, N. Court St., Cranston, R.I." He hand-printed this text with separate rubber stamps on his business card. He also placed a silver copy of the chess piece on his holster and strapped an antique derringer under his arm. So accoutered, he would appear at parades, the openings and finales of rodeos, auctions, horse shows, and the pony ring he once operated. From time to time at rodeos he would stage a western gunfight, featuring his quick draw and the timely use of his hidden derringer. He would also pass out photographs of himself and his cards at hospitals, drug stores, barbershops, sports shops and diners.

Between 1957 and 1966 Columbia Broadcasting System (CBS) produced a television series called *Have Gun - Will Travel* consisting of 226 episodes spread over three seasons. The series' main character, Paladin, was a professional gunfighter and a West Point graduate who, after the Civil War, settled in San Francisco's Hotel Carlton. He solicited his services by distributing his business card that read: "Have Gun, Will Travel... Wire Paladin, San Francisco" On the card was a picture of the horse-headed white knight chess piece. While on the job, Paladin would dress in black boots, pants, shirt and hat. The series was very successful. It was aired for eight years in it's initial run and licensed in various countries.

In 1957, Victor DeCosta saw the first CBS television production of *Have Gun - Will Travel*. Following he initiated an action at the District of Rhode Island for misappropriation of his Paladin live performance. The writers and network executives responsible for the series stated that the similarity to DeCosta's performance was pure coincidence. The United States District Court for the District of Rhode Island, Judge Edward William Day, J., entered a judgment in favor of Victor DeCosta and awarded him $150,000. CBS filed an appeal. On May 11, 1967 the court case *Columbia Broadcasting System v. DeCosta*, took place at the United States Court of Appeals First Circuit. The Court of Appeals, Circuit Judge Coffin, reversed the decision:

> "The story of this case - more bizarre than most television serial installments - is one of coincidence run riot. [...] [T]here comes a point where what is created is so slight a thing as not to warrant protection by any law. All human beings - and a good part of the animal kingdom - create characters every day of their lives. [...] Here, [DeCosta]'s performance consisted of two components: Appearing in public and passing out cards and photographs. No other action was involved, except an occasional quick draw demonstration at a rodeo. So far as his costume and menacing appearance were concerned, it was fully conveyed on the cards bearing his photograph - which also contained the chess piece, the slogan, and the name Paladin. The cards were passed out in great quantities over the years to all who would have them. So far as any action accompanying his personal appearance is concerned, whether it be simply riding a horse, or staging a quick-draw gun fight, these are hallowed shelf items in the tradition of the early West. In any event, the theme and plots of [CBS]' television series could not be said to have derived from anything created by [DeCosta] which was not revealed by his cards. The cards were unquestionably writings within the meaning of the copyright clause, and arguably were copyrightable under the statute. [...] The consequence is that the [DeCosta]'s character-creation was published [...] Not having copyrighted the cards, [DeCosta] cannot preclude others from copying them. [...]"

The court reversed the first decision and concluded that performances need to be fixed by notation or recording in order to get protection.

[See p.248]

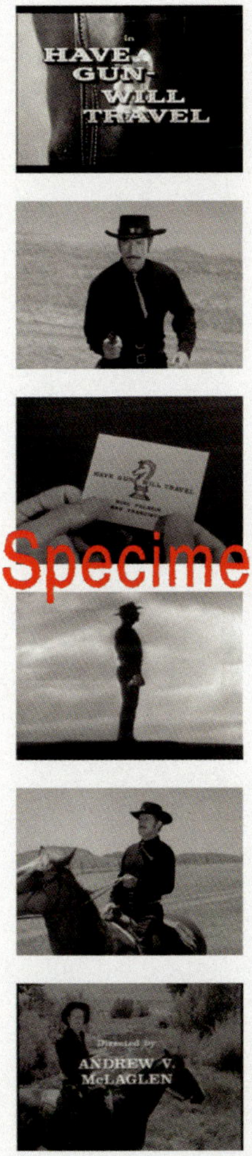

Thing 000815 (*Have Gun - Will Travel*)

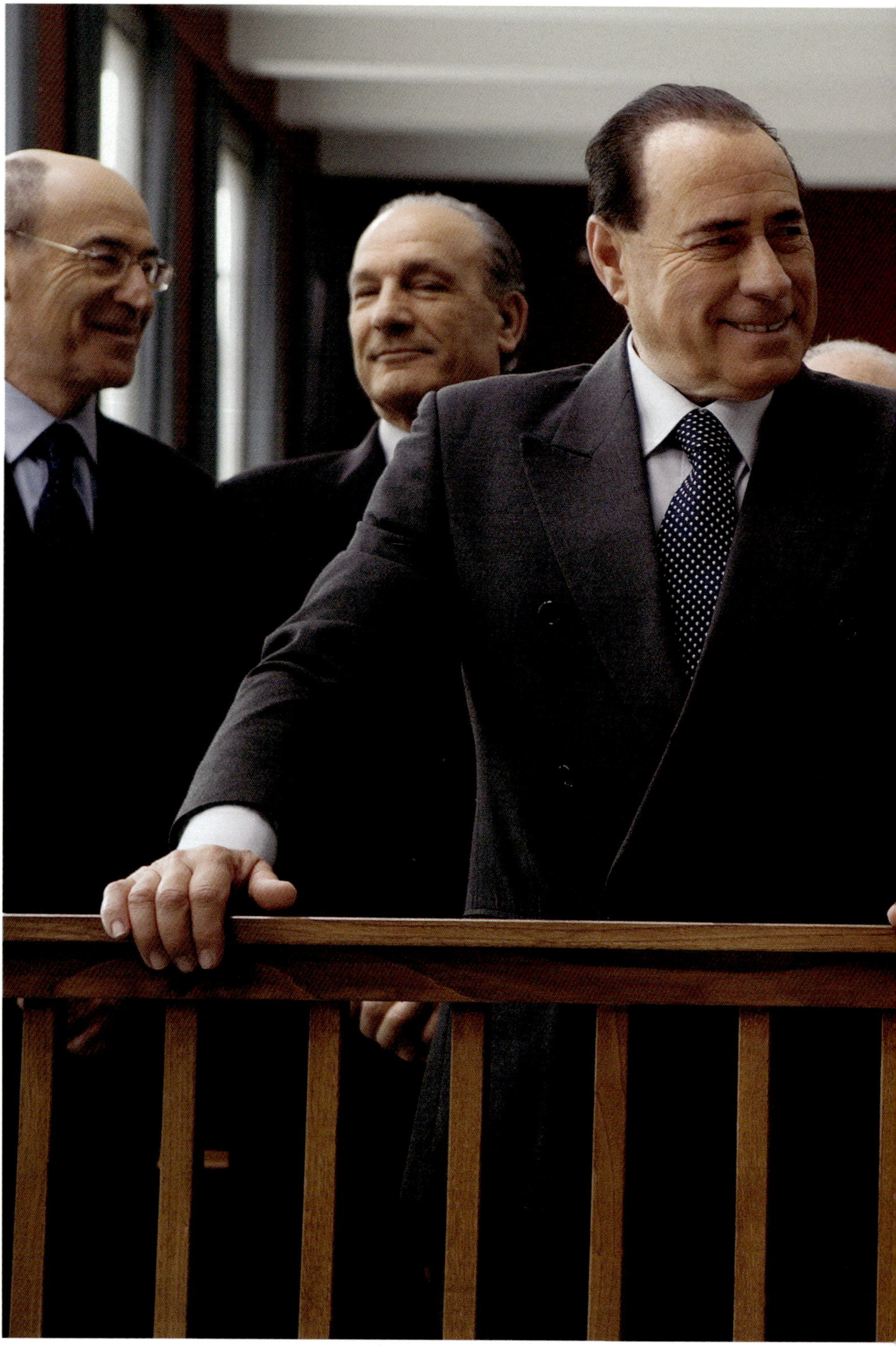

Aernout Mik, Production Still: *Shifting Sitting II* (2011). Digital video on harddisk / three channel back screen projection. Courtesy: carlier | gebauer. Photographer: Florian Braun.

[See p.249]

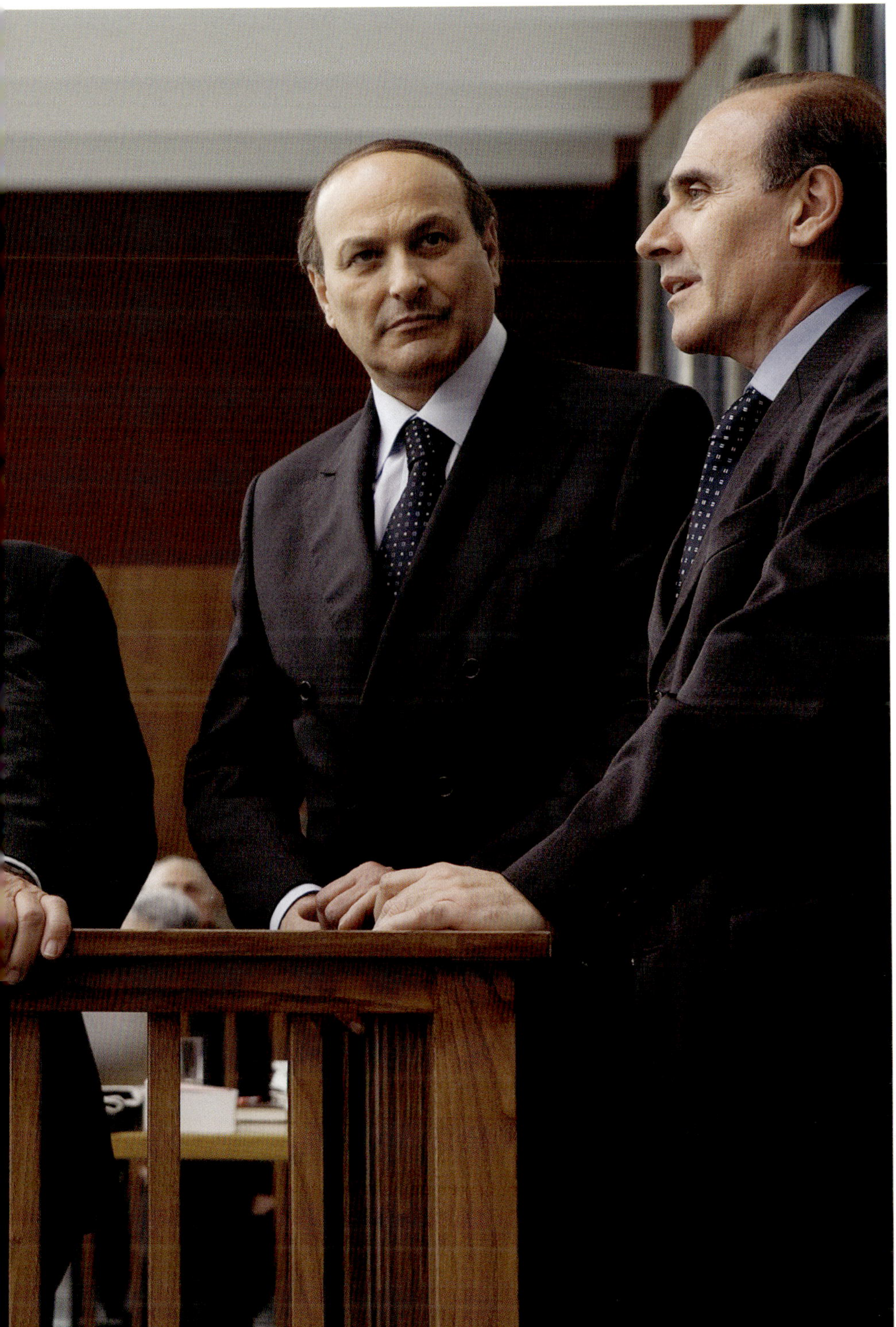

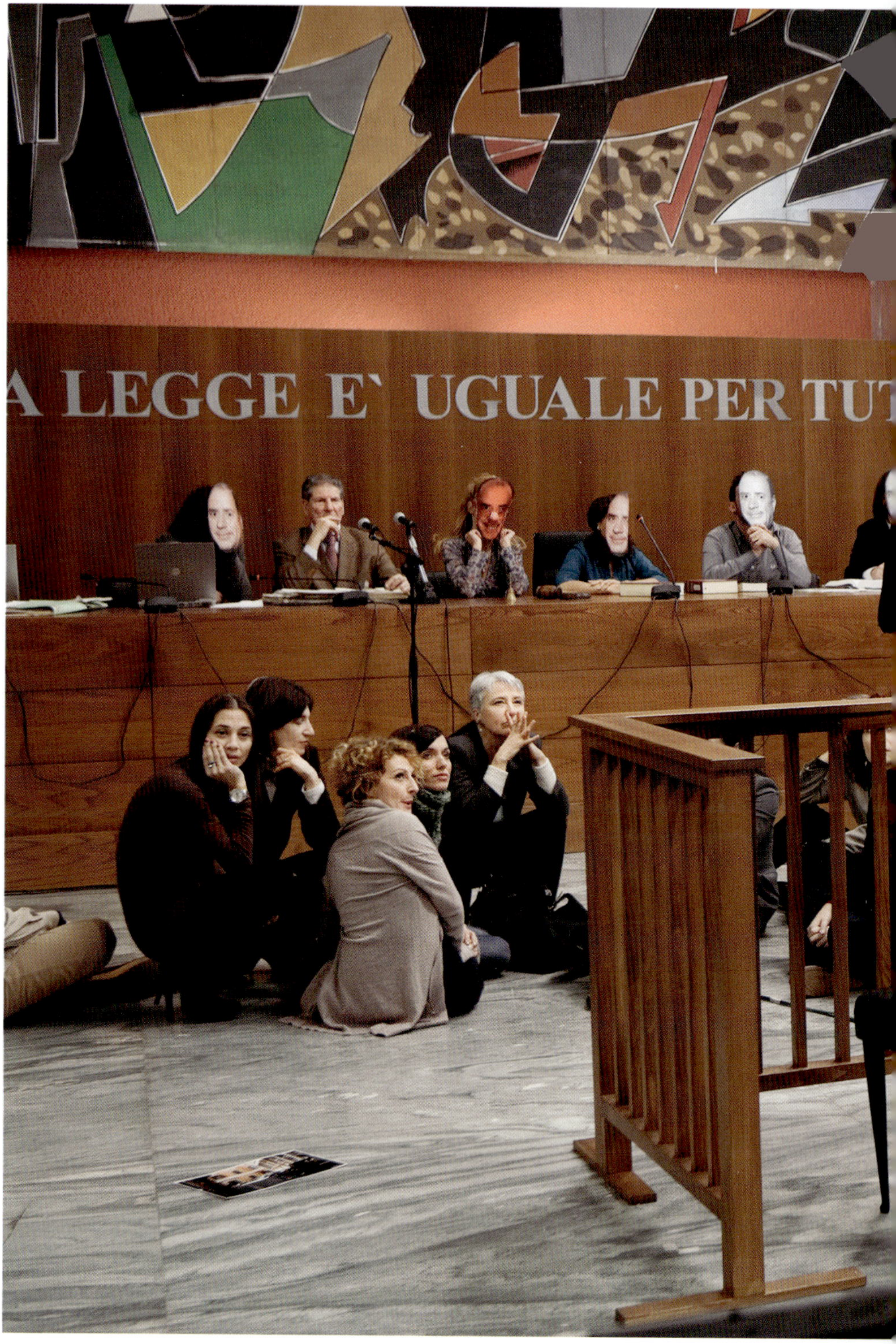

Aernout Mik, Production Still: *Shifting Sitting II* (2011). Digital video on harddisk / three channel back screen projection. Courtesy: carlier | gebauer. Photographer: Florian Braun. [See p.249]

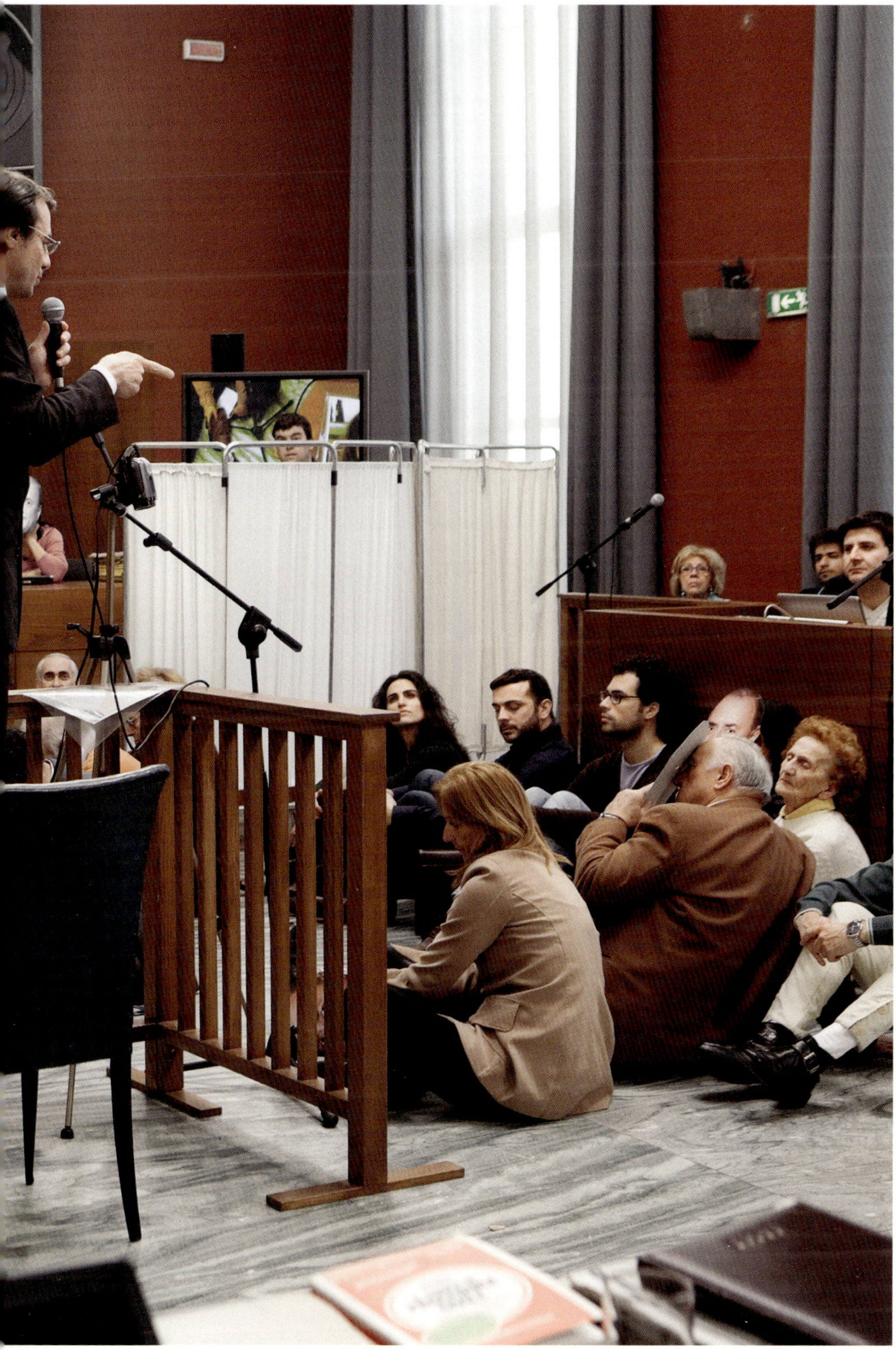

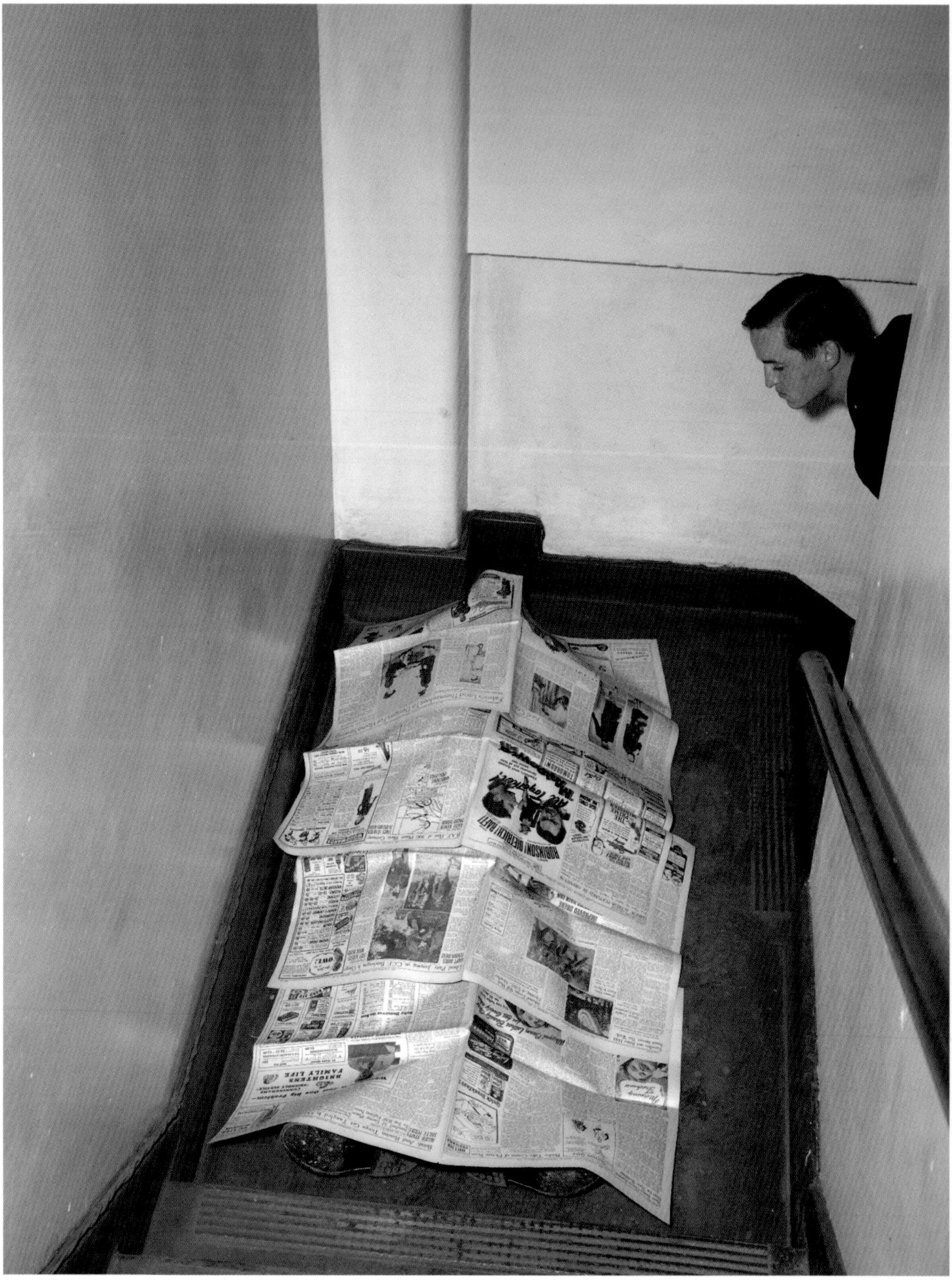

Stan Douglas, *Incident, 1949*, (2010).
Courtesy the artist and David Zwirner.

[See p.249]

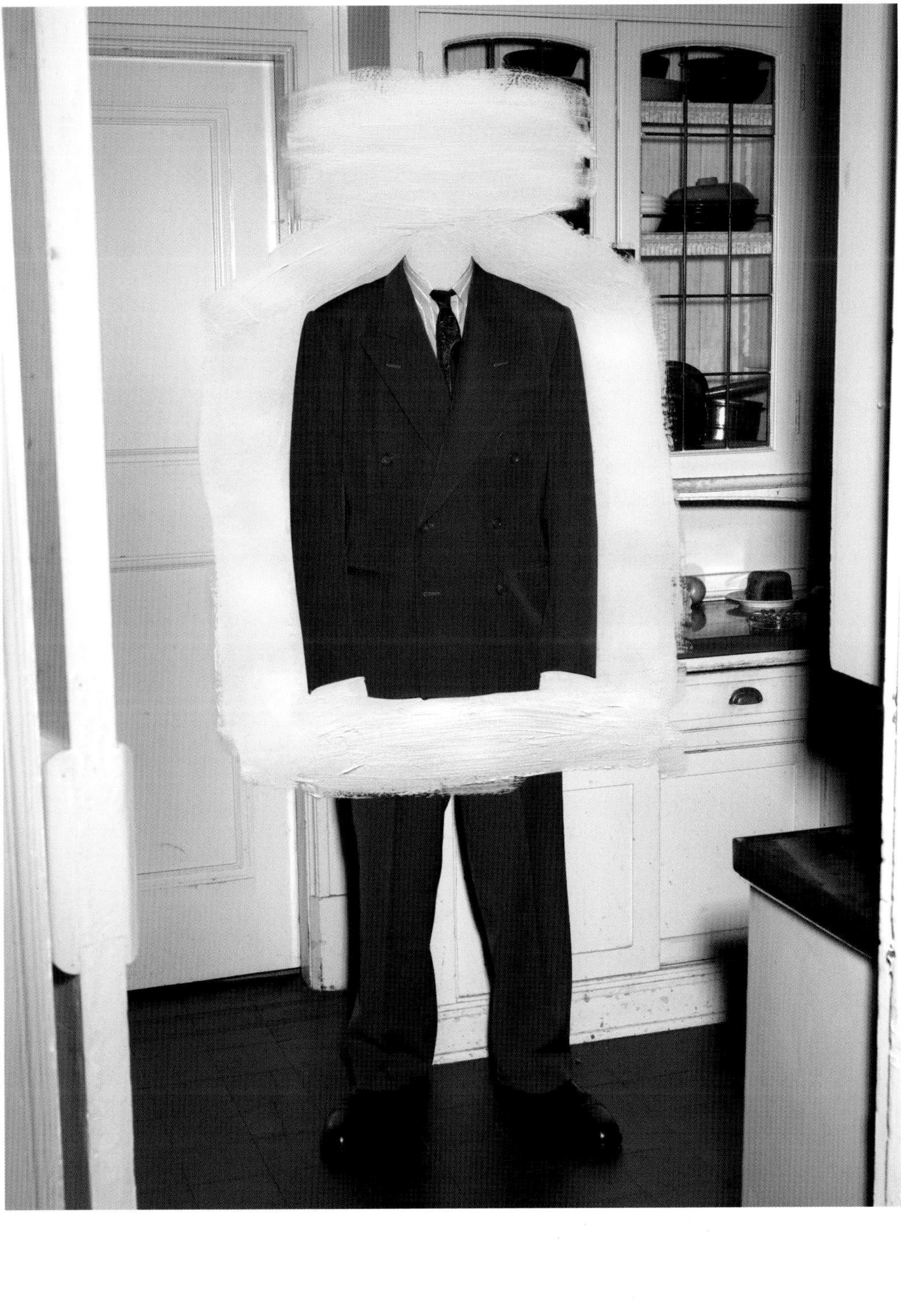

Stan Douglas, *Demobilization Suit, 1945*, (2010).
Courtesy the artist and David Zwirner.

[See p.249]

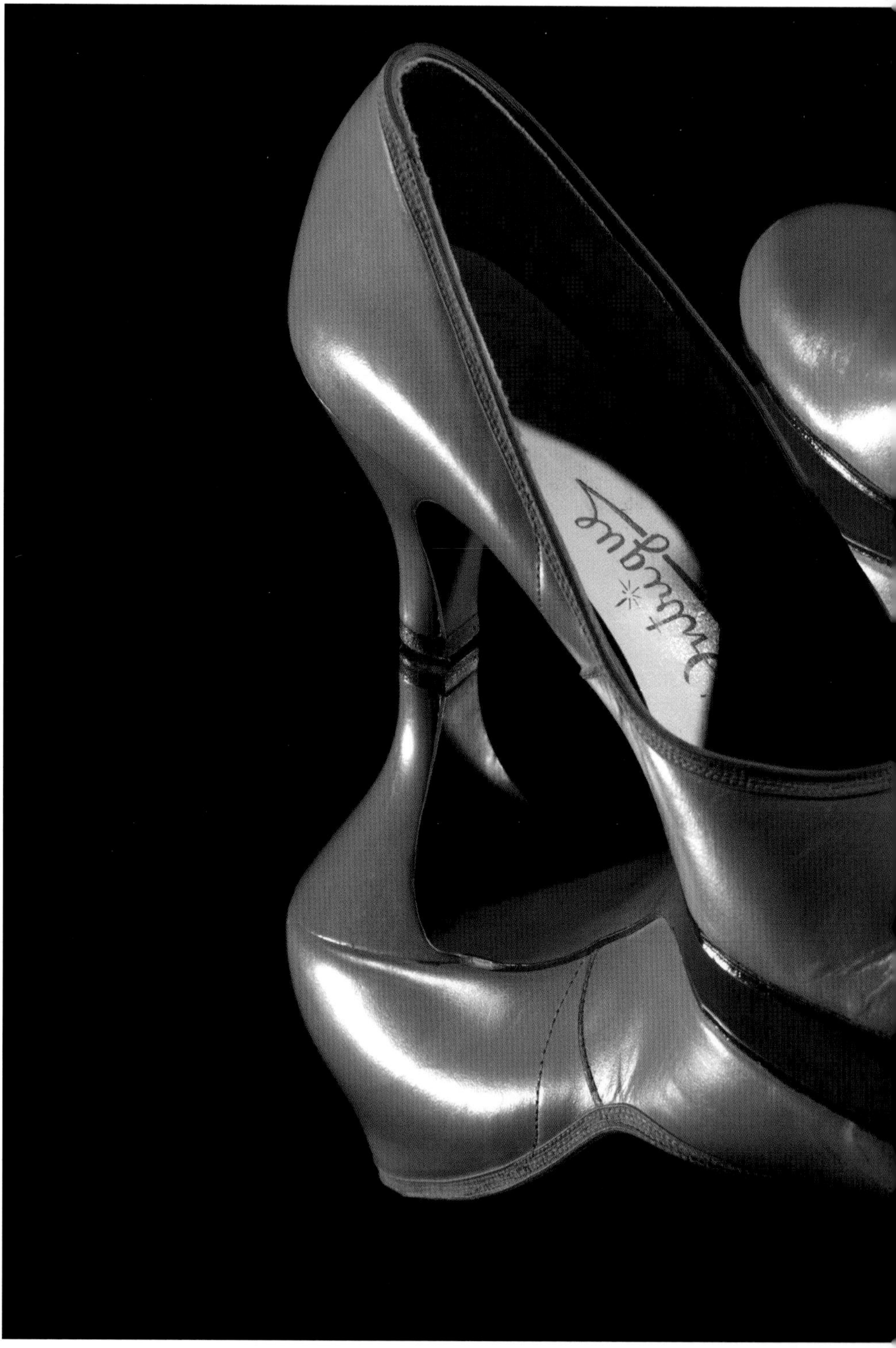

Stan Douglas, *Intrigue, 1948*, (2010)
Courtesy the artist and David Zwirner.

[See p.249]

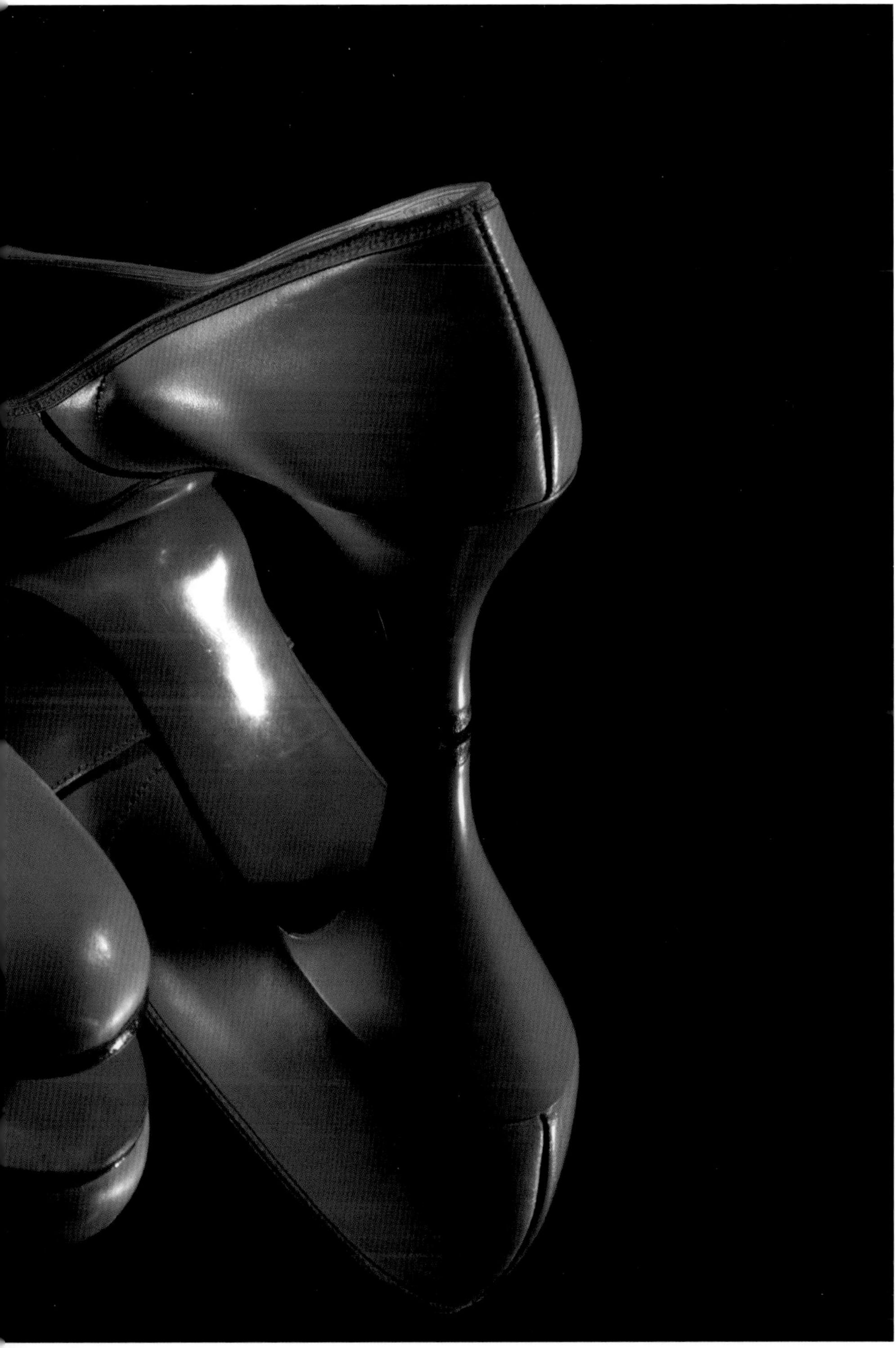

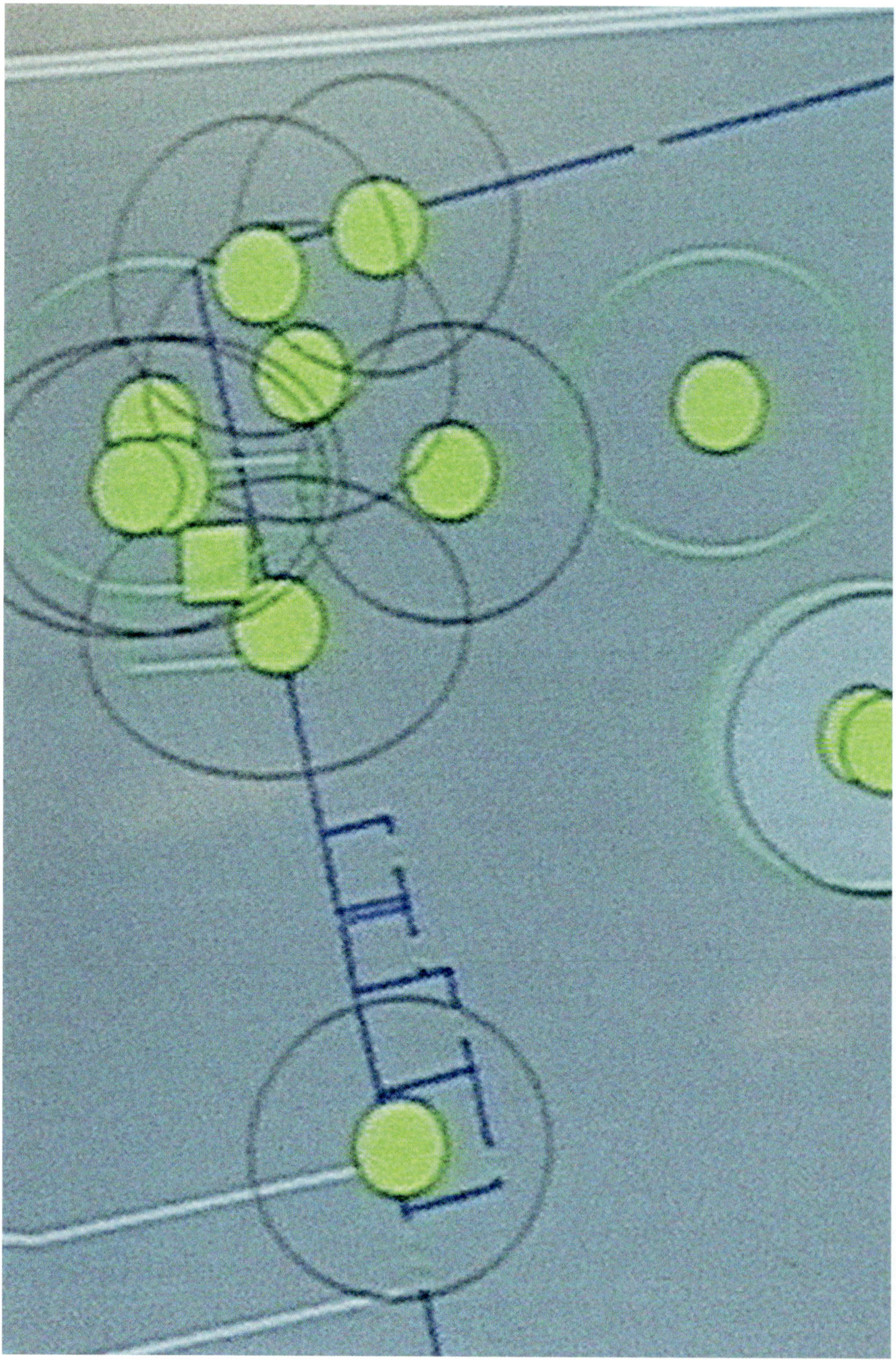

Harun Farocki, *Ich glaubte Gefangene zu sehen | I Thought I Was Seeing Convicts* (2000)
BetaSp, 23 min, Still. Courtesy the artist.

[See p.249]

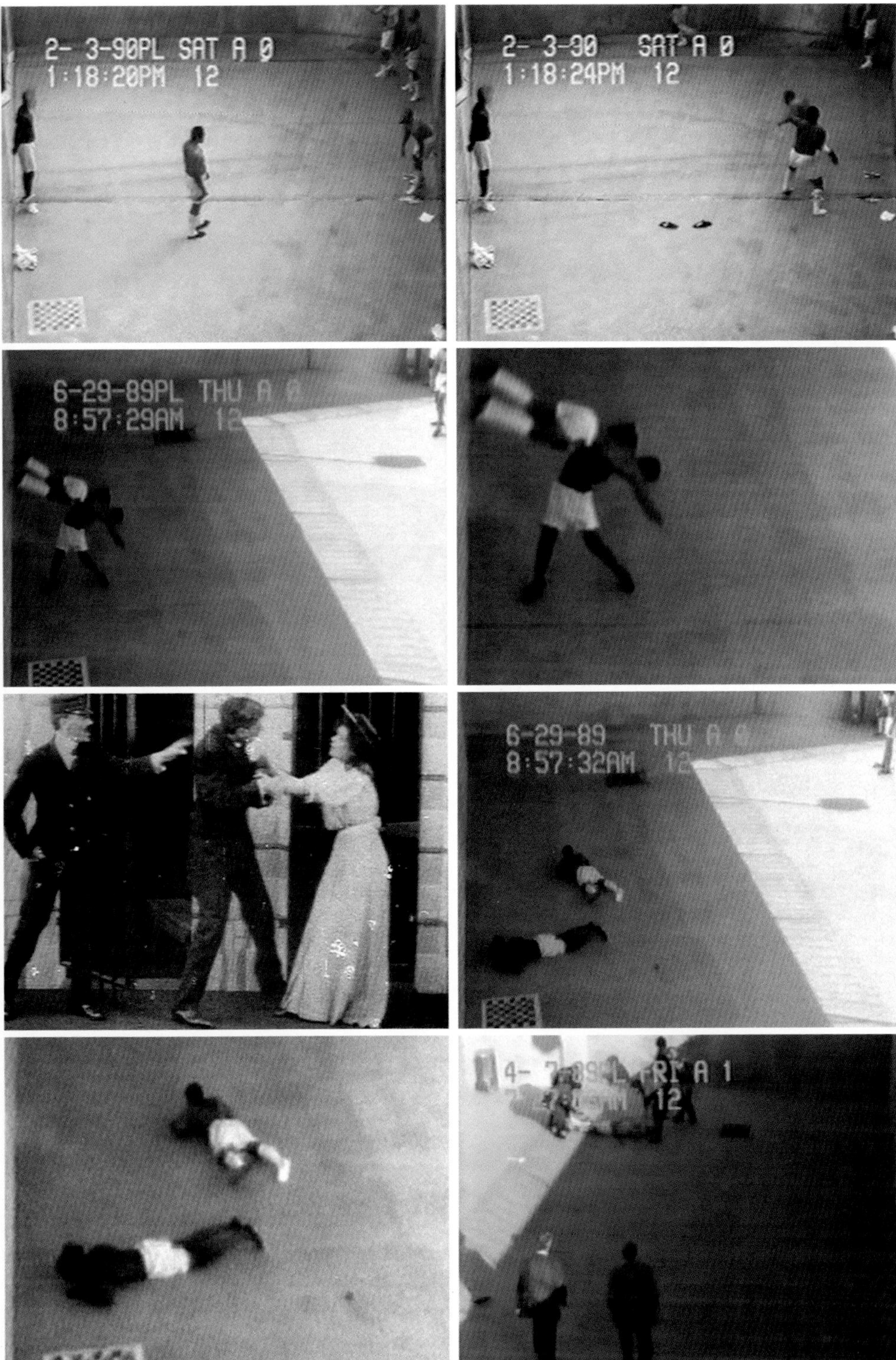

Harun Farocki, *Ich glaubte Gefangene zu sehen / I Thought I Was Seeing Convicts* (2000)
BetaSp, 23 min, Stills. Courtesy the artist.

[See p.249]

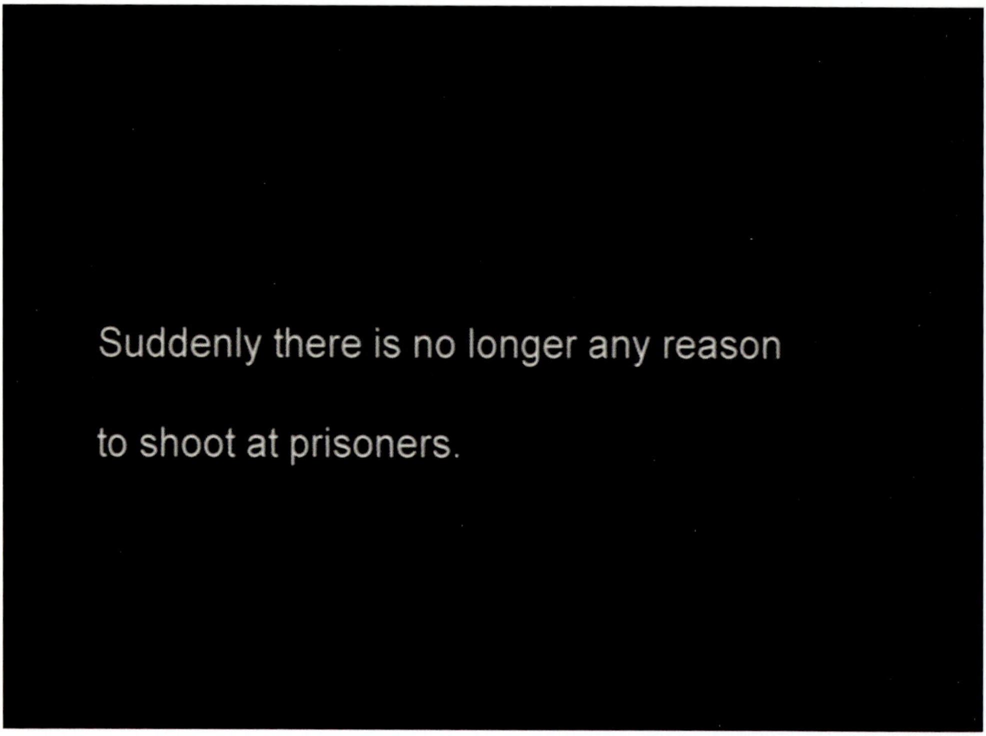

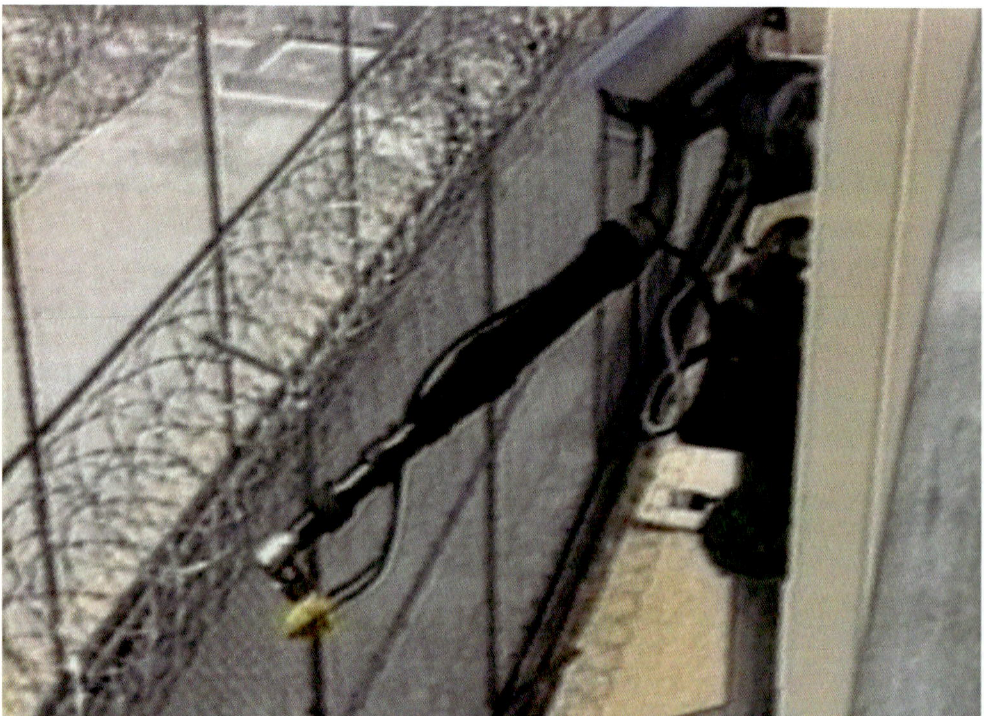

Harun Farocki, *Ich glaubte Gefangene zu sehen | I Thought I Was Seeing Convicts* (2000)
BetaSp, 23 min, Stills. Courtesy the artist.

[See p.249]

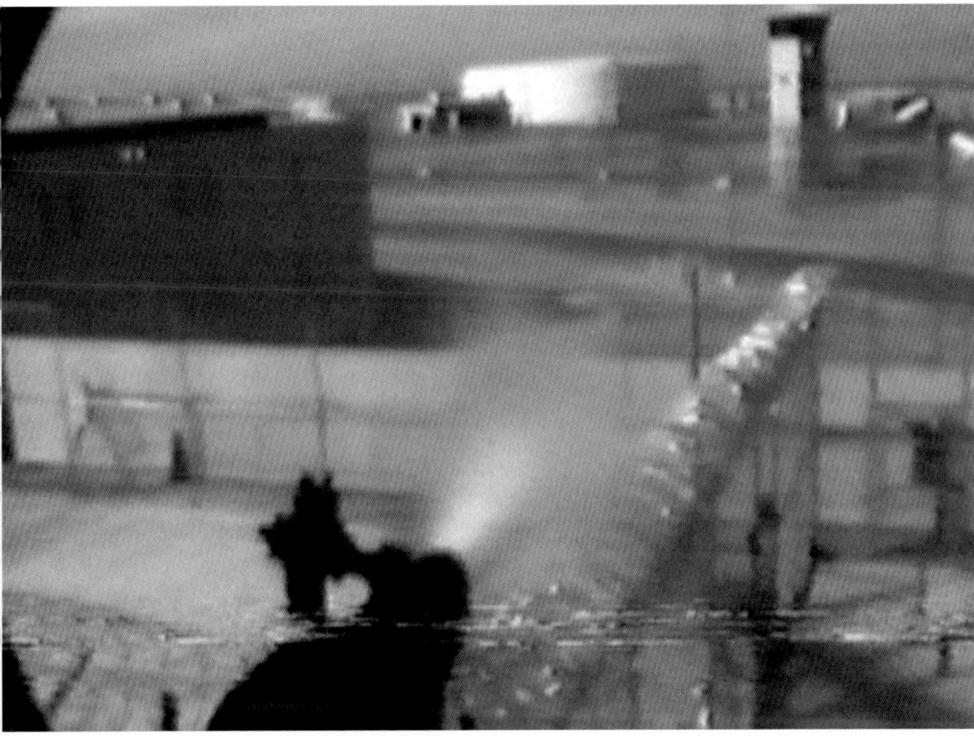

Harun Farocki, *Ich glaubte Gefangene zu sehen / I Thought I Was Seeing Convicts* (2000)
BetaSp, 23 min, Stills. Courtesy the artist.

[See p.249]

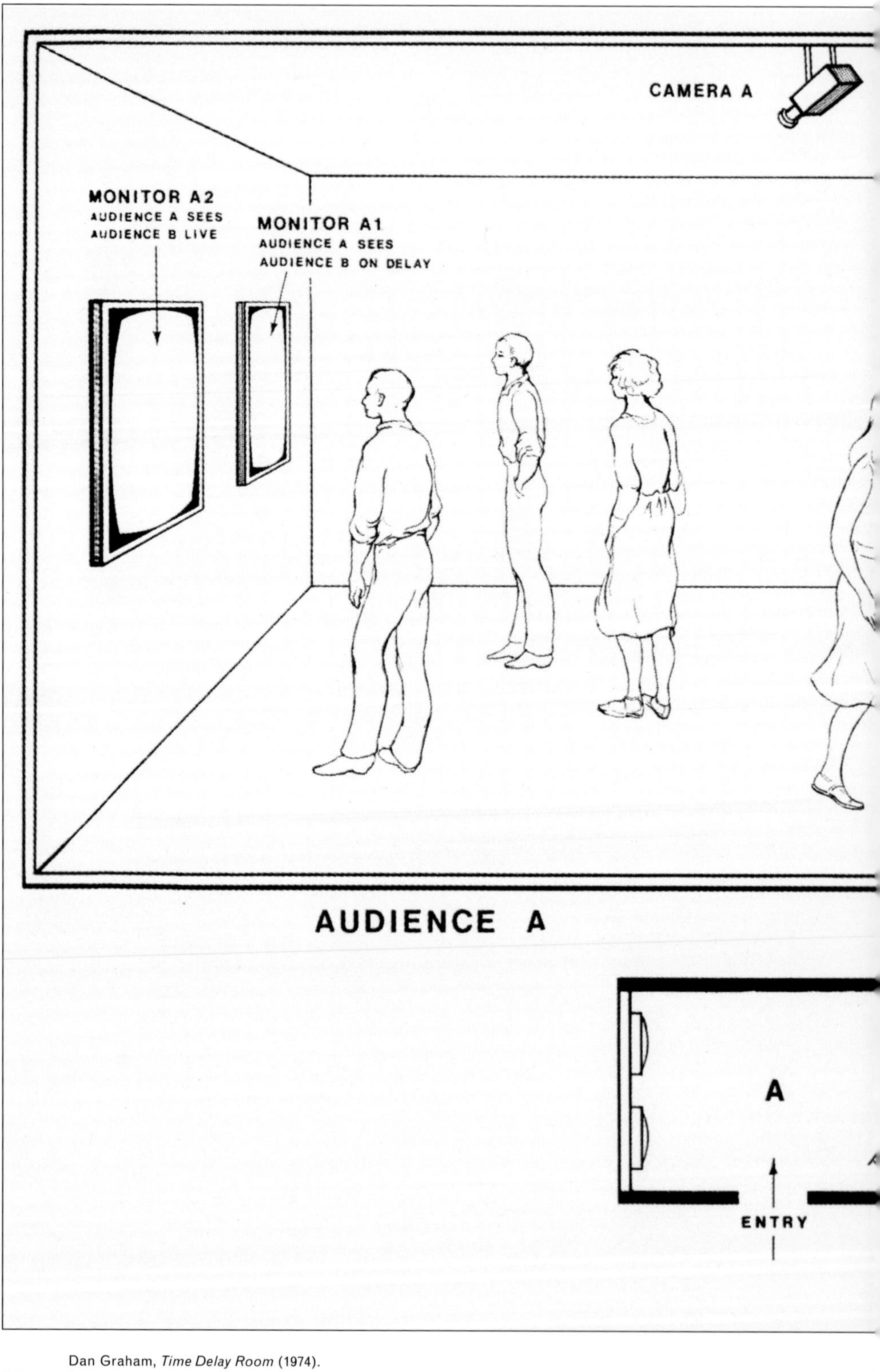

Dan Graham, *Time Delay Room* (1974).
Image courtesy the artist.

[See p.249]

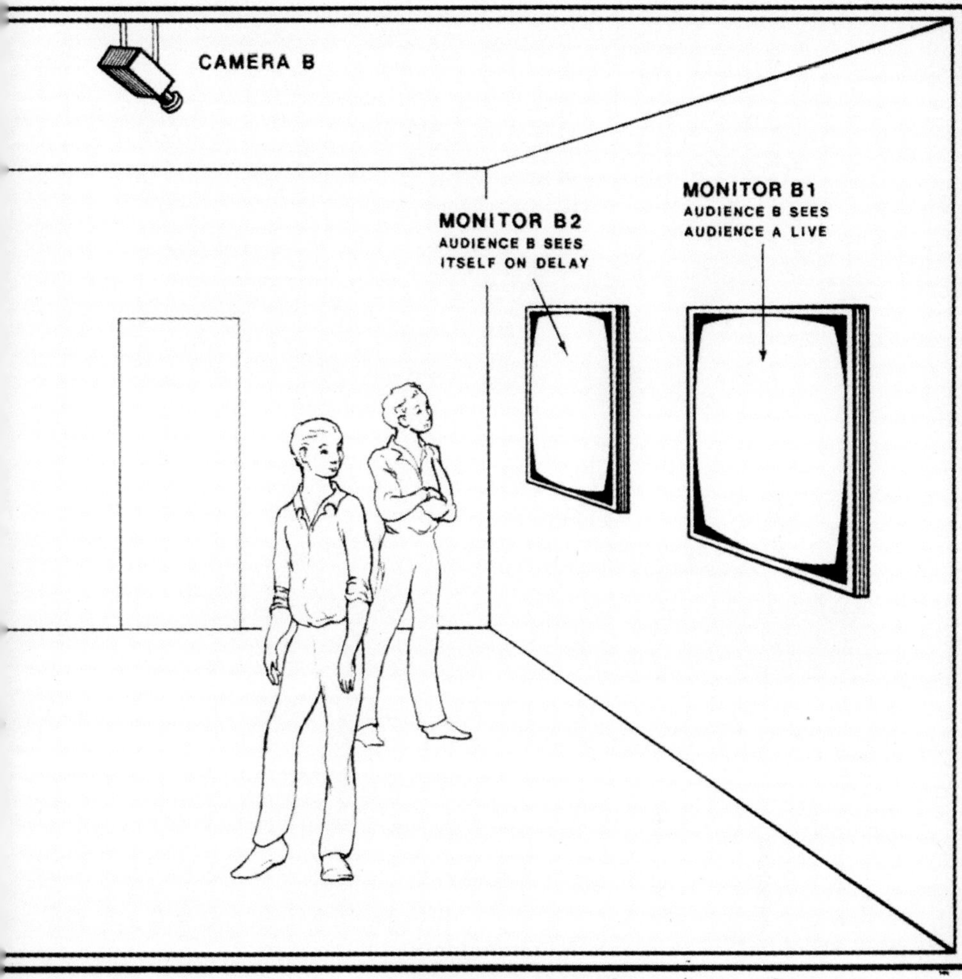
CAMERA B
MONITOR B2
AUDIENCE B SEES
ITSELF ON DELAY
MONITOR B1
AUDIENCE B SEES
AUDIENCE A LIVE

AUDIENCE B

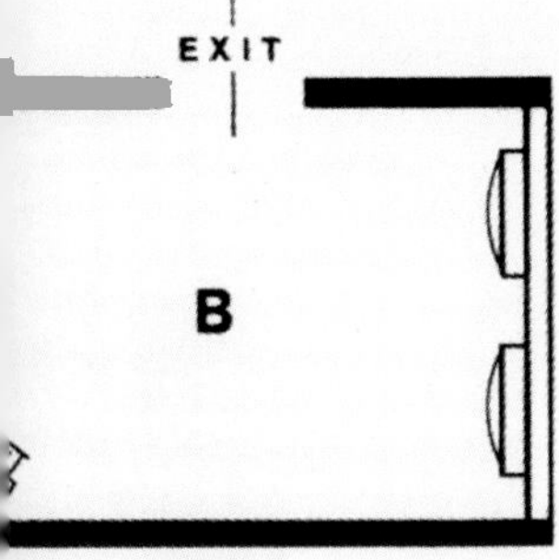
EXIT
B

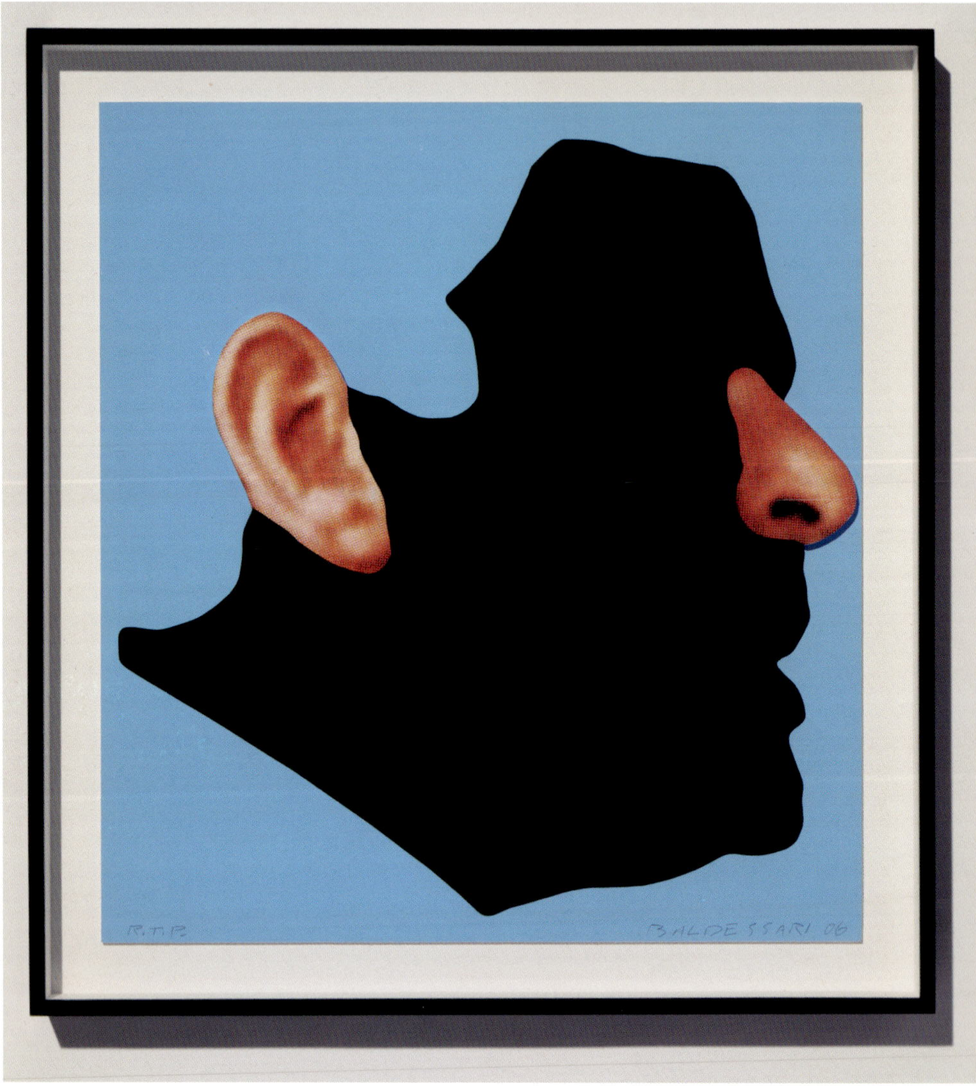

John Baldessari, *Profile with Ear and Nose* (2006)
John Baldessari and Gemini G.E.L. LLC

[See p.250]